Possessing Me

a memoir of healing

Jane Alexander

Wise Boar Media
SAN FRANCISCO

POSSESSING ME – a memoir of healing
by Jane Alexander

ISBN-10: 0-9830709-0-3
ISBN-13: 978-0-9830709-0-0

BISAC Headings:
BIO026000 BIOGRAPHY & AUTOBIOGRAPHY / Personal Memoirs
PSY022030 PSYCHOLOGY / Psychopathology / Bipolar Disorder
SEL020000 SELF-HELP / Mood Disorders

First published by Wise Boar Media
San Francisco, November 2010

www.PossessingMe.com

*To all those souls
who have ever seriously wondered
if there is anything at all about life itself
that might actually be worth living for*

TABLE OF CONTENTS

- PART ONE -

CHAPTER 1

QUARANTINE

It's not everyday that you come home to find your house has been quarantined by the government. But we had known it was coming ever since the engineers from the Environmental Protection Agency showed up. A relatively innocuous white pickup truck with low profile government logos on the sides pulled up one day and disgorged a couple of guys dressed in construction boots, helmets and flannel shirts handling clipboards and various ground probes and testing equipment.

It turned out that the grayish-white tiles we kids (and the dogs) were perpetually digging up in the backyard was asbestos. In fact, the property our house was built on had once been a dump for sheet asbestos, which is a heat insulating material that was used regularly in the construction of peoples homes during the early 1900s. Asbestos is somewhat safe, but the copious dust and fibers that are created by breaking and handling it causes a nasty lung cancer called mesothelioma. In accordance with the Clean Air Acts of the '60s and '70s, exposed asbestos had to be extracted and disposed of by trained specialists.

The EPA moved surprisingly quick when they realized the extent of the underground site. Our family (and several of the surrounding neighbors) were awarded by the federal and local government with enough money to acquire decent temporary housing for the length of the cleanup, a process that took several weeks. We moved into a nearby motel for the duration.

When I came home from school that day, the engineers were placing an enormous translucent plastic bag over our entire house. And not just our house, but also the houses to either side of ours and the one on the other side of the street. They didn't just bag up the houses but also every oak tree, willow and dogwood in the area. Even our jungle gym and the neighbors above-ground pool were enveloped in plastic.

Heavy construction machines descended upon our neighborhood. A tracked Caterpillar excavator dug an enormous pit on our property and dumped our backyard and all the asbestos under it into a line of waiting Mack dump trucks that carted off the toxic soil, away to places unknown.

Excavating asbestos requires extreme care to avoid spreading its carcinogenic dust into the air. EPA contractors were required to wear these thick white full-body protective suits that sported large transparent plastic domes and a closed-circuit air supply, which (along with the copious swathes of plastic sheeting everywhere) lent the entire work site the appearance of having been taken over by NASA. The job of the astronauts was to hose down everything in sight with torrents of water in order to prevent asbestos dust from getting off the ground.

The EPA crews did a thorough job, and as part of the landscaping deal we ended up with a freshly paved and widened driveway, a lush rolled-sod lawn and a line of young pine trees that delineated our property from the neighbors'. But what they did not replace was our nondescript two-story house, inside which another kind of toxin existed that was slowly but inexorably sickening our family. In the years before that creeping illness destroyed us, there was a lot of love and good cheer in our home.

My stepfather Tim was an Irish Catholic, a typical guy's guy in a lot of ways. He loved to watch his Red Sox, Patriots and Celtics games. For the World Series or Super Bowl he would break out the barbecue, the burgers and the Budweiser and invite some of his buddies to come over. They'd argue, sometimes loudly, about bad calls, cheering their favorite players when they scored, cursing them if they played poorly. But they never got rowdy or out-of-hand.

Tim seemed to delight in making things with his hands and he built a number of projects (with us kids assisting him at times) including a new porch, a club house for us, (complete with the requisite ladder and trap door), and a dog house for Christy and Sherlock, our golden retriever and German shepherd.

Tim also had a rich imagination and a natural gift for story telling. One of my favorite bedtime stories that I used to beg him to tell me was the one about a giant mythical bird called the Taka-taka. The Taka-taka lived at the side of the mysterious Lake Tanganyika. It flew as high or higher than any jet or airplane could. And when we were very little, Daddy taught us the secret call that could summon this magnificent beast:

Taka-taka-taka, Taka-taka-taka,
Put me on your back-a,
Take me to the mountain – to the mountain top.

With the understanding that if the Taka-taka bird heard our call, it would find us, and if it liked us, it would fly us to its home.

My mother Sarah was not the kind of woman who was given over to spontaneous displays of affection for her children. When we were babies and young toddlers she could be doting, but there was a cutoff point. Once we reached a certain age, about seven or eight years old or so, we outgrew her attentions and that was it, no more random kisses on the cheek, pats on the head or loving embraces unless we were really sick. Later, even that level of compassion would be beyond her abilities. But in the early days she definitely had her sweet moments.

When Sarah was in a good mood she became more creative, sociable and a lot easier to get along with. As her firstborn and the eldest of my siblings I tended to benefit the most from her expansive and euphoric personality phases. Once, when Sarah was in her inspiration mode, she spent an entire week painting a lovingly detailed, wall-to-wall and ceiling-to-floor panorama of a sea-side pier, complete with sailboats and seagulls, on one side of my bedroom. On the opposite side she painted a different background scene depicting verdant fields, deep evergreen forests and rolling, snow-capped mountains.

When I was little, it was not entirely uncommon for me to awaken in the middle of the night and be unable to fall back asleep. At times I'd get up and go to the bathroom. Not because I needed to, but because I was bored. I'd come out of my bedroom in my pastel yellow Loony Tunes footed pajamas and find the lights on in the living room. My mother was still awake, smoking cigarettes and watching television.

I would stand in the living room doorway, all blink-eyed and tousle-haired, and Sarah would say, "What's the matter honey, can't sleep?" I would shake my head and she'd say, "Me neither," and smiling she would pat the arm of the couch and beckon, "Come on over here and sit with Mama."

She would make room for me on the green cushions and we'd watch reruns of *Spencer for Hire*, *Magnum P.I.* and *Hart to Hart* together. During commercials she would brew us up some tea with honey or my favorite, hot chocolate with a daub of whipped cream on top. And sometimes she would share with me her favorite ice cream, "Heavenly Hash," a royal treat because it was her special ice cream and totally off-limits to everyone else. That I had had some myself was our little late-night secret.

In those days Sarah still entertained visitors in our house and one of those was her high-school friend June, who was my god-mother. One day Sarah and June took me with them on a day trip to Massachusetts. We went to the Boston Museum of Science, which was just paradise for me because I've loved science ever since I read children's books about it. We went to an Italian restaurant and had lasagna with eggplant parmigiana, an exceptionally rare and bourgeois feast for us back then.

My mother delighted that I seemed to take after her in all things. As a child I soon showed artistic talent and musical aptitude and my mother always encouraged me to draw, paint and take flute lessons and cultivate those abilities to my hearts content. We would go to Third Order Franciscan prayer meetings and sing hymns as she played her autoharp.

The early days were a time of innocence for all of us. We used to gather together in the living room to watch shows like *Lassie*, *Flipper* and *Little House on the Prairie* on our modest 18 inch TV. Mama still played her Beach Boys albums when she cleaned the house. Crucifixes draped with palm fronds and rosary beads and images of the Virgin Mary and St. Francis of Assisi adorned the walls in our house. We used to say Grace before dinner and Daddy tucked us into our beds at night.

As a family we dressed up in our finest to attend Saint John the Evangelist church on Sundays. After mass we socialized a bit downstairs in the reception hall and had coffee and donuts with the other parishioners. Then we'd all go home and after breakfast our parents would pack us kids and the dogs into our orange Volkswagen bus and we'd head out for the day.

In the spring and summer we would go to Greeley Park to picnic and play sports. On humid days we might drive to Robinson Pond for a swim. And every great now and then, if we were especially lucky, we'd go on a road trip to Canobie Lake Amusement Park or more rarely, Weirs Beach Water Slides.

During the cold New England winters we went ice skating and sledding and we used to have snow shoveling parties. We even went Christmas caroling during the holidays, knocking on our neighbors doors to sing them family renditions of "What Child is This?", "O Little Town of Bethlehem" and "Holy Night" like something out of Frank Capra's *It's a Wonderful Life*.

A lot of people remember The Eighties for the Big Hair, leg warmers, MTV, and the rise of cocaine as the social drug of choice. Growing up in the '80s, I remember that I worried quite a bit about whether I'd someday wake up to an atomic wasteland because the Soviets had finally nuked us during the night.

Back then, Sarah and Tim used to have occasional but terrible screaming fights with each other. Money woes and Sarah's ex-husband Andrew were two of the issues they battled over the most. In the early years they would kiss and make up after. Later on that stopped and the shouting and recriminations would eventually run down into an uneasy tension in the house.

Usually when they started screaming at each other I would run into my room, stick my head under my pillow and hold it tight to my ears until their terrible back and forth shouting stopped. One day, during another of their fights, I came out of my room to be on my mother's side and I asked Tim to stop being so mean and quit making Mama so sad. He turned and started screaming at me, "Go back to bed and mind your own business!" and I was shocked and devastated to suddenly be a target for his ire. In our house, screaming led to discipline which over time morphed into abuse.

I still remember a crayon drawing I made at that time, I was about six years old, depicting a scene where I lay dead on the floor with a knife handle and part of its blade protruding from my heart. Detailed and jagged streams of blood flowed away from me and pooled at the bottom of the drawing. On the backside I wrote down "Dear Daddy, this is how you make me feel." Then I placed the sheet, note side up, on my parents bed. This is my first memory of wanting to hurt myself.

When Tim came home from work and saw my message, he came into my room to hold me and to apologize, and things were better. But "better" never lasted for long.

Every time my brother and I left home to spend the weekend with my relatives, Tim and Sarah would warn us about being brainwashed by them. When we came back from those visits they would sit us down and debrief us about every last detail of our visit. If any incident came up they didn't like, my mother would be on the phone in an instant, screaming at my other dad.

The only brainwashing that occurred was the sheer effort Tim and Sarah expended trying to convince my brother and me that the other side of our family consisted of bad people who might "do things" to us. We were told again and again, "They are liars and you can not trust them."

They would seize and sometimes destroy gifts that my brother and I received from either our real father or our grandparents. Andrew (my real dad) once asked me what I wanted for Christmas and I wanted a calculator watch. He got me a Casio. At that age, I'd never owned something as expensive as that watch. There was no way my parents could afford something like it.

When my brother and I got home, I didn't divulge that I had it. I was afraid of what my parents might do. When Tim and Sarah heard the watch beeping they demanded that I surrender whatever was making the sound. I pretended not to know what they were talking about and so they tore apart my room looking for it. They would not stop screaming at me and threatened, "You will give it over to us right now or you will be punished!" Terrified, I finally showed them the watch and surrendered it.

Tim smashed it with a hammer on the dining room table in front of all the other kids. He tried to give us a lecture about how technology was ruining the world, "Digital calculator watches will make you kids forget about math and how to tell proper time," he admonished. Apparently, carpenter's hammers were not on the banned technology list. No doubt my stepfather would have defended himself by stating that Jesus was a carpenter. If a hammer was good enough for Jesus, it was good enough for him.

My grandparents bought us children's encyclopedias. We were allowed to keep the ones about ocean life, land animals and astronomy, but the volume of modern technology was confiscated by my mother.

"Give it to me," she said, when she noticed a picture of an atomic bombs' mushroom cloud.

"Why?" I asked.

"You guys are not old enough to handle this yet," she replied.

"Aw, come on Mama, why not?" I implored.

"Do not argue with me unless you are looking to get slapped, now give it over," she said testily.

In retrospect, I think it meant that it was she who was not ready for us to know about those things. Whether Sarah thought she was protecting us or just didn't want to deal with it, we never knew. Keeping us away from interesting things only made us more curious about them, despite the risk of punishment, a fact that my mother never quite understood.

When my grandparents brought gifts the next time for all of the kids (me, my brother Byron, stepbrother Sam and stepsister Alice), my parents confiscated them. They told us that we hadn't done anything to earn bonus presents this year. Then they took us all to a Secret Santa outlet for poor people and made us give our extra presents away. In truth they saw them as bribes to tempt us away from our loyalty to mummy and daddy.

Although Tim and Sarah encouraged us children to read and watch educational science programs that aired on public television, like *Nova* and *3-2-1 Contact*, they were paradoxically anti-technology. I remember asking Tim if we would get a computer someday. (The Apple II and the Tandy TRS-80 were quite popular in the early '80s.) His response, "There will never, ever be a computer in this home."

The lights in the house were not allowed to be on if no one was occupying the room. Tim saw it as a needless waste of energy, and hence money, to do otherwise. So we would get yelled at if we forgot to turn a light off upon leaving the room. Even my mother was not exempt and Tim would harangue her if she left lights on as well.

Winter was the worst in that regard because it was dark so early that a lot of lights needed to be on sometimes. Tim would come home from work and before the door was fully open he was demanding, "Why are there so many lights on!" As if we were supposed to huddle together all the time and move only as a group from one room to another.

Over the years I've given it a lot of thought and I doubt they thought of themselves as truly anti-tech. We had a toaster oven, a VCR, at least one, sometimes two automobiles. (But Tim boxed the remote control that came with the VCR, insisting that we all get up and walk to the VHS player and use the face buttons manually.)

Every piece of technology that my parents allowed into the home had to be carefully analyzed for its laziness-inducing potential. Then a list of rules would be drawn up, deciding who in the house could use what devices and under what circumstances. A washing machine was okay, while a dryer was regarded as too much automation. Thus our clothes were hung outside to dry and stiffen on clotheslines most of the year, every year. In the winter, elaborate clothes racks were set up near our cast-iron wood stove to dry our stuff.

My parents, Tim especially, constantly harped on us, the evils of technology and romanticized the virtues of labor and taking extra effort. But the reality was, that they couldn't afford to give us kids technological gadgets or even buy a clothes dryer for that matter. We never had a shower until we were teens. We bathed in a tub for years until Tim jury-rigged a hose and sprinkler-head at the end of a chrome pipe and installed a sheet of plastic for a shower curtain.

Our family could not compete with the middle-class advantages that some of my other relatives or even our neighbors enjoyed. The Birds for example, our nearest neighbors, had sports cars and a pool. Their only child, our friend Jimmy owned more cool toys than all four of us kids combined.

Tim and Sarah were probably very aware that they were not "Keeping up with The Joneses." Essentially they converted the dissonance of their dissatisfaction into the rationale that we didn't deserve those kinds of things and only spoiled, lazy people would want them anyway.

My mother had a fantasy about how she wanted to live. She has described it to me often enough: A wooden cottage on a quiet lake, surrounded by a white picket fence. Children playing in the yard, dogs and cats scampering. This was the burden Sarah dumped on each of her husbands and it was their job to make it happen.

Her first husband Andrew, my father, was pragmatic about it. His idea was to finish school, get his degree, go to work for a corporation, make some wealth and then go about buying a house and having a family. Sarah enlisted her parents to call my father and pressure him into joining a labor union which paid twice as much as the kind of part-time work my Dad was doing to help support us while he went through school. Sarah's folks insisted that there was nothing wrong with an honest, blue-collar job and it was expected that he set to work making their daughter happy. But Andrew steadfastly refused to drop out of school and give up his degree.

Perhaps figuring she had found a way to manipulate my father into dropping out and going to work full-time, she stopped taking The Pill without telling him. During that time I was conceived. Naturally, my father thought her conception was nothing short of a miracle. When Andrew questioned her about how it had happened, she told him she went off The Pill for religious reasons. Her parents continually reminded her that birth control was against Catholic catechism. Suddenly she couldn't stand the guilt anymore but somehow forgot to mention it. So it was my Dad's fault for knocking her up.

Instead of giving in, my father pinched things tighter, worked harder and more hours on top of school and still made ends meet though it was punishing him physically. Frustrated that she had failed to derail Andrew from his career plan, Sarah did it to him again. Sixteen months after I was born, along came my brother Byron.

Still, Andrew refused to drop out of college and one day, while he was on campus, he was served with the divorce papers. On the one hand, Sarah couldn't stand the accumulating Catholic guilt of preventing natural conception by using birth control, but on the other hand she apparently had no issues with getting a divorce. During this, I'm not sure Sarah ever once took a second to consider the welfare of my brother and I. It had become a bitter war with my father and his family on one side and Sarah and her family on the other.

During the process of the divorce my mother ensnared her next husband. Tim, my soon-to-be stepfather, was her case worker during the court proceedings and exactly what she wanted. Like my father before him he must have been enchanted by Sarah's curly red hair, her emotive freckled face and her overall passion for the arts, music, and religion.

Soon enough though, she bent him to her will. Tim quit his career as a social worker and became the blue-collar guy my mother wanted so much. We moved into the first floor of Tim's mother's house that had been built on the asbestos landfill that eventually attracted an EPA cleanup and removal years later.

Naturally, Sarah had to have his children as well and within two years of their marriage she bore my first sister, Alice. One of my earliest memories is of Tim digging the holes for the posts needed to support the white picket fence she cajoled him into building.

We lived a reasonably normal life in that house until about 1982. At that time I was seven years old and in first grade. My brother was in kindergarten, my sister in preschool. My youngest brother was yet to be born. It was also the year that my stepfather started whipping us.

CHAPTER 2

WELCOME HOME SANITARIUM

As kids we were made to understand that we were ungrateful wretches who refused to simply be good and behave. When Tim would go off and Sarah would wail about her impending nervous breakdown, the blame was always cast squarely on us kids. Being the eldest, I was made to bear the brunt of the responsibility.

Sarah had told us not to talk during nap time, but we whispered to each other through the cracks in our doors anyway. In a frenzy, Sarah burst into our rooms to give us a blistering hairbrush spanking over our bared buttocks and we'd be sent to stand in different corners of the house with our pants down around our ankles to face the wall until she said otherwise.

Swift, decisive punishment itself was never enough. There was always the threats and hysteria. Every punishment involved screaming, in-your-face speeches as well as humiliation in front of other family members. We felt like they were trying deliberately to crush our spirits and our will and of course we had no idea why.

We were ordered about the house like little soldiers. The expectation was, that when either parent gave us direction, compliance was immediate and total. We were not allowed to hesitate or stop to think about an order. More and more, if we were slow to comply or demonstrated any rebellious attitude, it led to some combination of screaming outrage and corporal punishment.

Banishment to military school was another famously overused threat they tried on us to scare us into behaving. We had no idea they never could have afforded it. These threats were for stuff like not doing chores thoroughly or because we would horseplay. If one of us ever made another of the kids cry because we were being mean or rough, we were in serious trouble.

As we got older the penalties for childish misbehavior were intensified and more severe. Gone were the ritualized spankings with bare hand, hairbrush and wooden spoon. Our parents took to all out assault and battered us for a variety of arbitrary and unpredictable reasons. The entire household existed in a growing state of anxiety and fear that seeped into the walls and the floorboards. A tangible aura of restlessness and poised expectancy, like helplessly watching a ticking time-bomb, slowly counting down to detonation.

Dessert became another form of leverage to use on us. If one of us was "bad," he went without dessert while having to sit at the table and watch the other kids eat hearty. I refused to be manipulated like that and eventually I stopped caring about dessert. The idea of "earning" dessert made me sick to my stomach and so I passed my portion to one of the other kids. In time I adapted to my mother's vengeful behavior and her manipulative games.

Once I no longer cared about treats and similar incentives it was one less leverage point that could be used against me by my mother. It was liberating to be freed of that concern. It was a coping behavior designed to out-wit Sarah, and it worked, frustrating her even more.

We were always in the process of trying to intuit the whimsical seeming rules of the game "Never make Mama mad." No contradicting her or making her defensive. Don't ever question her decisions or rules or ask, "But Mama, why?" Any of those things could and often would make Sarah go off on us.

Invariably, the penalty I had to pay for making Sarah lose her temper was be to be hit by my stepfather. She would report on all my little crimes to him when he came home from work. This resulted in being taken to the bedroom and subjected to one of his many leather belts.

When I became too big to be controlled over Tim's knee, he abandoned his belt in favor of battery. Tim was a robust and muscular man who performed physical labor ten hours a day, six days a week. He could effortlessly pick us up with one hand and throw us bodily through the air into walls and furniture which he did with zeal and wrath.

My traitorous siblings would turn me in and rat me out for real and false accusations in an attempt to gain standing with either parent. I would be in my room listening to music, reading science or fiction and into my room my parents would burst like a SWAT team, Tim or Sarah or both.

One of my mother's favorite tactics was to grab me by my hair or ear and drag me all over the house while screaming at me. Then she would foist me off to my stepfather who then dragged me into other rooms to whip me. The crying and screaming was contagious. Once I started begging my folks, "Please Mama!", "Stop Daddy!", my siblings would start sobbing one by one and as the background sounds increased in volume my parents would scream to the other kids, "Go to your rooms!"

Whenever they flew into these histrionics they would preach the Bible at us. Always the Ten Commandments and their cherry picked sermons, "God commands that children honor their father and mother!" Spare the rod, spoil the child. Any disobedience was seen as a sin that must be punished for our own good in order to save us from going to Hell.

When we were little, Tim actually threatened to drive us there. He would get his jacket and keys and tell us all to get out of bed and get dressed because he was going to take us to Hell and leave us there. We all had seen the color pictures of Hell in the children's Bible story books and we believed it was real. We didn't know that it wasn't possible to simply pack us into the bus and drive us there.

Only after several of us were half in and half out of our coats, crying and clinging to my stepfather's legs, begging not to be taken to Hell, would he finally relent and send us back to bed. We were scared to death and would promise him anything to give us another chance to be good. I used to have nightmares about it.

All of us kids showed signs of stress and mental distress caused by living with our maladjusted parents. We all developed strange behaviors and idiosyncrasies. My youngest brother Sam was not at all talkative. His silence was a kind of survival technique to avoid being noticed. He had a hard time mastering toilet training.

My sister Alice used to steal food and hide it in her room. One time my parents got really upset about the missing Hershey's chocolate syrup we used to spike our milk with sometimes. We all got interrogated and my sister broke down under the burden of guilt. My parents raided my sister's room and found a cache of food under her bed.

She had taken jars of peanut butter, fluff, fruit preserves, honey and the Hershey chocolate syrup. My parents paraded these discoveries and kept yelling at my sister, demanding to know why she did it. Alice never answered with anything but, "I don't know!" followed by crying. We all watched as my parents shamed and humiliated her in front of the whole family. She would continue to wet her bed in the night into her teens.

Of course it was not only Alice and I who got into trouble. If my brother Byron happened to be the focus of my parents' anger, he would lock himself down and freeze in place. His face lost all expression and he became unresponsive when my parents screamed at him. That only infuriated them even more. When they started hitting him he would drop and curl into a ball and ride it out. This made it harder to strike Byron satisfyingly and that infuriated them too.

At one point he was diagnosed with attention deficit disorder because he had a hard time concentrating and his school work was sub par. Byron was treated unsuccessfully with Ritalin for a few months. He just lost weight that he couldn't afford to lose and he had no appetite.

Sarah, witnessing the effects of this methamphetamine analog on her child, in a rare moment of insight and protectiveness, discontinued him from the drug despite the insistence of school administrators that he be made to take it. They punished her and my brother by forcing him to repeat the first grade. Without doubt he was one of, if not the most intelligent of the kids at his grade level. But it can be hard to concentrate in class with the fresh memories of recent dramas and the reoccurring threat of violence hanging over our heads that was always just hours away.

Byron and I never had problems with toilet training. We never stored food in our rooms or developed compulsive eating disorders like Alice. Unlike my chubby stepsister, Byron and I were quite thin back then. We looked like we didn't eat. The truth was, we were so stressed out we just didn't gain weight no matter how much we ate.

Cumulative stress chips away at your body's defenses and so we developed health problems. Before we were kicked out, Byron came down with stomach ulcers while I used to have chronic diarrhea and strange dermatitis. The diarrhea cleared up as soon as I left the family as did the skin problems later on, all by themselves.

We all had these different reactions, coping strategies and abnormal behaviors that grew out of life in my family. For one thing, our self-esteem as children was so low that we became targets for bullies at school. Byron and I in particular suffered from bullying because we were perpetually living in our own worlds and we didn't socialize well with others.

Alice had a different strategy. She was a joiner. In the social dynamic of the family life she was the tattletale. She broke down first under far less pain and pressure than my brother and I could take. Whenever Alice thought she could gain standing or reprieve she would not hesitate to finger us for alleged misdeeds. She liked the temporary protection of being on my parent's good side.

My parents knew it too. If they wanted to get to the heart of the matter and my brother and I stonewalled, they applied pressure on her, knowing she would turn us in sooner or later to save herself a beating. We hated her for it. My brother and I excluded her from our conspiracies because we knew she'd rat us out. We told her to her face, "That is why you can't hang out with us." Alice didn't know how to keep a secret.

My own reactions were just as alarming, perhaps more alarming than my siblings'. I did not freeze under fire nor try to save myself by revealing secrets and pointing fingers. I learned to conceal my emotions from my parents but became increasingly violent behind the scenes.

We didn't get to have a lot of nice things as kids. I had a metal lunch box with considerable decoration on it and it was brand new. In the first grade there was a kid having a temper tantrum during which he kicked a line of lunch boxes. When he did, mine was forced to slide on it's decorated side across the pavement, instantly defacing it.

Enraged, I picked up my lunch box and began running as fast as I could up to the kid who was still red faced and fuming. With my full momentum I swung my lunch box directly at his head, hitting him in the temple. He never saw it coming. He spun completely around, fell to the ground and lay there, unmoving. Some of the other kids started saying that I had killed him. I fled from school on foot, quickly outdistancing the pot bellied yard monitor that chased me. After about a block I realized I was running straight towards the police and fire stations and I surrendered to the teacher pursuing me and let him bring me back to school rather than risk getting into trouble with the cops.

Of course the school principal called my folks to tell them I had assaulted another student. Before, during and after the corporal punishment that followed, my parents continuously threatened me that if I ever hurt anyone ever again, the punishments would be far, far worse.

They kept screaming maniacally like a broken record that I had to turn the other cheek because I was Christian. Over and over again they tried to program me with the same mantra. *Turn the other cheek, or else! Turn the other cheek, or else!* Strange that they never did turn the other cheek themselves when we made them mad.

In the third grade my parents pinched their finances tighter to send me to Catholic school, hoping it would help my attitude and keep me on the straight and narrow. We had one particular teacher there, a nun by the name of Sister Bernadette, who regularly threatened the students with corporal punishment for interrupting class.

Once she caught me passing notes to another student and announced to the class, "Pass notes in my class one more time and I will beat you over my knee with my shoe." The next day I brought to school a pocket knife I scrounged from Tim's workbench at home and told her, "Sister Bernadette, if you ever touch me, I will stab you."

The religious school experiment did not work as hoped, so by the fifth grade I was back in public school. There was a boy named Jason, who kept tormenting me in class. He'd throw pieces of paper at my hair, launch rubber bands into the back of my head or knock my books off my desk as he passed by. I finally got him busted for it and he got detention. He then told his older brother, who was in high school. The older brother stalked me on the way home from school soon after, and threatened, "If you ever rat-out my little brother again, I'll kill you."

The next day I started carrying a steak knife up my sleeve while walking to and from school in case I ran into him again. Which I did. At the time, showing him the knife in my hand was enough to keep this boy at bay. He in turn told his mom what happened, and she called the cops.

A detective came to visit my family to see what was going on and I explained to him that the older boy had threatened to kill me, that my parents refused to let me take self-defense classes, and I needed to protect myself. The detective advised me, "The responsible thing to do is to tell an adult that you've been threatened." But I had done that before, during previous fights, when I had been bullied and my parents always blamed me for making those kids mad at me and not the other kid's parents for not teaching their children that it was wrong to hurt others.

My folks had a strange rationale for this, stating: "It takes two to tango." People didn't just pick on or start fights with me for no reason, they explained. I must be doing something to provoke them.

To the bulk of the kids that preyed on me, their reason seemed to be that I was a vulnerable, disheveled, socially awkward little four-eyed geek who always had the correct answers in school. I was the student who always walked up to the teacher's desk to turn in my test paper first and spent the last forty-five minutes reading Orson Scott Card or Anne MacCaffrey without worrying at all if I had scored less than an "A." These kids couldn't academically beat me in the classroom so they'd physically beat me whenever I wasn't in one.

You see, it's okay to be smart and excel at school if you are from a middle class family, dress in the latest styles, are popular, live in the suburbs and show school spirit. If you are one of the beautiful people, you are encouraged to succeed and cheered when you do and you gain self-confidence in the process. You are allowed to pull ahead of the pack.

But if you seem unselfconscious that you are dressed out of fashion or wearing cheap clothes, then you are not cool. Compound that with an introverted personality that finds more satisfaction in reading sci-fi or fantasy books than in going to a pep rally. Add that you don't have any idea (and couldn't care less) who is running for class president, then you are labeled a loser. A dork. And in lieu of dropping dead so the other kids don't have to suffer from the sight of you, you are supposed to at least be invisible.

It got so bad at one point that there was a small gang of local kids on BMX bikes who routinely ambushed me on the way home from school like a pack of jackals, and threw rocks at me, yelling: "Teacher's Pet! Teachers Pet! Hey! Where are you going? Why are you running away?"

As soon as the detective left, my parents started in on me with their predictable tirades and out came the leather belt but neither that cop nor the punishment that followed was a deterrent because what happened soon after this incident was that I became obsessed with weapons, especially knives. Eventually, I started sleeping with one under my pillow.

At the time ran public awareness commercials about child abuse on television. I remember seeing a sorrow-eyed child crying over a soundtrack of verbal abuse coming from unseen parents. If that had been filmed in our house it would have been a documentary of sorts. I recognized it one day when all of us kids were crying and standing in the corners only to be sent to our rooms without dinner later.

I turned away from the uninspiring limbo of counting and re-counting all the tiny yellow and white flowers of the peeling wallpaper I was facing as punishment one day, to try my hand at guilt-tripping. I spoke to Sarah defiantly as she sat at the table, browsing the slick pages of a Bible-thick Sears catalog, ignoring the sobs coming from all four of her freshly spanked children and the piles of unopened junk-mail and unfolded laundry that sprawled across the table like an invasive species.

"This is abuse!" I accused, as I glanced over my shoulder at her sidelong.

"Oh poor baby," Sarah dripped mockingly. "You think you are being abused? Well at least we don't lock you in the closet and burn you with cigarettes, so count your lucky stars," tapping the smoldering end of hers into the ashtray meaningfully.

"Now shut up, turn around and face the wall," she commanded as she continued turning the pages of her catalog.

One day, Tim tasked me with raking the front yard of all the leaves. It had to be done after I got out of school and before he came home. I waved the rake over the lawn here and there, largely ineffectively, while day dreaming about living on another planet.

Sarah came out and noticed that the lawn was barely raked at all. "When your father comes home and sees that you have not raked the front lawn, he is going to kill you." she told me resignedly. "Not that you don't deserve it, you were warned." And she went back inside.

Adrenaline surged into my bloodstream and I began furiously raking the lawn. I didn't even know what was meant by "doing it right." When I saw Tim's truck coming down the street, I dropped my rake and fled. I ran away from the house in fear of my life. I ran on foot clear into the next town where I tried to locate my friend Danielle's house. A place I had only ever been to by car.

Danielle's mother turned me in by calling up my parents when she saw me and I ran from her house. I used to run cross country and track and I easily outran the adults but my friend's mom sent her older daughter after me. This girl was in her late teens and was a top track and field athlete in her high school. She chased me for some time and together we hurdled porches, low fences, and hedges, until she finally caught up. Danielle's parents drove me back to my family's house and all the while I kept begging them not to.

My mom came out to the car and talked with Danielle's mom while I was fearfully casting about for my stepfather. I wondered if he would slay me right here in the driveway or wait until they left and take me out back. I wondered where they would bury me and if I would get a funeral. Poised to run again, I crept out of the car. There were police cars in our driveway. As long as there were cops with guns maybe my stepfather wouldn't be able to kill me. If I was to be arrested and jailed for being a runaway, so be it.

Sarah charmed and smiled away Danielle's folks, and the police too, and brought me inside. I couldn't stand to be in the same room with Tim, I was so terrified of him. My parents realized that I had over-reacted to their threats and they tried to play down the severity of the punishment I was supposed to receive for not raking the entire lawn within the allotted time. They were kind to me for a couple of days. All too soon it was back to the usual drama.

* * *

My parents poisoned holidays for me early on. To give an example. Sarah would not let us Trick or Treat on Halloween. Flocks of costumed kids roamed our neighborhood with satchels of candy and she wouldn't let us outside. My mother was one of those people who fell for the Halloween Candy Tampering Scare that lasted from the late-60s to the mid-70s. To refresh the minds of those that lived through that and to inform those who missed out, the Candy Tampering Scare was in essence a moral panic. Three completely isolated and unconnected events led up to this hysteria.

In 1964 a mean spirited New York housewife gave out Halloween packages containing steel wool and ant poison. In 1970 a child died after eating his father's heroin stash. To cover it up, the family invented a story about poisoned Halloween candy. In 1974 a young boy from Texas died, eating cyanide laced Pixy Stix. His father was later found guilty. In an attempt to misdirect police he had given out cyanide laced candy to other kids during Trick or Treat, and some of them died. He was later executed.

In my mother's mind, people we didn't know in our neighborhood might be putting razorblades in candy apples, so to protect us, she refused to let us Trick or Treat like all the other kids. That's what she told us when we asked her why we couldn't join the door-to-door kids. To avoid such a calamity, Sarah would pack us into the family bus and drive us to three or four select homes of people she knew from church groups, and allow us to receive candy from them. That was the extent of our Trick or Treat, every year, for as long as we remained a family.

There have been many more rumors of tampered candy over the years, but only one other real incident occurred in Florida, in 2008. Between 1974 and 2008 nearly every subsequent report of tampered candy was found out to be a hoax, often perpetrated by the child who "discovered" the tampered candy. In thirty years there had never been any cases of candy tampering in my hometown, rendering my mother's poisoned candy conviction into something more akin to a fixation. An exotic neurosis, at best, and a paranoid delusion possibly, at worst. Because ultimately her concern was never realized in the lives of any other children we knew or went to school with all the years we were growing up.

Christmas was another time I grew to loathe. Christmas Day was supposed to be sacrosanct. It was the one day of the year when we had a family truce. My parents were least likely to physically punish us and scream at us on Christmas Day. Why they couldn't act that way all the time, and why they seemed bent and determined to fake it on Christmas, eluded me.

Then came the year Sarah and Tim tried to buy my good behavior with one present. I was twelve years old and it was gift giving time around the Xmas tree. I had begun to wonder if my parents had finally made good on their threat to pass me over during Christmas because that year I barely got any presents while my younger siblings all had small piles at this point.

Then my stepfather produced one comparatively large present that had not been under the tree with the others. I don't remember their exact words, time having scrambled precise recollection. All I can do is loosely reconstruct what my parents said to me after.

At first, they were not going to give it to me. I had been rebellious and unruly and far too evil that year to earn such a special and important present. So I hadn't done anything to deserve it.

After much debate they had decided, well, maybe if they gave me this really grown up present I might show some gratitude, try to behave better and be a better role model to the other kids.

At that point, I didn't want their gift. Previously we got gifts because parents do that for their children if they celebrate Christmas. There had never been strings attached, it was just: Here you go, Merry Christmas! I didn't know what it was yet, but I already felt sick in my stomach about it. Being good meant being a little drone that had no will, that only obeyed. But that wasn't me. They didn't think I was ready or mature enough for such a gift but they had decided that, despite all their misgivings, to give it to me anyway.

I knew what it was as soon as they handed me the box. I set it aside to unwrap after I watched the others open some more presents. I was not going to appear eager after their speech. Then, without any emotional reaction, I unwrapped a $100 stereo cassette player.

This pretty much amounted to their entire Christmas budget for me. On one level I was quite happy because I had really wanted one for years, but when I finally got one, it was tainted by the blatant guilt-trip and the bombastic appeal to virtue that came with it. That sabotaged my Christmas forever after.

* * *

That same year I lost the hearing in my left ear. My parents were both predominantly right-handed, so when they slapped me, it was the left side of my head that got hit the most. When children are struck repeatedly in the face and skull by full grown adults, their developing cervical vertebrate are whiplashed again and again. For some kids it results in chronic weakness in the ears, nose and throat, which makes them more susceptible to infections.

I was sitting in first period class in my seventh grade year when the tinnitus struck me. All day long this incessant ringing and buzzing permeated my skull. It was infuriating. No one else heard this sound. It got progressively louder as the day wore on. By evening I was worn out and fatigued and much to my entire family's surprise I excused myself to go to bed early.

The next day I awoke to a hallucinogenic nightmare. The ringing was everywhere. I was in a boat on a stormy sea or so it seemed. My bed was rolling. The floor was undulating. My book cases, stuffed animals and furniture, each seemed alive and quivering. The walls were moving. Everything had an orbit and an element of unreality. I couldn't keep my eyes open for longer than a second, the urge to vomit from the vertigo came so fast that it was almost unstoppable.

It was late morning and my mother was gone to her job as a school bus driver, taking my siblings with her. I couldn't recall if Sarah had attempted to rouse me for school. I allowed myself to slide out of bed onto the floor and started crawling inch by inch along the floor of my bedroom. Navigating blindly, through sheer memory, I slowly crawled through the living room, then across the kitchen floor, and finally into the bathroom at the opposite side of the house.

Still keeping my eyes shut for dear life, clinging to the toilet, I used the last of my strength and hoisted myself upright. That effort was the last straw and I began vomiting convulsively into the bowl. Around that time my mother came home.

I mentioned that Sarah was a school bus driver. Once the youngest of us was old enough to go to school, she was forced to go to work to make ends meet. Her job required she work for about three hours in the morning and three hours in the afternoon. Around ten or eleven in the morning she came home and found me half unconscious on the floor with my head in the toilet bowl.

At once she began screaming at me as though she was channeling the then still-incarnate ex-preacher-turned-comedian, Sam Kinison.

"What are you on? What drugs did you take? Answer me, dammit! What did you get into?!"

Her reaction was so over-the-top hysterical, it might have been funny if I wasn't so sick and if her words hadn't came like out of a megaphone much too loud. Ow! Owww! Her voice was like a hammer on my nerves. Hypersensitive to every sound and sensation, her yelling was a shockwave that shattered my brittle and overheated brain with each syllable.

She was angry and disgusted with me that I had fallen ill. I tried to babble something like, "I'm not on drugs Mama, I've never tried drugs. I am just sick."

"Well at least you didn't vomit all over the floor, because there is no way I am going to clean up after you," she acknowledged grudgingly.

Sarah briefly touched my forehead and nodded to herself. "Yeah, you got a fever, you can stay home." She was glad I chose Friday to be sick. "You had better get over it by Monday because you are going to school regardless," she warned me. I tried to walk back to bed, holding onto walls and chairs and collapsed several times, much to her ongoing tight-lipped disgust.

I barely remember that weekend. I was totally laid out and spent much of it asleep or otherwise fevered and unconscious. By Monday I was famished from three days of not eating and I was able to keep down a piece of toast and some oatmeal. Sarah touched my forehead: still warm but not hot. Good enough. I could eat, speak and was no longer feverish. Off to school with me.

I tried to make it through the day. I could walk, as long as I did so carefully and did not jar my head or turn it rapidly. Stairs were another thing entirely. I had to ascend and descend flights of stairs in between classes and I kept falling down. The constant vertigo, the nausea and incessant ringing in my ears made me so dizzy that I had to close my eyes and feel my way up the stairs, using the banister.

A passing faculty member, a teacher I did not have, noticed my difficulties walking and asked me if I was sick and I said "I think so." She helped me to the nurses station and the nurse immediately realized I was sick. "You should not be in school," she stated. "We will contact your mother."

I dreaded this, but it couldn't be avoided. Sarah asked to speak with me. In a tightly controlled but still venomous voice she stated that because my stepfather couldn't be reached she would have to change her plans and come to get me. "You will pay for this," she assured me. Telling me to be standing outside the school and waiting for her arrival, she finished with, "Do not make me wait around for you." Then she hung up.

Propped up by the flagpole I waited for her outside. The gusty wind threatened to knock my rubbery legs out from under me but I stood anyway, refusing to show my weakness. She pulled up in the station wagon, angrily gesturing for me to get in.

The whole ride back home Sarah ranted about how I dared inconvenience her. She had been enjoying her coffee and cigarettes with the other bus drivers after their routes were done and I had interrupted this. Spoiled ungracious child was I. Not satisfied until she had a nervous breakdown and on and on she went with her incessant recriminations.

I remember contracting chicken pox years earlier at school while in first grade. Back then Sarah had commiserated with me and told me about the time she had had the disease as a young girl. She had waited on me while I suffered at home during two weeks of itching. She had bought me a stuffed animal, books, and generally tried to make me feel better. She didn't get angry with me or try to make me feel guilty about getting sick. Something had happened inside her mind in the last five years for her to have become so selfish and mean.

Needless to say, being exposed to physical abuse and psycho-emotional histrionics did not make us kids into model students or children. Far from it. The behaviors of abused kids are well documented. Failing grades, talking back, running away, stealing, lying, violence, aggression, destructiveness, combativeness, antagonistic, sadistic, self-injuring, anti-social behaviors, confrontational with authority, health problems related to stress and hypervigilance, the list goes on.

Byron and I had been in on-again-off-again counseling ever since the last custody hearing, but that didn't seem to stymie our behavioral issues. The family court judge had ordered my brother and I to attend therapy as a consequence of the upheaval caused in our lives from my mother's divorce and remarriage and subsequent custody battles with our biological father. But more and more, money was an issue and so after a few months our parents stopped making appointments.

Psychology, prayer and all the love and mercy she showered down on us all failed to change us. Faced with the reality that her children were becoming little monsters despite her best parenting and modeling efforts, she sought help.

Sarah now turned to the parent gurus. Highly recommended by one of her fellow bus drivers (who was also a mother to several teens), Sarah brought home a book titled *Tough Love* (written by Phyllis and David York) and it made our lives even worse.

"When you can't reach your teens, can't even live with them . . . it's time for *Tough Love*."

Armed with permission from the authors, the abuse in our home reached even new heights. "You guys have had it far too easy," Sarah explained to us. "This is now going to change."

My mother identified herself as a parent under siege from her difficult children. York's book granted her a license to cast off whatever restraint she possessed and give herself over to ruthlessness. It was time for Sarah to take back control of her family. On occasion she had tried to restrain my stepfather's violence. Now she not only gave him free reign but actively encouraged him to hit us. Whatever it took to get it into our heads, "WE are the adults and YOU are the children. You will all learn to listen, obey and respect, one way or another."

Our entire house was in distress. Every day was punishment day. If we talked back, we got hit. If we got bad grades, we were yelled at and threatened. If we complained, we got hit. If we got too happy, we obviously needed work to occupy ourselves. If we moped around the house, we got screamed at to count our blessings and how dare we act depressed when we were so lucky to have a roof, three meals a day and good, loving, Christian parents.

In one recurring incident my stepfather would go to the kitchen to get a glass of water or a bowl for his orange sherbet. It was my job to wash the dishes after dinner. Being the easily distracted person that I was back then, I had no patience for chores and tasks. I did them haphazardly so I could get back to my books which were vastly more interesting than kitchen drudgery.

Inevitably sometime in the night, Tim would find a spotted glass, a still greasy bowl, and come after me. He would burst into my dark room, grab my ankle while I was still asleep, drag me out of my room, across the house and into the kitchen. Then he turned on the overhead lights blinding me and dazing me.

Florid faced, Tim would scream at me, "Do them again! All of them!" He would throw all the dishes back in the sink and make me wash them again. If there was a single dirty glass, I would be smacked and had to do them all over again and again, until I learned to take chores seriously and do them attentively. I didn't understand the level of detail they expected from me when it came to chores and so I learned nothing and it was only a matter of time before this confrontation repeated itself.

On more than one occasion, after a round of screaming, threats and repeated bouts of corporal punishment, I considered killing my stepfather. I never could quite think about killing my mother. There was a time, when Sarah used to read me Bible stories, and share some of her favorite ice cream, "Heavenly Hash," with me. I cherished those few moments when I was very young and my mother and I were really close. I always felt she would do better if Tim was dead.

I once read about a Russian scientist named Ivan Pavlov who had trained his dogs so that they would salivate whenever a bell rang. It came to me one day as I was walking home from school that I was being behaviorally conditioned in some way too.

Just as I would come around the last bend in the road I would be able to see our home from about a block away and my whole skeleton would turn to lead. My stomach would knot and coil. Sometimes my legs would start shaking and my heart would pound heavily. I would slow down and take my time covering that distance.

I realized that I had been having this reaction for some time. The dreaded last block before I walked into hell. If by some chance my stepfather's truck was visible, if he was home early, my dread would surge to full panic. It meant the punishments and dramas would be starting a bit sooner this evening.

During the dread walk I would steel myself. I would cloak my thoughts and build walls around my feelings. My face would turn to stone, eyes squinting into a penetrating stare, my voice came hard and cold. All my senses would come alive in anticipation of attack and I would dare not show any emotion or hint of my internal readiness as I walked back to the front lines of our domestic war with each other.

CHAPTER 3

RESISTANCE

I remember the day when I told my parents in front of all the other kids that I didn't believe in God anymore. Sarah's hand, carrying the fork to her mouth, froze midway and she stared at me and my stepfather put his food down. For several long moments there was total silence. Then my mother dismissed the other children from the table.

Tim was, at first, uncharacteristically quiet. He just sat there brooding under his storm-cloud eyebrows, stroking his curly brown beard with one hand and let my mother grab me, get in my face and yell at me until she was shaking and out of steam. Then he started in on me while Sarah sat there chain smoking her Benson and Hedges deluxe ultra-lights, muttering the Lord's Prayer under her breath, recovering from the first of many more rounds of bad cop-bad cop style interrogation that night.

They would put their face inches from mine, their spittle hitting me.

"So suddenly you don't believe in God?" Sarah accused.

"You think you are smarter than us now?" Tim demanded.

They glanced at each other questioningly and asked, "How did we not see this coming?" And gazing up at the ceiling they wailed, "Lord, where did we go wrong?"

I had just recently become more of a skeptic about some of the contents of the Bible on account of how much time I spent alone in my room with nothing to do but read science books and encyclopedias. I knew I was probably stepping into a minefield to bring such heresy to the dinner table but I could not have predicted their completely over-the-top reactions or the show they put on that night with their Inquisition.

At some point that year Sarah was at her wit's end. Therapy, church, tough love and punishment did not have the intended effect on me. Instead I became more distant and belligerent. Around then I had my last "quality" one-on-one time with my mother. She decided to take me on a field trip. Just me. I would have to miss school, but this time for an actually important and worthwhile reason besides being sick or being suspended.

Sarah drove me to Rhode Island to attend some kind of Catholic convention. We went to an impressively huge cathedral and participated in a day long mass that was done mostly in Latin. Sometime during the service and after communion Sarah led me to be blessed and prayed over by the priests and bishops. She desperately hoped this would drive the demons out of me. It failed.

At around the age of thirteen I became convinced that healthy normal parents did not act like mine and their children did not act like us. My survival instinct, my rage and indignation and sense of rightness finally overcame family loyalty and protectiveness. I went to my school guidance counselor to report my parents for child abuse.

It is a strange thing to plot against your own parents and attend secret meetings with adults. To think in terms of exposing them and opening up the family business to the scrutiny of outsiders. For me the bond of family loyalty had been strained past the breaking point. I was very fortunate to have a sympathetic counselor who took the time to listen to me. I poured out my story, from the screaming fights between my parents to the whippings of the belt.

I explained, "Whatever love and closeness our family once had is long gone. We live in a state of siege against our parents and each other. I have had enough and I think it is time for a sane, intelligent adult to take an interest in what is going on inside our house."

"I am required to file a report with the local Child and Family Services." he said, "That report will most likely cause a social worker to investigate." That, of course, was what I wanted.

Sure enough, within a matter of weeks, a social worker from CFS was sent to my school to talk to me. She interviewed me in the guidance office and I commenced to pour the whole story out. I told her about the yelling, slapping, and being thrown around the house. I told her that I thought all of us kids were being abused by our parents.

The social worker's attitude then became grave. "Accusing your parents of child abuse," she informed me, "Is not something anybody is going to take lightly." This was serious business, getting a state agency involved in investigating a private home. "You have to be very sure of your allegations," she advised me, "Because once set in motion, the process will be served." But I had never been more serious. "My brothers and sister and I need help," I implored.

Shortly after that meeting, my parents received a notice by mail that a social worker would be stopping by to examine the house and interview the family in about a weeks time. We had never seen such a frenzy of industrious maintenance from our parents before.

Holes in the walls were repaired. Crucifixes were hung back up on the walls. Piles of laundry that had lain stagnant on the floor were washed, dried, and put away. The carpets were vacuumed, the linoleum floors were cleaned. All the broken toys, dog feces and debris scattered about the backyard were picked up and removed.

The other children were coached in what to say and in what not to say. You might think it curious that the investigating agency would give my parents advance notice. The only way the agency could perform a surprise inspection would be if there was evidence or reason to believe that one or more of the children were in imminent danger. Since none of us had burns, broken bones, or were malnourished, they had to do it by the book.

My stepfather had once been a social worker himself. When Tim struck us, he knew not to hit us with a closed fist, so there were no black eyes or split lips on our faces. His preferred method of attacking us was to batter us about the head and body with an open hand and then throw us into walls, furniture and other objects. The slaps would daze you, but it was falling into walls, the cast iron wood stove and other objects which did the most injury.

What damage occurred seemed entirely accidental. Everyone knows kids are always falling down and having accidents.

The social worker, Ms. Hafidi, came at her appointed time. She wore a business suit with a skirt and heels, her hair was severely pulled back in a bun. She walked around our house and took a look at the backyard and came back to my assembled family. She spoke with my parents. Ms. Hafidi interviewed each of the children separately. Everyone performed perfectly. My mother characteristically took the lead. She dissembled, deflected and denied.

The social workers findings? There was no abuse going on here. She saw us as the typical Christian, hardworking, all-American family. "You are so fortunate to live in such a model family," she assured me. Their masquerade as a loving and functioning family had worked.

It was kind of like in one of those slasher films, when one of the victims calls the police and tells them that there is someone in the house trying to kill her and when the cops show up they don't find anyone and then leave. Only to have the killer come out of the shadows moments later.

You feel betrayed by the ineffectiveness of the good guys but you also realize that the bad guys are too good at being bad. The foundation of a lifetime of cynicism was laid down that day. It was not the first time it had happened to me. It happened before with the kids at school who bullied me for being socially inept. But this was the first time it had been so serious and had such high stakes.

Ms. Hafidi went on to make recommendations to my parents, suggesting that I now needed counseling. There was concern that I would go to such lengths to make up things to get attention. All the adults involved believed that I was a liar. The social worker left, never to return, and I despaired.

The next day, after us kids had come home from school and my stepfather from work, my mother called a family meeting. Sarah explained to my siblings what all that preparation and theatre the day before had been all about. Namely, that I had tried to tear the family apart by telling lies and that I had done this because I no longer wanted to be in the family.

Sarah then declared that I was no longer part of the family. From now on, nobody was allowed to speak to me. From henceforth I was to be banished to my room. The only times I would be allowed out was for school, for the occasional weekend visits at my grandparents house to visit with my real Dad and if I absolutely needed to use the bathroom. Alice was tasked with bringing my meals to my room. If anybody was caught talking to me, the same thing would happen to them.

For a while the other kids stayed away, yet eventually, one-by-one, each of them would come and visit when they thought they could get away with it. They would knock softly and whisper to me through my door, "How are you doing?" Each time I told them, "I'm fine," and I forbade them from coming back, so that they could avoid what happened to me.

The thing is, this was not really punishment to me. It was a kind of relief. I wanted to be left alone and my parents were finally ignoring my existence. I no longer had to deal with my brothers and sister, so that stress was gone too. Nothing could be better than to come home from school and be allowed to read my books and listen to my music without any interference. I was finally able to think in peace and relative quiet. This punitive exile was working out entirely in my favor.

Over time the strictness of this banishment lessened as new circumstances led to more exceptions. For one thing, my parents finally found some affordable therapy for me in the next town over. They said it was my responsibility to go to my therapist appointments and they allowed me to use my bike to get there. So I had a two hour round trip bike commute twice a month and that was total physical and psychic freedom from the house.

Another issue that occurred was that our golden retriever was capable of opening two different locked doors in order to let herself out. Once escaped, Christy would raid all the neighbors garbage cans and make herself a nuisance. I knew the neighborhood and since I was the oldest and the fastest runner of all the kids, it was always my job to bring her back home. There was a learning curve and eventually that dog got better at opening the doors and ran away with greater frequency. Not that I blamed her in the slightest.

Usually we kids came home from school before either parent did. One day I arrived home in time to catch the dog trying to escape. I began to encourage our golden in her efforts as it gave me a reason to get out of the house. Eventually I simply began letting the dog out of the house deliberately.

She escaped quite a lot in those days. Especially once I hit upon the idea of simply timing the "escape" to occur shortly before my mother got home. I would leave a note on the table telling my mother that Christy had escaped again and I would be back as soon as I found her.

It became a game. I would give that dog a good head start only to find her waiting for me a short ways up the road. We would escape the madhouse together and go on walks through the neighborhood.

After a few months of this exile a couple friends that I hadn't seen in awhile began to show up asking for me and one day my mother relented. She came into my room in her usual manner of not bothering to knock or announce herself first, to tell me that someone had come to visit me and that I could hang out with them for awhile. But once they were gone it was back to my room.

Long after the failed investigation by Ms. Hafidi I wondered how I might exonerate myself. If I could get some kind of evidence, it would prove that I wasn't lying. It wasn't as though I had the resource (and the ability) to put spy cameras all over the place. Compact cell phones with video recording capability wouldn't be around for another twenty years. Nevertheless, I still had the stereo cassette-tape player with a built in microphone that I received for Christmas.

I hit upon the idea of recording the ambient sounds next time my parents decided to go off on me. It was somewhat hard to set up in advance, because as a result of my exile, I was no longer part of the daily drama. Consequently, the next person in line to be targeted by my parents wrath was my brother Byron. It wasn't long before his screams replaced my own. My parent's tag teamed on him, as they systematically tried to crush his will, physically and mentally.

So it was, that I was finally able to collect evidence, that both of my parents were rampant child abusers, by secretly tape recording an assault in progress. That recording eventually became known as *A Two Minute Glimpse Into Hell*. The recording features clearly audible sounds of impact as my stepfather strikes my brother, and his subsequent moaning.

At no time was I ever unaware that I was deliberately betraying my family privacy and loyalty by recording the secret truths about life in my home. Yet, I felt deep inside that I was more like a revolutionary freedom fighter. A resistance movement consisting of one. What was going on was reprehensible and I am as sure today as I was back then that I was right in documenting and exposing it.

* * *

As awful as it seems, to be ritually cast out of your family by your own mother, it really was not so bad. It was a vacation from the awfulness of being a participating member of my family. While I did spend long hours in isolation it actually helped me create my own identity.

It gave me time to think, to ponder, to contemplate deeply the important things, like questions about religion and philosophy, science and spirituality. It gave me time to read undisturbed and think about what I had read. In my isolation I read and reread all my books, dozens of them.

Every single day was self-directed study time. I was really quite fond of the current arrangement. As a result I was quietly becoming even more of my own person and increasingly a real stranger to my parents and their way of thinking. As time went by, I formulated my own thoughts and opinions about things and I found myself wishing I could debate my parents and challenge their views about life and the world as they knew it.

That year and the year before I had read hundreds of books. I read over a hundred of them in less than two months for the an-

nual Multiple Sclerosis Read-a-thon and won an outstanding
achievement award from school for it. That was far, far more
books than I had ever seen Sarah or Tim read on their own combined while I was growing up.

I never did get a chance to challenge my parents and debate
them. Family life as I knew it was soon to change forever. The
plan for summer of '88 had been to spend a few weeks instead of
the odd weekend at my grandparent's house. This would coincide
with my father Andrew's arrival and visit from his home in Hong
Kong. I'll never forget when my father asked me, completely unexpectedly, "So, what would you think about going to Hong Kong
and staying at my place for awhile?"

"No way. Are you serious?" I replied, disbelieving. "Because if
you are serious, I'd love to go."

To which he replied, "Well good, because you're going to
Hong Kong." I'm sure I must have shrieked to hear my good fortune. He went on, "It took a bit of doing, but I convinced your
mother to let you go for the summer."

It was my first time in a 747 airliner on a transoceanic flight. I
vividly remember our plane coming in at night and the city was
like a jewel of neon lights. All that light reflected off of dark wa-
ters as we flew over ferries, floating restaurants, and long
container ships, all slowly moving in and out of Hong Kong har-
bor. There were skyscrapers everywhere you looked. Many were
adorned with colorful and brightly illuminated corporate logos
immediately recognizable in the air from a distance, like Kodak,
Sony and Coke. Most were in Chinese and what they might mean
presented a tantalizing mystery to my excited gaze.

To go from a small town in an area known for its concentration of conservative Christian and Caucasian people to a place
with a completely foreign language, an alien culture, and different
religions, was intensely educational. I got to see Buddhist temples
and I learned about Taoism and Hinduism. It was there that I first
saw tai chi being performed and it was something thousands of
people did outdoors as a totally normal morning exercise. People
did tai chi while waiting for the bus. To my young eyes it looked
like silent prayer performed with your whole body. I was power-

fully magnetized by tai chi. It spoke deeply to me on some level and I knew that somehow, someday, I had to learn it.

My father made it clear that while he had no problem fronting the expenses, if I wanted to play tourist and go shopping in the extensive indoor and outdoor malls, then I would have to earn my own shopping money. To that end, Andrew, who was the managing director of a semiconductor plant at the time, put me to work with some of his technicians who taught me how to assemble test products for his company. I punched in and out with a time card printed mostly in Chinese and I took my breaks in the break room with the other rank and file employees.

To top that off, Andrew taught me how to use the subway and bus system, with the expectation that I was going to be able to go home from work at his plant in Kowloon to his apartment on Hong Kong Island by myself. It was scary the first time but I handled it no problem and I never got lost on the first or subsequent trips.

Not too bad for a thirteen-year-old the first time out in a foreign country. I grew up in many ways as a result of that trip. I can never forget it and I have always been grateful to my father for bringing me out there so I could have a prolonged experience of life in a previously unknown country and culture. It broadened my horizons and lifted many scales from my eyes.

* * *

My aunt Myra had finally dropped me off back home with just a day or two to spare before school started, thus ending the wildest summer of my teenage life. A summer that saw me spending about ten of twelve weeks away from home. As soon as I stepped inside the house, I sensed something was wrong. The house seemed different and at first glance I couldn't figure it out. When you have lived in a place for so long, certain things seem permanent. Then it hit me. About half of everything was missing.

I sleuthed around the house quietly, letting my eyes report back all the nuances, trying to piece together the puzzle here. Like a detective trying to analyze a crime scene. Slowly, realization dawned. My mother was gone and she had taken just about every-thing she owned with her. In addition, it also appeared as though Sarah had taken my younger brother and sister with her too. There was no one home when I came in.

I looked around to see if perhaps my mother had left me a note explaining what had happened, but nothing. Something major had come to a head and a breaking point had been reached.

My mother had abandoned the household and broken up our family of eleven years. She had taken with her the two children that she had with Tim, leaving me and my brother to deal with our stepfather by ourselves even though he had no legal or guardian rights over us whatsoever.

My grandparents had gone away for the Labor Day weekend. The only relative I could contact, my aunt Myra, had just left here twenty minutes ago and I knew she wouldn't be near a phone for awhile. Eventually I did contact her and informed her of the cur-rent situation. I also had only a day or two before school started and I still needed some supplies and clothing.

The next day she came back down to pick me up and take me school shopping, a responsibility which should rightly fall upon either of my parents. As aunt Myra dropped me off back home for the second time in as many days, she told me, "If things get out of hand or dangerous, call me or your grandparents up, and one of us will come and get you."

As I roamed the partially empty house, I analyzed my feelings about the whole thing. Technically, no one had ever told me that my exile was over. It was my mother who had initiated my banishment and it was fear of my mother that kept the excommunication going. With Sarah now gone I considered her policies null and void. In fact, the lack of her presence made the aura of the place a bit lighter. As though a vortex of darkness had gone away.

To be honest, it was a great relief to have her gone. It seemed I could breathe easier. It was also a bit of a relief to have my younger siblings gone as well. I was no longer responsible for them and no longer had to role model for them. It was no longer possible for them to try to get me into trouble. Nor could I be blamed for their actions and that was a burden off my shoulders as well.

Sarah was gone, and good riddance I thought to myself. We'd been held hostage to her emotional states and her irrational, screaming hysterias for so long, it was hard to imagine the house being quiet. While it seemed far too small for a six person family, it was possible that there was now just enough room in this dwelling for the three of us that remained.

It wasn't until late in the evening of the next day, that Byron and my stepfather finally came home. For the most part, Tim and I avoided each other. I was just as happy keeping to my room as I'd been doing for months.

When I noticed that chores weren't getting done, I found myself doing work around the house voluntarily. I took over the care and feeding of our dogs and in the process they became my dogs. The golden retriever and the German shepherd both came to sleep in my room at night. Because my stepfather often kept my brother with him during non-school hours, on those evenings and weekends when my stepfather stayed at his new girlfriend's home, it was just me and the dogs, guarding our house.

In some ways, the school year from age thirteen to fourteen was the most turbulent of all my teenage years. My trip to Hong Kong and the subsequent partial dissolution of my family combined with the weight of responsibility changed me, and I could barely relate to kids my own age anymore. So I hung out with older kids instead.

Tim explained the new rules to me. I had a copy of the house key and unless the weather was inhospitable I was to be outside any time he wasn't home. He didn't really care what I was doing, so long as I was not in the house or getting into trouble with the law. Unless it was raining or snowing or dark out, if his delivery truck wasn't home, then I was not allowed to be inside.

That may sound harsh, however, like with my mother's banishment directive, it was actually not so bad. It worked in my favor because now I had tons of unsupervised time with full permission, I just couldn't spend it in the house. I could do anything I wanted.

I spent more time with my friends during that year than any other year that I can remember.

I had discovered the fun of role-playing games and most of my older friends played them, including the now ubiquitous and well known Dungeons and Dragons franchise. I didn't even have a specific curfew. Sometimes my stepfather came home really late or not at all. On those days I could stay out if I wanted or I could come home, provided it was dark. On weekends, as soon as I was up I had to leave the house and go hang out with my friends.

I got used to the new routine quickly. The change from being so limited, overprotected, a virtual prisoner in my room to having no structure at all was incredibly liberating. It almost seemed like some kind of test. I was on my own, responsible for getting myself up and to school. I had my chores I'd always hated doing. Now I was the only one doing chores at all. No one was even home while I was doing them usually.

When I talk about our standard of living back then, I don't mean to exaggerate our household economic conditions. We were certainly not dirt-poor or in abject poverty. There was always enough money to have lived in better conditions with a higher rate of consumption than what we had.

My biological father, Andrew, was court ordered to send child support payments for my brother and I. These checks could have paid for better clothes that didn't fall apart. It could have allowed the entire family to eat something other than macaroni, hot dogs and peas for dinner all the time. The money could have paid for a proper shower installation or for a laundry machine that actually worked most of the time. It should have gone into dentist visits, which we never had.

Instead we had coupon clipping parties and consumed endless bowls of tasteless puffed wheat cereal for breakfast and bologna sandwiches on crumbly white bread for lunch, practically every day, for years. Because we were all slaves to my mother's dream home. An idyllic fantasy of a cottage nestled in the woods with the white picket fence and dogs playing out front.

After failing for weeks to find a plot of land that was affordable, my parents decided to pray and use faith in God to find a place to build my mother's fantasy house. They closed their eyes, and, hand in hand, moved a pen in circles over a state map like it was a Ouija board. Then they stopped and the place where the pen stopped was apparently where God had decided for us to have a home.

Marlborough is a rustic little town in the middle of Cheshire County, a heavily forested area in the scenic Monadnock region in southern New Hampshire. Deeply rutted dirt roads wind through the forests around Marlborough and it was somewhere along one called Stone Pond Road that the pen had stopped. As luck would have it, land was for sale and my parents bought a small plot there.

My mother christened our homestead "Maranatha," an Aramaic phrase which means "the Lord has come," in a hand-painted wooden sign she nailed to the trunk of a tree in letters large enough to make out from the road. The cost of simply preparing the lot for a house was prohibitive and my parents forced us kids to spend several summers clearing brush, trees, deadwood and boulders, while the black flies, mosquitoes and horse flies ate us alive. I remember excavating the pit for the outhouse and building the stone retainer walls around the hill that our home was built on.

Next came the drilling of the artesian well. It was expensive to drill through bedrock. They ended up drilling far deeper than was originally estimated to get to the water. There wasn't enough money to pay for the expensive pumping system we needed to have installed to bring the resource up. Consequently, we never had running water in the house and had to walk a half mile to Stone Pond to fill up gallon jugs with water to bathe and cook with.

I found out later that much of the building of the house relied on the child support payments that my brother and I never received benefit from. I remember my stepfather arguing with my mother over money and how they couldn't afford to install the roof until "Dingbat's check" comes in. At some point I figured out that *Dingbat* was my real Dad and *Dingbat's check* was our child support payment.

Over the years, until our family broke up, we spent several summer months and holiday vacations living in that house without

a bathroom, shower, or toilet. In leaving Tim, my mother abandoned her unfinished dream home that had so sabotaged our cost
of living, hijacked our child support money and stole our summers
playtime with endless manual work projects.

From what I understand, that house and property became a
huge financial burden to my stepfather and he couldn't sell it for
many years afterward. The property tax alone gnawed away at his
finances for a long time. Proof, perhaps, of some kind of karma in
the world?

The drama didn't end with Sarah's disappearance. It did lessen
considerably, as she had been the prime mover of the daily punishments routine. She was no longer around to give Tim the
laundry list of all the heinous sins we had committed. As a result
there was no reason to start the rituals of meting out punishments
for all. He would come home later than ever before, and watch
sports on TV until he fell asleep on the couch. As long as no one
was interacting with another there was an uneasy but much needed
peace to the house. It was those interactions which always spoiled
the truce. It would go something like this:

I would come home and find something missing in my room,
like one of my music tapes. Given the unlikelihood that my stepfather would've taken it, the only possible candidate was my
brother. It was one thing to have my parents, who had no respect
for my space, go through my room taking or destroying whatever
they felt like. They were a juggernaut, the unstoppable parents.
But to have my own brother going through my stuff was intolerable. Since he had no respect for my space I had none for his. In a
fury I would burst into his room and start searching it. Sooner or
later not only did I find what I was looking for, but also several
other things that he had taken.

Fuming, I waited for my brother to get home. Then I would
commence to replay the same kind of confrontation that I learned
to model from Tim and Sarah over the years. I would ask him if he
knew where a certain item was. He'd deny any knowledge of that
item. Then I would produce that item and demand to know why it
was that I had found it in his room along with all these other
items.

At which point, no explanation from him would be sufficient. I would interrupt whatever he was saying and just commence hitting him. I would threaten to attack him again if he took my stuff or if he complained about the beating I just gave him. It was unfortunate, but we were seemingly destined to repeat that ritual time and time again.

* * *

The trip to Hong Kong had emboldened me in many ways. After seeing tai chi chuan in Hong Kong, a seed of obsession about learning the martial arts had been planted deep inside me. There was no way my stepfather would pay to let me take self-defense classes. I had asked a couple years earlier and when my parents asked me why I wanted to take karate classes I told them it was so I could fight back when I was bullied by groups of kids. Needless to say, learning to fight was against their fanatical "turn the other cheek" policy they had tried (unsuccessfully) to program into me.

Spending so much of my time alone and unsupervised, I decided that I would learn martial arts any way I could. The first book on self-defense that I ever owned was called *Stand Firm* and I stole it from the school library. It had instructions and pictures and some basic drills. At home, in my bedroom, I secretly began trying to learn self-defense, and that is when I gained the ability to train myself without peer support and encouragement. I was deeply motivated to learn to stick up for myself and fend off attack at home and at school.

I had a new crowd of friends. Kids in their late teens, some in their early twenties. When they found out that I wanted to learn martial arts, a couple of them took time out to teach me things that they knew. Some of my friends had parents that did pay for their karate or taekwondo lessons. Some of them had been to basic training in the Army. Others were successful in brawling at school or on the street. Whatever their experience, they took some time to teach me different things and to encourage me and we sparred together.

As soon as I began to exude awareness and confidence, the harassment and bullying at school stopped. It also helped that word had spread, that I was hanging out with kids from high school, many of whom were older siblings to the kids in my grade level.

All of this new confidence, some physical prowess, training in the martial arts, a clique of older friends and constant, unsupervised autonomy helped build up my ego. I was no longer willing to tolerate any form of nonsense or disrespect from Byron and I was beginning to stand up to Tim. For that matter I was no longer taking crap from students or teachers at school either. It was because of this new chip on my shoulder that the less frequent physical altercations with my stepfather became more violent and prolonged when they occurred.

My brother usually kept his mouth shut after one of those confrontations over respecting bedroom sovereignty. What got us into trouble was if our confrontation became loud enough to alarm my stepfather's ancient and hunchbacked mother who lived alone upstairs. If Nana heard a ruckus she would tell him about it. When that happened, Tim would fly into a rage upon coming home from work, bursting through the door and slamming everything in sight.

His screaming rants would go something like this, "So I hear you two like fighting, huh? You want to hurt each other? Well how do you like this? (Slap-strike-slam!) And this? (Smash-slam-strike!) How do you like fighting now? (Slam-slap-smash!) You like that?" He would go to me, rinse and repeat, then go to my brother, rinse and repeat. I doubt we ever went past two weeks of peace before there was a confrontation between some combination of the three of us.

I was just as happy either in my bedroom listening to music loudly or being out with my older friends, driving around, playing RPGs and even going to parties and concerts occasionally. Once I was outside, there was no parental supervision of any kind and no parent, no adult, had any idea of what I was doing on an hourly or daily basis. For months and months I did what I wanted, when I wanted to.

Late one evening I was deliberately mouthing off to my stepfather, standing up for myself. He came running after me, burst into my unlit room and started throwing me around, battering me into furniture.

At the side of my desk there was a stack of mirror tiles, some of them broken and irregularly shaped. Tim pushed me backwards into the stack and in the darkness jagged slivers of mirror tile pushed into my lower back and kidneys, and I felt a warning pain. My blue denim jacket with its thick heavy-metal rock band logo patches sewn all over it had provided just enough armor to prevent a puncture.

In that instant, as I felt the searching shards of glass pressing into my back, my last shred of loyalty to my stepfather and to the notion of family was destroyed. I knew he had no idea of the danger that I was in. And I realized that this most certainly was not even close to punishment for my own good, this was battery. This was assault for his own ego, to make himself feel better and in control.

My absent mother sure as hell wasn't going to save me from daddy. There was no guardian angels or spirits, no superheroes on their way to save me. This was not metered justice; this was an attack and I was in danger. In that moment I absolutely, profoundly understood that the only person I can ever truly believe in and count on to save me was me.

In a burst of adrenaline I pushed him back enough to get clear of the tiles. Tim paused for a moment to regain his footing, and breathing heavily he inquired, "Have you had enough yet?" I could see him fairly well, my eyes had already gotten used to the dark. I turned my body slightly away from him and lowered my head and eyes.

In the primate world this was a gesture of submission. I did it deliberately to lure him into thinking just that and also to conceal that I was winding up. I summoned up all the years of wrath and helplessness. I channeled all my suppressed anger into my fist and I punched him, with perfect precision, right in the sweet spot, on the top of the heart but below the diaphragm.

He forcefully expelled air with a whoosh! His facial expression was hard to make out clearly but his eyes were wide with disbelief. He staggered back, then fell to the floor. The bedroom door's hinges were weakened from repeated slamming over the years. Tim took the door completely off the hinges and it fell with him onto the floor.

I advanced forward in a martial arts-like stance and looked down at him for a long moment, ready for anything or to press my advantage. He just sat there, legs akimbo, hands by his sides, wheezing, trying to catch his breath but unable to. In the slanting light coming in from the next room I could now see that his whole face was a mask of shock and amazement, and I smiled.

I stepped back away from him, into the shadows of my room and turned my back on him as a sign that he was no longer a threat to me. Finally I heard him get up and as he did I called out softly, "Don't ever touch me again."

"You are a lost cause," I heard Tim mutter back as he walked out. "I give up, there is no more hope for you."

That was the first time I had ever decisively won a fight in my life. The kids at school were not scary to me after that. This explosive, hateful strike, aimed to the most vulnerable places, became my trademark answer to an escalating confrontation. I began using it on kids at school that tried to mess with me.

Whenever I got angry, the hate would flow like lightning through my limbs and I would slam desks, walls and doors. It had felt great to give in to my anger and hit my stepfather with everything I had. I would intercept the detention letters from school in the mail, burn the notices in the fireplace, show up at detention on time and repeat when necessary. I accepted the consequences, such as they were, in the event that I got caught or ratted out in the ever increasing number of provoked assaults that I got involved in. Serving detention for fighting was a kind of badge of honor compared to the stigma of being seen being picked on and helpless.

I learned from my social mistakes and adapted. I sat at the back of the classroom with the miscreants and underachievers. I turned in my test papers with the others when the end period bell rang. I never did homework anymore, which dropped me down to a "C" student. I developed a reputation for being crazy as I would go off on students and faculty alike. Sometimes my acting out resulted in hijacking long minutes in a given class, posturing and threatening a teacher that was giving me direction. Oddly enough this actually made me more "cool" in the eyes of some students.

That's how my life was for awhile. I was always in the dark about all that was happening and couldn't tell if my parents were legally divorced yet. About once every three weeks the other two kids would come stay for the weekend. Some semblance of a routine arose from the aftermath of my mother's flight from home. Things were about as normal as they were ever going to get again. The holidays were strained that year and I spent them with my grandparents.

One day, as I was going through the remainder of my mother's personal effects, I spotted an abandoned black purse. Thinking to myself that it might have small bills or change at the bottom, I dug it out of the closet and rummaged through it. In addition to some coins, my fingers found a folded up letter.

The letter was addressed to a man named Dominic and the writing was in my mother's elegant cursive. In the letter she was trying to explain to Dominic, how his desire to watch porn videos made her feel uncomfortable when the two of them had sex. The letter went on at length, filled with Sarah's concern for the future of their ongoing tryst. This was solid gold. As I read that letter, I distinctly remember thinking to myself, "My life is a bad soap opera."

My mother. The same pious woman who took me with her to attend Third Order Franciscan prayer meetings and was so quick to urge us all to go to Confession. She was the same person who quit taking birth control pills, out of supposed "Catholic guilt," all those years ago. Sarah swore to us all that she would never divorce again, yet she was cheating on my stepfather. And judging by what I was reading, it had been going on for some time. Probably long before she fled the house.

Well, I knew right away what I was going to do with it. I read and reread it several times. Finally, I walked into my stepfather's room, unfolded the letter and placed it on his bed for him to encounter when he got home from work. Later Tim would tell me in passing, "I know you put that note on my bed like that to hurt me." He was right.

Winter went and spring came. Summer was fast approaching with a mere month left of my last year in junior high school. It was just an ordinary average day, the last day that I spent in that house. My brother and I were both home from school. As usual we were arguing and antagonizing each other over this and that. When my brother kicked my door, I used my new martial arts on him to open him up and I struck him again and again, forcing him to retreat to his room. We engaged in a shouting match and I told him he was weak and that there was nothing he could do to touch me that I could not stop him from doing.

The little son of a bitch says to me, "Except when you are asleep, then there's nothing you can do."

I cannot accurately transmit in text the level of darkness and wrath that swept over me when he said that. My little punk brother knew some of the same ambush tricks I knew and it was only a matter of who was going to get whom first. There was no way I was going to live in fear of my younger brother killing me in my sleep. Not after winning against my stepfather and bullying back at kids at school.

I did not take this as a joke or posturing on his part and I flew at him in a rage. It was just us two down here and that's what I would tell the cops. It was the truth. So I began to systemically beat him. I quickly gained the upper hand and I mocked him as I punished him for daring to threaten me. Bit by bit Byron crawled from me, trying to get to the outside stair case in order to scream for help from Tim's elderly mother, Nana. I would let him crawl up a few stairs at a time before dragging him back down by his leg.

Nana finally heard the ruckus, opened her door and began shouting from the top of the stairs, "Stop hitting him!" Over and over she screeched, "You're crazy!" and "You're evil!"

I roared back up at her, "I am evil!" Despite her demands I began kicking him in the head. His murderous thoughts came from his brain and I was not going to stop until he was no longer capable of thinking those thoughts. All the years of repressed anger at him came out then.

This was for all those times you went into my room when I was not home.

This was for all the times you lied and got me in trouble with our parents.

This was for stealing my stuff and on and on as I kept hitting him.

He wasn't just being punished for being my bratty, competitive younger brother, but for everyone else in the family too, and for the kids at school who had hurt me when I had been a weak and easy target. It was not Nana's threats to call my stepfather at work or the police that stopped me. It was the sudden and instant recognition of my behavior as being the same as my parents'. I had become exactly like them. I was putting down my brother for defiance in the same way that my parents had done to me. That was what brought me to my senses and caused me to stop. As I stepped back away from him and walked down the staircase, Nana yelled after me, "You are not to spend another night here. Do you hear me? I am telling Tim when he gets home. You are too dangerous and I want you out of this house!"

I knew that there would be serious drama when my stepfather got home. Amidst the ongoing threats to my safety from both brother and stepfather, I knew I couldn't stay here any more and I called up my aunt Myra. The first thing I said was, "Do you remember last summer, when I said that one day all hell might break loose and that I might need emergency extraction?"

"I remember," she replied.

"Well it just happened ten minutes ago and it is going to get worse when my stepdad comes home. This is it, the balloon has gone up." Just like that, she was on her way down.

School ended early that year. I went to live with my grandparents. At first, things were much improved. It did not last. Once I left the house I grew up in, my life spiraled out of control. I never really regained the same level of control that I had at this point until I was a legal adult.

By summer's end of '88 I had returned from a glorious vacation in Hong Kong to a broken family. Within a years time I would be locked down in a psychiatric hospital and diagnosed with incurable mental illness.

CHAPTER 4

ANOTHER BRICK IN THE WALL

The first couple of weeks living with my grandparents were great. I was on my best behavior and they treated me like a guest. It was a welcome change from being treated like crap or ignored all the time.

The grounds here were far more upscale than what I had grown up with. Everything inside the house was clean and well organized. Their home had been remodeled several times over the years. There were new devices and appliances and furniture wherever you looked.

When I moved in, my new hosts had to be made aware of certain reactions that I had. The first time my grandmother put her hand on me when I was in a deep sleep, my survival instinct was triggered and before I was fully conscious and aware of where I was and who was touching me, my right hand had snaked out from under my bed covers and grabbed her by the throat.

For her own safety I recommended she never touch me and to knock softly before entering. It would be best if they did not come into my room at all when I was sleeping. (I slept with my hand on a knife under my pillow and that was not something I wanted them to know because I was certain they wouldn't understand and they'd be worried.)

My grandparents adapted. If they wanted to wake me up, they would knock on my door and call my name. If they knocked too sharply or called out my name loudly, it caused me to leap out of bed screaming, adrenaline pumping, pulse pounding and shaking. The years of living with my rageaholic parents and the bullying from school had screwed up my fight or flight reflexes badly.

Soon enough the newness wore off. Trouble started with their nagging and assigning me chores. My grandparents had been living for years by themselves, taking care of things around the house just fine. I asked myself: Why is it that, now that I live here, they can no longer empty the kitchen trash or vacuum the house?

They offered me an allowance and that helped motivate me somewhat. An allowance was not enough to get to me to take those chores seriously. It wasn't possible for anyone to find the perfect incentive. I never gave chores a high level of attention back then, because my mind was going a million miles an hour and it was my ideas, imagination and memories which occupied much of my attention span. Besides, I wasn't their kid, who were they to tell me to do anything?

All my friends were now far away. I no longer had a gang of likeminded people to hang out with whenever I wanted. Calling one of my friends up back in the 1980s cost a prohibitive long distance charge. I once rang up an enormous phone bill, trying to stay in touch. When my grandmother got the bill in the mail, I had a lot of explaining to do and I was forbidden to call long distances again.

My grandparents lived in a quiet neighborhood. The neighbors to either side were all senior citizens. I didn't know where the cool kids hung out and what the delinquent kids did in the area to alleviate boredom. I didn't know anyone my own age for miles in every direction.

I enjoyed some perks while I lived with my grandparents.

They were a thousand times more permissive than my parents had been.

They let me watch anything I wanted on TV.

They told me to help myself to whatever food I wanted if I was hungry.

I did not have a bed time, just a midnight curfew.

On some level I was grateful for this, but it wasn't enough to pacify me. It was not enough to offset the mounting pressure from my grandparents. They were always criticizing me for every little thing.

"Could I please bring my laundry to the basement instead of letting it accumulate in my room?"

"Would I please use a coaster with my drink on the coffee table?"

"Would I turn down my music, they could hear it downstairs?"

"Could I take off my shoes instead of tracking across their white carpet?"

"Would I not set this down there, please?"

"Could I not do this, that and the other thing?"

In the Hell House, we'd had very few possessions of great value. We had grown accustomed to living with dirty, broken and neglected things. Compared to my grandparents middle-class sensibilities, I was practically feral. Details, details, all these little things that they wanted perfect. Always nagging me about some ridiculously insignificant thing that I couldn't possibly remember the next day. Which of course meant they were going to bug me about it again, sooner or later. It's frustrating to know you're going to be harassed again and that nothing you can do is ever good enough.

My grandparents wanted their entire two-story house to be perfectly clean every single day. It was laughable that they actually expected me to remember their list of dos and don'ts. Why should I even care? It wasn't like the world was going to end if I spilled something or broke something or set something down over there. Nevertheless, they wouldn't get off my back about it.

A simmering resentment for them began growing. I had enough anger and hate as it was and now this. Couldn't they perceive it was not wise to get me mad? None of my coping behaviors were satisfactory. I scared them when I slapped the walls or counters or furniture in imitation of my parents. My hard stares and generally hostile and uncooperative attitude in response to their attempts at communicating with me only made things worse.

All sorts of dysfunctional behaviors and neuroses began to resurface. The old patterns of paranoia and suspicion returned. I started taking notes of the precise locations of a variety of my personal belongings, and sure enough, I found evidence that my grandmother was periodically searching my room and going through my stuff when I wasn't around. I had beaten my brother into the floor for doing that to me.

At the next opportunity that presented itself, I searched the entire house, everything, from top to bottom. I went through my grandparents bedroom and closets. *You do that to me, I do that to you and see how you like it.*

I began to creep in the halls and stairways, positive I would catch them talking about me behind my back. As expected, my grandmother was complaining about me to unknown people on the phone, discussing the litany of horrors I gave them and debating what to "do" about me. Thankfully, I had tons of practice eavesdropping on my parents and it came in handy as I listened, fuming, to my grandmother's surreptitious complaints about me.

Things finally reached a head when my grandmother handed me the phone to speak with my father who was calling from overseas. He was low voiced and threatening and that was not how you started communicating with me back then unless you wanted major drama in your face.

"My folks are getting desperate with you." Apparently the stress was too much for them and I was going to give them both heart attacks. "Why do you persist in fucking with my mother and father, after everything they have done for you, taking you in and giving you good food and a nice place to live?" I didn't reply. "Have they ever laid an unkind hand on you?" he asked.

"No," I answered sullenly.

"Then I swear," he promised, "if you continue to hurt my parents, I will personally come back to the States and make you wish you'd never been born."

I had already been there and done that with my other parents. One parent had fled, the other I knocked on his ass. I tended to hold lasting grudges back then, so my respect for my real dad plummeted several notches for many years afterward. I tuned him out, seeing red, my knees wobbled from the adrenaline, my hands trembled from rage. Flashbacks from physical battle with Tim and Sarah, replayed in my mind. I had been delivered from my parents only to have the other side of my family turn on me too.

The foundation of deep cynicism that had been poured a year earlier just kept getting harder and harder as it cured. I learned that all I needed to do to trump any argument or confrontation was raise the stakes until the other party was convinced of their imminent danger.

Both my fathers resorted to this tactic. My mother had done it. My grandparents had used it indirectly by using my father as their proxy. You can control a person through the power of fear. I learned that lesson well, and effectively intimidated people as a result.

I retreated to my room for hours. I went out of my way to avoid interacting with my grandparents since I had no idea what I would say or do next and whether they would have an aneurysm as a result.

Even so, for awhile things smoothed over a bit. By the middle of the summer I had a job, working part-time as a dishwasher at a nursing home. I finally got into karate classes, rode my bike everywhere and swam at a local town pool. I had found ways to be busy and entertain myself. I had no complaints per se but my grandparents continued to nag me over the little things.

Towards the end of the summer, an entire string of events occurred which destabilized things further.

First, my grandparents discovered all sorts of their property outdoors that I had damaged after storming out of the house in a rage.

Then they found my stockpile of knives and weapons and naturally had no clue why I had them.

Finally, my grandmother caught me losing my virginity in my bedroom with someone I was dating from work.

The rounds of criticisms and recriminations resumed.

"Why do you spend so much time in your room?"

For that matter, "Why do you always keep your room so dark?"

"Why are you carrying knives all the time?"

"What in God's name is the matter with you?"

"What are you thinking?"

"Hey, are you even listening?"

I couldn't tell which made them more uncomfortable: that I wore all black, carried weapons and slept in until noon every day or that I'd been having sex in my room with someone. The sex thing really disturbed both of them and I could not fathom why.

Losing my virginity was inevitable. It had to happen sooner or later. My bedroom was the safest, cleanest and most obvious place. I wasn't old enough to own a car with a backseat for that sort of thing. Where did they expect me to do it?

The next mistake they made in dealing with me was to demand that I go to church with them. Sunday was the only day of the week that neither of my grandparents would be home. They no longer trusted me in the house alone and they thought that going to church would be good for me. Attending was not an option and if I refused to go with them it was made clear to me that it would be the "last straw." That didn't sit well with me at all.

What they didn't know was that God and I had a kind of messy divorce going on. They were not aware that I had once sat doing devotionals for hours by myself as a child. They had no idea that I was once a member of the Third Order of Franciscans. They didn't know that I had once been an all-star bible studies student.

They certainly could not have been aware that I had prayed to God, every day and every night for years, trying to get God to make my parents stop fighting each other.

I had prayed that God would save us kids when my parents began turning their aggression on us.

I had begged for him to stop the mean kids at school that had bullied me. None of my prayers were ever answered.

My family broke up. My parents divorced. It wasn't until I took matters into my own hands – by learning to fight and becoming a bully myself – that I stopped being targeted at school for harassment.

The next Sunday mass was the first I'd been to in years, since I had walked away from my church devotions at the age of eleven or twelve. I remember it as one of the most grueling hours I had ever endured in all my life.

Listening to so many people praying to God made me sneer with derision and disgust. Listening to the sermons had my stomach in knots. I twisted the words of the prayers I once had known by rote. I changed every instance of the word "God" into "Satan" and every instance of "Holy Spirit" into "The Devil."

I muttered my prayers to Satan to deliver me from this. I began staring at the pictures of the saints on the stained glass window and imagined every window in the church exploding. I would stand and sit according to the liturgical missal but I refused to kneel and there was no way my grandparents failed to notice that detail.

My body was so agitated, so hot, I thought I would burst into flames. I was sweating with barely suppressed rage as I muttered my twisted prayers to Satan and tried to avoid eye contact with anyone. Surely God must be offended that I was here. Something had to happen when you prayed to the devil while inside a church. Maybe the priest would start speaking backwards or the giant crucifix behind the altar would spontaneously ignite. I kept looking around for signs of angelic or demonic presence. Nothing was happening.

Somehow that infuriated me even more. One would think that if you tried to summon Satan into God's house during a Mass there would be some kind of fantastic special effects display from one or the other, but alas, nothing supernatural happened. I had only contempt for my grandparents for forcing me to come to church. How could all these people in attendance, my grandparents included, make it into adult age and still believe that there was a higher power listening to their prayers?

As the rage gradually subsided, it left me physically drained, yet restless. The dark depression that compels you to fantasize about and dwell on intricately detailed self-harm scenarios had rooted into my being a long time ago. It was incidents like the one I just described that brought it back full bore.

I was sick and tired of never being able to satisfy my grandparents. I was guilty with the knowledge that I had helped destroy my family and I knew that somehow I was destroying my grandparents too. It looked like I was probably going to get into a physical altercation the next time I saw my father. Family war was starting all over again.

No one is on your side. Face it. You are alone.

Maybe I was some kind of monster, just like everyone said. Maybe there really was no hope for me. It was obvious that no matter who my parents were, I could never do anything right by them. People simply could not leave me alone and let me be myself. What was the point of even waking up when every day is a struggle?

The struggle will never end, you know that. And you know what to do.

My grandmother was chain smoking now because of me. My own mother had blamed her inability to quit smoking on how much I stressed her out. I was the source of everyone else's problems. It was clear that the world would be a better place without me. Things could only keep getting worse, they never got better for long.

The more time I spent dwelling on all this, the more simple, logical and obvious the solution seemed.

The only way I could ever stop hurting people, or being hurt by people was to kill myself.

If you take yourself out of the equation, you solve your problems and theirs.

My grandparents owned firearms and I knew where they were located. At any time I could have used one, but I did not. There were a couple reasons why I didn't. Ironically, one of the reasons was because I didn't want to traumatize my grandparents. Additionally, handguns already had a bad reputation in connection with suicide. I visualized a scene where my grandmother came into my bedroom only to see blood and brain sprayed over the walls. I knew they would probably never get over it, in the years they had left to them. I knew that they would probably blame themselves for leaving loaded handguns accessible to a troubled teenager. Mostly, I wanted to die in peace. I wanted to have some grace on my way out. I wanted the spiritual pain to end. I had always envisioned that an overdose would just put you to sleep. I didn't want to inconvenience anyone anymore.

I didn't know which of the many different kinds of drugs that were in the house would be the most fatal. They all had warnings about overdoses on them. I rummaged through my grandparents endless bottles of pills, taking a few of these and a few of those. To this day I don't remember what I took. I did not want to take too many from one particular bottle so as to not short supply them of a needed medication.

As far as overdoses go, this one was weak but it was no mere gesture. I genuinely believed that the warnings on the packages were accurate. In my naiveté I thought this stuff would really kill me. I only took twenty or thirty pills. It seemed like a daunting number to swallow at the time. To make it less formidable, I crushed them up into a giant pile of powder and poured it into a glass of milk.

Before the ordeal I made certain preparations. I cleaned my room and put away all my things. I wrote my first suicide note. I had dinner with my grandparents and pretended everything was fine. If I seemed less talkative than usual, they didn't mention it. What was there to say? All I could think of was that I would not be alive by this time the next day. I was caught up wondering what the aftermath would be like in the house.

Then I went back upstairs to listen to music and brood until I was ready. While I was dwelling on what Hell might be like, I remembered a commercial about suicide prevention from TV. It was called "The Nine Line." *When you feel like ending it all, call 1-800 and keep on dialing nine.*

On impulse I called the number. I wanted to tell someone candidly and without self-censure that I planned to kill myself and listen to what they would say. I guess I had hoped the person on the other end of the line would be an older person, preferably female, but the voice was a young man's. I cannot forget what a completely unsympathetic and condescending asshole he was.

As soon as I told him that I wanted to kill myself, the tone of his voice changed from conciliatory to patronizing. I wondered whether his strategies for talking me down were his own or something he was reading from some kind of scripted formula.

Within seconds he terminally pissed me off. He told me, suicide was a cowards way out. He inquired as to whether or not it had occurred to me that what I was going to do was extremely selfish. What this complete idiot didn't realize was that I fully understood and identified with being selfish.

For years, hardly a week had gone by without either parent constantly reminding me that I was the most selfish child in the world. I knew that already. Of course this was selfish! This was entirely about me and my wants and of course I was thinking only about myself! He wasn't finished though.

"Has it ever occurred to you that you are going to hurt your family?" he asked earnestly. "Don't you care how they are going to feel?" He was dead serious. I didn't know whether to laugh or scream. I began insulting him in short bursts of unbridled fury. I cursed him roundly with the most colorful profanity I knew at that age. I was so irate I could barely speak intelligibly.

Bitterly, I informed him, "It is because of my family that I am planning to kill myself. It is my intention to hurt them as much as myself. They are supposed to feel guilty, it's part of the plan!" They were supposed to wonder where they went wrong and what they could've done to make me feel like I was wanted, valued, loved.

I followed that with, "You have no idea what you are doing. No way anyone could understand me, not even the person at the end of a suicide prevention hot-line. You failed to stop a suicide this evening. Thank you for making the choice that much clearer." I hurled more profanity at him before hanging up. Way to go slick.

My next phone call was to a priest. At the time I had only been a heretic for a little over a year or two. Now, faced with death, my newfound skepticism was not enough to overcome all the years of belief. I needed to cover all my bases, just in case I was wrong. Pascal's Wager I believe it is called.

I asked the priest, "Do you really believe in Heaven?" "I do," he replied. I asked him if he really believed that even a murderer could go to Heaven if he or she truly asked for forgiveness. And he said something like, "If you are willing to put yourself in God's mercy, all things are possible." So I asked him to hear my Confession and to give me the Last Rites.

He realized to some extent what was going on. I told him that it was futile to try to talk me out of it. I had made up my mind and there was nothing that he could possibly say to me that would make me reconsider. Could he please just give me the sacraments so I could rest in peace? And he did.

After I got off the phone with him, I sat on my bed, collecting my thoughts for awhile, listening to "Brain Damage" and "Eclipse" from Pink Floyd's *The Dark Side of the Moon*. There seemed no point in procrastinating further. I thought about my grandparents downstairs and how they had no idea what they were doing to me. I wondered which one of them would find me first.

I took my glass of milk, stirred up the pill sediment from the bottom and drank it down as fast as I could. Then I stretched out on my bed, laced my fingers over my breast, closed my eyes and waited for death to come. I was so tired of my existence and the futility of it all. It was an incredible relief to know that it was all going to be over soon. As I closed my eyes, my body finally seemed to unwind from its state of perpetual tension, knowing that it all was over now.

When I woke up it was past noon. I didn't understand how I was still alive. Strangely, I felt quite peaceful and rested. I went downstairs and found my grandmother seated at the table and smoking cigarettes. I had barely been up for a few minutes when she started haranguing me about something.

I interrupted her in mid-spiel. I don't remember exactly what I said but it was something along the lines of, "You sit here, judging and criticizing me. What would you do if I was gone? What would you do if I wasn't here anymore? You don't care about me and how I feel. You'd probably be happy if I was dead."

She responded with a growing look of puzzlement, "What? What do you mean? What are you talking about?"

"I mean," I began levelly, "that I shouldn't even be here right now, I almost died last night and you just sit here, telling me about how unthoughtful I am."

"What?" she exclaimed incredulously.

"Last night I tried to kill myself with an overdose. You sit here nagging and criticizing me with your trivial concerns and you don't even know or seem to care that I should be dead right now."

"What are you talking about?" she demanded.

"If you go to my room upstairs," I answered evenly, "You will find a glass with the residue of all the pills I took last night."

She stabbed out her cigarette in the ashtray and left the room. When she came back downstairs she had the glass with its bluish-white sediment of pills crusted at the bottom. Then she was on the phone talking in urgent tones with whomever was on the other end. Good. Maybe she would think twice about bothering me now.

Back at the table, I noticed right away that her attitude had changed into something I had seen before. It was the "I've thrown up my hands in despair because I am all out of ideas as to what to do with you" attitude. Sure enough, the first thing out of her mouth was, "I don't know what to do with you."

Why is it that parents are always driven to do something about you?

I'd heard this before from my own mother.

I was enough to drive you crazy.

I was enough to drive you to drink.

I was enough to give you a nervous breakdown.

Hearing this come from another person, knowing I had caused it, just proved everyone's point about how awful I was.

She asked me if I would go to counseling if they set it up. I told her it was a waste of time, I'd already been to several counselors before. My attitude and outlook on life had simply continued to worsen as time went on. Then it was I who suggested that maybe I belonged in an insane asylum because that's where crazy people are put.

My grandmother even agreed with me about the asylum being helpful. She voiced the opinion that it was clear that I had a lot of problems. She suggested, "Perhaps that it is for the best." Maybe the doctors would be better able to help me. "Things have to change," she told me, "Because I can't cope with this situation anymore." An echo of the same things my mother used to tell me.

The next day she took me to a family psychologist. We talked for a while. He asked me about some of the concerns that my grandmother had told him.

"Did you really try to kill yourself the other night?" - *Yes.*

"Would you consider yourself depressed?" - *Yes.*

"Can you think of a particular reason why?" - *No. It was more like everything, life itself was depressing.*

"Is there anything anyone could do to help?" - *No. There was nothing anyone could do to help me.*

"Is it possible that you would attempt suicide again?" - *Yes.*

He took down his notes and sifted through files. While he made various phone calls, I scanned his bookshelves and looked at all the titles in the event that he had something interesting about psychology. Then I spotted a book called the **Diagnostic and Statistical Manual III**. I asked him in between phone calls if he would mind if I looked at it. He said, "Help yourself."

First thing I did was scan the table of contents looking at all the various names of the mental disorders. I was surprised to see so many sex related disorders. Skimming those entries superficially was entertaining for a few minutes.

It was the behavioral, mood and thought disorders which fascinated me the most. When he got off the phone he asked me, "Did you figure out your problem yet?" I told him, "According to this book, I have at least two or three dozen mental disorders." He chuckled knowingly and told me that they warn you about that in psychology courses.

The symptoms under the heading of Post Traumatic Stress Disorder had me riveted. Never before had I seen my own behaviors laid out in such clear clinical terminology. My pulse quickened as I identified myself under that entry. Those symptoms: flashbacks, nightmares and anxiety were exactly my experience of life. It said, that in order to be diagnosed, the symptoms needed to persist for at least four weeks. I'd been experiencing those symptoms for at least four years.

When I mentioned it to him he disagreed, and informed me that it was highly unlikely I could have that syndrome and not to worry about it. Baffled, I asked, "How do you figure that?" and he responded, "PTSD is a veterans problem and since you have never gone off to war, it's not really an issue." (This was back in the late 1980s.)

He gave his dutiful recommendation, based on the mental illness symptoms that I presented in his office. The withdrawal, the lack of motivation, the apathetic responses, the suicidal intent and the morbid thinking all pointed to clinical depression. Armed with his professional recommendation my grandmother was able to admit me to a psychiatric hospital for the first time.

She had been my legal guardian soon after I had come to live with them, so it was she who signed me in. At the time I was as much interested in getting some help as she was in getting it to me. Although I was depressed, I was looking forward to getting analyzed and treated. I had faith in the idea of psychological help and therapy.

I found myself on the child and adolescent ward, the "Special Treatment Unit" of Charter Brookside Hospital, located in an outlying industrial area in southern New Hampshire. The clinic was situated at the end of a one way street in a wide open lot with new pavement and a landscaped frontage.

When I was admitted to the ward, I noticed right away that it was nothing like wards I'd seen on television. For one, it didn't look like a hospital. From the outside it could've been a corporate headquarters or a small campus. From the inside it looked like a hotel or a college dormitory. This was a private psychiatric facility, modern and state-of-the-art.

My grandmother then told me she thought this was for the best and she felt that I would finally be able to get the help I needed here. Then she left for the long drive back.

As soon as I was escorted onto the ward I faced an alternate reality. There was suddenly a new world of mental illness over-awareness and nonstop supervision. The first thing they asked me to do was sign a "safety" contract with the staff. I was amused by the idea. If I felt like trying to off myself again I would want it to be private, on my terms and in a place of my choosing, certainly not here.

Nevertheless, I had to sign a written contract which stated that if I felt like hurting myself, through self-mutilation or suicide, that I'd seek out staff attention right away. After signing this contract the next thing they did was search through all my personal effects.

Ostensibly the reason for it was to find and secure all contraband and "sharps." They were looking for drugs, legal and illegal and anything remotely blade or knife-like. I'd have to sign out scissors or a generic, institution supplied safety razor from the Sharps Closet and return those items promptly when I was done with them from now on.

Meals were served cafeteria style in a spacious dining area. The food itself was prepared and served by caterers. The facility had a contract with Marriott Hotels to provide meals, which were generally good.

The day to day life was a structured program, completely spelled out on a wall mounted chalkboard in the common area.

First was morning wake up call.
Then roll call to round us up for breakfast.
After breakfast there was group therapy.
School classes came after that, followed by recreation time.
Next was usually "quiet hour" where we all had to be in our rooms.
Then there was group therapy again, followed by dinner.
TV time came followed dinner time and preceded bedtime.
That was our daily routine from 7 am until 9 pm.

The one size fits all "school" was a joke. Two different teachers taught all the basic subjects between them. Classes were shorter than in normal schools, everything was condensed. The classes were not challenging and a total waste of my time but minors are required by Federal law to attend a certain number of school hours.

There were also regular "art therapy" classes, another joke. Have you ever seen art created by a dozen morbidly depressed teenagers? I deliberately never created meaningful art of any kind while there. You don't manufacture art on command just because someone says, "It's now mandatory art therapy time." A mental institution was not a place where I could generate muse.

The last picture I'd drawn about how I felt inside had dramatic results. My emotional expression through art had only elicited horror and negative attention from those that had seen it. I learned my lesson the first time on that issue.

Recreation was a different matter entirely. Going outside meant walking around a paved area about twenty feet on a side, surrounded by chain-link fence at least ten feet high. The kind with the points sticking up at the top instead of bent down. By contrast, the facility did have an indoor basketball court. A volley-ball net could easily be dragged across the center. The walls were white painted cinder blocks. The gym was lit by giant fluorescent lights descending from the ceiling.

The first day I spent on the unit was quite an introduction to the machinery of acute mental health crisis care. I was put on sui-cide watch. What that means is, that a nurse is assigned to watch you constantly for the first seventy-two hours. They take your shoes and belt away. You are not allowed out of the sight of that staff person. She follows you everywhere, including when you go to the bathroom.

For the remainder of the week I was on a restricted status, called "restricts" in ward-speak. That meant I spent all my time on the ward and was not allowed to go off the unit for meals or exer-cise. Meals were wheeled to me in the common area. I didn't get a choice of what I wanted.

By the next week things had settled into a routine. I was no longer on suicide watch, so I didn't need to be within ten feet of staff at all times.

There was always a nurse whose job it was to do thirty minute checks. These "safety checks" were performed twenty-four hours a day, seven days a week.

The experience probably doesn't sound too bad on paper. But being there, experiencing the aura of the place, living in it, makes all the difference.

The single worst part of being there for me were the restraints. Restraints always led to screaming and screaming always led to being restrained. Once you have heard the screams of fear, helplessness, and rage of a child being ganged up on by a half dozen unfamiliar adults, you never forget it.

I was quite reactive to interpersonal drama and confrontation. It'd been a constant feature of my family life for years. The histrionics usually involved components of verbal, physical or psycho-emotional abuse. Because of all that, I had become extremely sensitive to threats to my person and intrusions of my body space. Raised voices, yelling, and threats, always seemed to lead inevitably to assault at home (and at school) and it was no different in this place, despite what the staff chose to call it.

Restraints usually involve one patient and four, five or even more attacking staff. Restraints could happen at any time of day or night. The very first restraint that I ever saw badly triggered me and it happened on the first or second day of my inpatient stay. The screams of this nine-year-old little boy, as he bravely tried in vain to fend off his adult assailants, kicked in my adrenaline glands. I sat there twitching, trying to restrain myself from running to his aid as I visualized myself blitzing the staff from behind while they were focused on him. He broke free long enough to tear through the unit to the main door.

With a desperate kick to the bottom, he popped the magnetically locked door open. I didn't realize until then how easy it would be to crash through those doors if the need arose. He ran right into the arms of more staff that had been summoned from other units to assist in the restraint. Eventually they immobilized him, at which point he was forced bodily into the Quiet Room where he stayed for a long while before returning to the general population.

Witnessing this, I became immediately paranoid and distrustful. Though I was sitting still, my pulse was pounding in my ears. I couldn't concentrate on anything but my heightened sensory input.

Watching the staff assaulting that little boy less than twenty feet from me triggered my fight or flight reflex and I experienced flashbacks of the violence I grew up with. I became increasingly doubtful that I would receive actual benefit from being here, in an environment where this sort of thing happened in plain view.

At the time I possessed a heightened awareness of where every patient and staff were. A detailed mental map that included everything in my view and a rough visual simulation of where everyone was that was out of my line of sight. My eyes constantly monitored every doorway for additional threats.

The mental experience of hypervigilance was not too dissimilar from the appearance of some video games. The radar and tracking software in my mind assigned anyone near me with a threat potential value and color-coded them accordingly. Green subjects were inert teen patients slouched on the couch. Red targets were every single adult. Numbers indicating their approximate weight, height, movement speed and current distance from me floated next to the status bar positioned over their heads.

It was like having *Terminator* vision. Body language, tone of voice and intensity level is how you rapidly discriminate the threatening people in a room full of strangers or family. The restraints were a deeply disappointing and disheartening feature of institutional life. I got all too used to seeing it happen and I never felt safe in places where this was done to people.

So how was subjecting yourself to the institution experience supposed to make you better? Interspersed throughout the day were various therapies and attending them was not optional. Actual one-on-one psychotherapy or counseling was surprisingly limited. I was seen by two different psychologists once a week each. The sessions were psychological assessments, not actual behavioral therapy.

Before I had arrived at this place I had imagined that I would receive daily counseling. I figured that being inpatient meant being on vacation and taking a respite from the life that had driven me here. I thought that there would be a line-up of different psychologists and that I'd be allowed to choose the ones that I felt I wanted to talk to based on the vibes I got off them.

Then reality hit home hard when the experience was anything like I'd imagined. It was like being a kind of prisoner. Don't do this. Don't do that. Don't say this thing and that thing. Don't go there or over there, go here. Get up now and go to this meeting, go exercise, go to class, go to your room, come out and sit in the common area. It was not a safe, sane healing environment.

When you consider the amount of freedom and latitude that I had enjoyed since I was thirteen, the inflexible structure of this place, the rules and regulations got old real fast. I had played along at first when I thought that I would actually get real help, but after the first two weeks I wanted out. The place was too threatening with all the other teens and their issues, with the rigid program structure combined with the daily restraining of the patients. I had better things to do at that point then spend another day there. The inpatient life was not the road to getting over my problems and I knew it.

Part of the issue was also their forced therapy. I don't know who first invented group therapy, but I would like to mention just how useless and futile it was to me. Try to imagine a room filled with emotionally disturbed teenagers, all of them strangers to each other. They all have some kind of behavior issue as a result of their upbringing. Most of them are not even ready to talk about why they're here. Consequently they are not willing to open up and spill their guts to a group of strangers in such a vulnerable and exposed setting.

I, for one, had nothing to say in a group. Unfortunately, nonparticipation is considered noncompliance. It is automatically misinterpreted as the deliberate sabotage of one's treatment goal rather than an indication of psychological reticence.

On my third week as an inpatient I was subjected to a lot of testing. First, I had to take a complete intelligence test followed by the Rorschach Ink Blots, the MMPI and an extra-long session with a psychologist who wanted me to give a condensed version of my life at that point.

At one point I was administered an EEG. As I was coming back to the unit afterwards, I observed one of the nurses walking out of my room with my stereo cassette radio in hand without my permission. I'd pretty much tried to be invisible so far. I had never antagonized anyone or acted out in the slightest. Until now, there had never been a reason to flip out or "go off" in ward-speak.

I recalled past incidences when I had attacked my brothers and sister for touching my belongings and I thought to myself, *this lady must be insane*. I rushed to intercept her as she was opening up the sharps closet. In the most venomous voice I could muster I inquired, "What exactly do you think you are doing with my radio?"

My radio was one of my major therapies. I listened to my cassette collection to escape the present and pass the time. When my mother had banished me at home, I had had the company of my radio. When my grandparents began starting in on me, I could always go to my room and listen to my tapes. It was a critical anger management strategy for me.

"You didn't make your bed today," she answered. I'd agreed to the rules when I came here and one of the rules was to make my bed every day which I had always done until the EEG night. I had not been allowed to go to bed on time the previous night. I'd been forced to stay up until past midnight in order to allow me to sleep during part of the EEG.

When I was summoned to take the EEG, it was like four, maybe five o'clock in the morning. I had no idea that the procedure would take so long. I assumed that I'd be allowed to resume sleeping after I had returned to the unit, get up later and make my bed then. It was just an unmade bed, no big deal. Only it was a big deal, because the morning shift nurses had come on duty while I'd been in the lab. At some point, the nurse that did safety checks had noticed that I had not made my bed and I had caught her confiscating my radio for seventy-two hours.

Once I had heard her puerile explanation, my anger surged. And before I could think twice about it, I punched the wall next to the sharps closet extremely hard. That strike was meant for her and I wanted her to know that I'd spared her a broken nose. The blow impacted the wall hard enough to put a significant dent in it and attract the attention of staff and patients alike.

I had come here for help. I expected to be treated with respect. I certainly did not expect to be punished by complete strangers with so arbitrary of an excuse. I fantasized that I would receive some deferential treatment for having so many troubles. I thought that being a mental patient meant that I'd have no stress, no pressure. I guess I had hoped to be left alone in a comfortable chair on a porch overlooking an idyllic garden or a tranquil lake, to chill out. But what I did not know was that that kind of treatment for the mentally ill had been mostly phased out by the end of the nineteenth century.

She informed me then that I had "really done it now."

"For physically acting out, you have to go to the Quiet Room for a time-out, immediately."

I rolled my eyes at the silliness of the idea. I was too old to go "stand in the corner" anymore. And she was not my mom. So I walked back to my own room where I knew I could calm down as long as there were no more threats. But she followed me a moment later.

"You have no choice but to go to the Quiet Room."

"I'll be fine," I insisted. "If you will just leave me alone."

"Well I am sorry but I can't do that," she said. "You've broken program rules twice and now there have to be consequences."

This was getting sickeningly similar to the power dynamics between my mother and all us kids before she had split. I was not going to be "punished" by some bitch psych nurse who had herself started this encounter with me by laying hands on my stuff. I sat down on my bed and tried to marshal my calm.

Then she proceeded to escalate the situation even further by doing a countdown before summoning other people to "help" me get to the Quiet Room. Now both my parents liked to do "the countdown" before exploding on us kids. I was conditioned to go off when that happened.

"If you do not come out of your room and go into the Quiet Room willingly in fifteen seconds," she informed me, "Then the choice to go voluntarily will be taken from you."

As soon as she threatened me and started counting down, she put into motion an irreversible series of events. I went into defense mode and began sending the signals to my body to attack, as though my life depended on it. She was no longer a nurse. She was just another one of Them.

"Ten seconds," she warned.

My heart was pounding now as I held to my resolve.

"Five seconds," she droned.

Unbelievable that they call these places "hospitals" I thought to myself as I braced for incoming violence.

"Last chance. Are you coming out?" she asked.

"No," I glared at her as I stood up, legs shaking, ready to fight now.

"Have it your way then."

She gestured with her hand up the hall to the triage station and shortly a ward code was announced over the speakers. *Calling Dr. Brown to come to STU immediately, please.*

"Dr. Brown" meant summoning staff from other units to assist in a major restraint. They never called "Dr. Brown" unless they thought it was going to take more than six people to handle a patient.

They actually locked down the ward, and all the other patients were sent to their rooms. Staff began pouring into my room and into the hallway outside it. Gradually they backed me into a corner and when they got too close, I gave one verbal warning, "Stop!" and launched a controlled shot across the bow of a male staff member by jumping into the air and performing a spinning crescent kick to the space in front of his face.

Then they attacked me en masse. There was no sportsmanship or honorable combat. This was no even match. Nor was it a video game sequence of attackers. Instead of facing me one-on-one or even two-on-one, with an exchange of attacks they all rushed me together. Each staff grabbed a separate limb in an attempt to immobilize just that, then they tackled me to my bed.

I fought them. Years of pent up indignant, righteous rage that I had only ever dared to release in small doses engulfed me. I gave myself over to the fear and the rage and I let it have me. I fought harder and longer than any other restraint I had witnessed anyone else go through before or since.

As I fought, I continuously surged against them. I played tricks, suddenly relaxing and pretending to be worn out and then I would renew my fight with twice as much fury.

I became so violent that they couldn't sedate me. I was like a live electrical power line and I thrashed unceasingly while I screamed and cursed at them. I was in awesome conditioning at the time. I didn't smoke or do any drugs. I did karate, swam in a pool regularly and biked everywhere. I had endurance and my legs were quite strong for a teen.

I managed to kick two psych nurses in the face hard enough for them to be propelled away from me and they had retreated, covering their bloody noses and mouths with their hands. More staff took their place and continued to try to immobilize me.

Eventually, my own body began to tire and one by one my limbs were restrained. When I could not strike them any longer, I used whatever means I had left. I screamed primal rage at them and spat at everyone involved until a towel was finally forced over my mouth. I lay there with a half dozen adults holding me down and I shook like a wild animal with unconstrained wrath.

They were not going to walk me out of here like most restraints I had seen so far. Out of the corner of my eye I could see the psych techs bringing in some kind of contraption. Every second that I lay still, my muscles were recharging and my anger had not even begun to be tapped. If anyone even so much as wavered slightly in their restraint I would send a surge into that limb again.

When they had enough staff in the room, I was lifted up for a few moments. Underneath me they placed something called the safety blanket. It was a heavy canvas, sleeping bag-like affair, so-called apparently because once an aggressive patient was restrained inside it, everyone else could feel a lot safer.

Once I had been lowered into the bag, I was again lifted quickly and set down upon a canvas web of boards, each over the length of a yardstick. The result was that once the bag was zipped and the canvas was strapped across I was encased in a sheath of wooden boards running nearly the full length of my body from the neck down, which made it impossible to move my elbows or knees. Bound as I was in these boards I had absolutely no freedom of movement at all other than my head. I suppose I could also clench and unclench my fingers and toes. That was it.

Then, on a count of three, a half dozen staff, three on a side, picked me up horizontally, walked down the hallway and into the Quiet Room where I was finally set down. By attacking me they had caused something to pop loose inside my body. I had no idea that I had so much killing rage inside me. It was like a living entity, a dark force I could feel moving in my blood and bones tangibly. A demon must have somehow got inside me, I felt so completely possessed by this wrath.

It was suffocating to be in this thing. When you exert yourself strenuously you need open space around you to breath, to gasp, to let your chest expand deeply. Several psych nurses were on either side of me, far too close, and I thought I was going to die because it was so hard to draw breath, severely immobilized as I was. Thinking I might suffocate in this bag, I begged them to kill me. I dared them to.

"You have no choice!" I screamed. "If you don't kill me now, if you ever let me out of here again I will kill you all." Glaring balefully into each ones eyes I promised, "I will remember your faces, your names. I will find out where you live and kill you!"

Then I warned them against killing me. I said, "If you kill me now, I will haunt each of you to an early grave. Before I whisper the words that distract you from the oncoming traffic, I will have driven you insane. Do it! Kill me here and I will haunt you all until you are all dead! Each of you that dared do this to me! That dared touch me!" They would all pay the price for what they had done to me that day.

During my restraint they took the opportunity to force blood draw on me. For three weeks I had refused to cooperate with the blood nurse as she wheeled her cart through the unit. I was scared to death of needles and especially intravenous blood draw. I was also scared that there might be some sort of organic marker, a gene or some such, that could prove I was nuts. I didn't want it to be as easy as that.

They told me, "We have to know if something is wrong with you and a blood test may give us needed information." I shook my head from side-to-side in negation, "No!" and they ganged up on me again, releasing the straps only so much as needed to pull one arm out, sit on it and forced me to accept the needle into my vein. I hollered at the blood nurse over and over:

"I will kill you for this!" For violating and injuring me. "You have no right!" For taking my bodily fluids from me by force. "You're filth!" I spat at the nurse as my blood drained out of my arm, down the tube, into her vial. "You can't do this!" I hissed at her. "I said NO!" as she took off the tourniquet.

"I will kill you!" I continued to scream after them as they finished up. "I will find you!" Until finally, with blood drawn, in total restraint, they left me there in the Quiet Room. My voice was nearly useless from so much screaming and I just lay there trembling and panting and whispering over and over, "*I will find you.*" The nurses did their checks, peering at me through the tiny wire mesh and hardened glass window set in the steel door that blocked the only way out.

All this was brought on by the intractable standard operating procedure of mandatory Quiet Room time as an automatic and nonnegotiable consequence of hitting a wall out of anger. This, because some stupid psych nurse had laid hands on my personal belongings in order to penalize me for not making my bed. It was just as irrational as my parents' discipline had been.

Eventually they took off the safety blanket and I did get out of the Quiet Room. A few days later I was called into my psychiatrists office. Initially I was almost excited. This was what I had come here for, to find out what was wrong with me. My psychiatrist, Dr. Wasser, was quite thin and had shoulder length curly black hair. She wore a pair of enormous spectacles on her face and came with the obligatory condescending air of intellectual superiority. As it turned out, there was nothing in my blood which indicated any biochemical or neurological reason for my behavior.

Dr. Wasser told me that after analyzing and collating the admissions paperwork, the psychiatric testing batteries, the input from psychologists, relatives and group facilitators from the Special Treatment Unit, a diagnosis had been made.

She laid it all out for me. The suicide attempt, the withdrawal and self-isolation, the self-harming behaviors and prolonged apathy, all pointed to clinical depression. Fine, I agreed, there was no doubt I was depressed. This had been an established fact for most of my life.

Then she told me about all the little things that I had never considered to be a flaw. Apparently my staying up all night, the intensely obsessive focus on things of personal interest (like my fixation with weapons and martial arts) and my general state of irritability were all symptoms. One by one she rattled them off. "Pressurized speech, flight of ideas and grandiosity," she stated, "all point to disordered thinking brought on by mania."

What Dr. Wasser was talking about, this "mania," was nothing less than my inner sense of power. It was why I was so intense all the time. The inescapable, continual sensory awareness of everything around me combined with the thousands of data streams and internal dialogue generated from the chorus in my head. It was the source of my imagination, inspiration and psychic ability. I was born this way. So when my psychiatrist began to talk about mania like it was a disease, I immediately became suspicious.

"With the presenting symptoms and your psychotic episode on the unit the other day," Dr. Wasser lectured, "The evidence points to manic depression illness."

"Well," I asked, "how long does it last?"

She answered regretfully, "Manic depressives are diseased for life."

When I asked her how I had contracted it, she replied, "You didn't contract it from a pathogen, so you mustn't think of it as such. But it is a disorder. A manifestation of genetic expression that has a high degree of heritability." I thought fleetingly about my mother's mood swings. My face must have given away my confusion and disbelief because she added, "It isn't some personality flaw."

"Don't blame yourself," she commiserated. "It's not your fault, it's caused by a chemical imbalance in your brain." Back then the term "bipolar disorder" was still fairly new, and "manic depression" was still often used interchangeably. At the time, bipolar disorder was a heavy diagnosis and it was rare to diagnose a young teenager with it because it was considered an adult illness. At her words a deep sense of foreboding came over me and I sensed some kind of danger was imminent.

While it was convenient that my symptoms matched this "bipolar disorder," I sensed that it was not the beginning nor the end of what was wrong with me. My gut feeling became even stronger when she tried to explain to me, why it would be better to think of it as being bipolar as opposed to the older name, manic depression.

According to Dr. Wasser, this whole thing was a cycle. The mania would inevitably lead to depression. "Typically, most people with bipolar disorder learn to accept medications in order to prevent going to the extreme 'poles'." she explained and added, "With medications and therapy, a lot of people with bipolar can lead an almost normal life." But even with ongoing psychiatric help there was no guarantee that I would not need to be rehospitalized again in the future.

"But I am not always depressed or manic or both," I said. "There are times when I feel just fine, normal."

"That is to be expected," she answered, "It is those times when you are feeling normal that you will be convinced you no longer need medication." At that, I grew even more skeptical. "Inevitably," she informed me, "going off medications will lead to suicide attempts or manic episodes which will probably land you straight back into acute psychiatric care."

"Without medications, therapy and support," Wasser prophesied, "You will forever lead a life of morbid depressions and florid manias." She apologized to be the one to have to tell me, "Without treatment, manic depression is really a disability."

I stared at her, frankly incredulous. She went on to tell me that because of my psychosis they would start a new treatment with me, involving psychiatric medication.

"I am not psychotic," I protested.

"Not according to the staff that were present during your restraint episode the other day," she countered. "Look, it's like this," Wasser said, "Delusions, grandiosity, a belief that you have special powers, those are all elements of mania." As she scanned my assessment paperwork she queried, "Here you stated that you hear voices telling you to kill yourself?" I nodded. "Those are some of the symptoms of schizophrenia. It's not all that uncommon with mental illness to present dual diagnosis. It's not the end of the world though. We are going to give you some help with that. Tonight we are starting you with an antipsychotic."

Clearly, admitting to hearing voices was a mistake. Fortunately, I had not confessed to the other related phenomena. While the mood swings had been ongoing since I was a child, hearing voices was a more recent development. For the last year or so, ever since I got really involved with the occult and meditation, I had been occasionally hearing other people's thoughts.

Sometimes it was as simple as looking at someone and knowing exactly what they were about to say a moment before they said it aloud verbatim. But every now and then I could hear voices murmuring, calling my name and talking about me just barely out of earshot, even when I was alone. I somehow knew that my own thoughts were broadcasting telepathically and I worried that if I could hear other people's thoughts, then what was stopping them from hearing mine?

I told Dr. Wasser in no uncertain terms, "I am not a junkie or a pill head. I do not believe in drugs. I am against the very idea of taking drugs and I will NOT be taking your drugs, period."

At that she finally raised her eyes from her notes and met my gaze. She told me in equally certain terms, "You have no choice. None whatsoever. You will be started on it tonight."

"And if I refuse?" I asked.

"If you refuse," she replied over the frame of her lenses, "then you will be restrained and injected, every single time, until you learn to accept it."

At that, I quietly snapped inside. To me she was no longer a psychiatrist. Dr. Wasser was simply another one of Them. She was my enemy, another target. I saw a vision of myself smoothly standing up out of my chair, leaping across her desk, picking up a pencil and jamming it deep into her neck. The urge was overpowering and the rising inner clamor of the voices demanded it.

Do it. Do it now. Stab her. Get up. Move. Move now. You must move now. Get up. Do it now. Stab her. Do it now. Stop wasting time. Get up and do it before it's too late. Do it. Get up now. Move.

She was soft and unfamiliar with fighting, dirty tricks and desperate violence. Sitting just mere feet away from me, the doctor was severely disadvantaged.

I visualized myself behind Dr. Wasser, choking her out. She must never be allowed to share my diagnosis or to tell the nursing unit that I was to be medicated. She could not be allowed to walk out of this room alive. She was the most dangerous person in my life, and sitting there with her glasses and hairdo and skirt, she couldn't stop me if I wanted to come after her.

Dr. Wasser went on to describe the function of an antipsychotic drug. She told me, it would take two to three weeks to work. She mentioned a small sample of possible side effects, like drowsiness, minor weight gain, and diminished sexual arousal. None of which sounded appealing to a teenager.

When I asked, "How long will I have to take meds?" she said, "In all probability, forever."

Desperate and deeply afraid, I tried to conceal my inner violence and I asked in a voice just a few shades above pleading.

"Why can't we do counseling? I just need more of it. That would help. I like counseling."

Her answer was something I'll never forget.

"Well, there is really no point right now because we are just talking to the disease," she stated. "Perhaps we can start therapy in a few weeks, once you've adjusted to the meds."

Almost I leaped out of my chair at her, almost. In that moment I understood that they wanted to chemically change my personality against my wishes. The psychotic maniac they were so afraid of was me, the real me. It was my spirit. It was a fundamental part of who I was as a person. It was my rage against the machine. Sure, by their reckoning, the suicidal depression and mania was a serious problem but I didn't feel like I was at the mercy of a biochemical disease. I think I realized then that psychiatry was probably bullshit. They had no idea what they were doing.

That night, along with the other patients, I heard my name called at the nurses' station for meds for the first time since I had been admitted. I was given a small plastic cup. In it was 8mg of a clear liquid called Trilafon.

Its temperature was cool and it had an industrial chemical odor to it and tasted far worse than it smelled. I remember it as the smell of death and I would come to know that horrible smell and taste in my mouth, my sweat and my body odor for months. There was an awful lot of things about that chemical that I should have been made aware of, but was not. Facts that were deliberately omitted so as not to "agitate" me.

For starters, the dosage I was given was the maximum dosage prescribed to sedate violent behavior and to quell delusions in full grown adults. The drug itself was not recommended for people under the age of twelve.

I had to take the drug in plain view of the med nurse who had me open my mouth so she could see that I had swallowed it. Then I calmly went into the bathroom and immediately stuck my fingers down my throat trying to induce vomiting but couldn't get my stomach to heave.

I started panicking, desperate to get that cold chemical out of my body and afraid I'd be unable to. I tried inducing vomiting again, only to fail. Then I realized, that even if I succeeded, I would have to do this every day, perhaps several times a day, until further notice.

Sooner or later I might get caught. I might not always be able to go vomit immediately after med time. What would I do then? Obviously, the sooner I vomited after swallowing it, the better; too late and it would no longer matter. Being caught would no doubt result in assault, restraints and injection, exactly as my psychiatrist had threatened me.

Bullying I could deal with, I could fight back. A hostile parent, sibling or patient I could deal with in terms of self-defense. But there was nothing I could do about being attacked by six, seven, eight or more people, with nowhere to go, no weapons, nothing and no one to back me up. The indignation of having to fight half a dozen full grown adults, over and over again, was something that I could not possibly survive psychically.

Voluntarily taking their toxins was fractionally more palatable then forced injections. Choosing a course of voluntary action over fighting tooth, claw and nail was undoubtedly the most difficult decision I had ever made in my life at that time. After flooring my stepfather I refused to submit to anyone or anything. I had a new choice in life, which was to fight back against my oppressors with everything I had. Now, being forced to have my mind poisoned, either by violence or because of threat of violence, and fully aware of the fact that I could do nothing about it, made me more suicidal in that moment than I had ever been previously.

If I thought I had a right to feel sorry for myself before, it paled in comparison to this new situation. Desperation and lack of workable options is the guaranteed formula for suicide. They were trying to erase the most important part of my identity, the unique aspects of my mind and personality. The best parts of me. All because I had punched a wall out of anger. *This could not possibly be my life and my reality*, I thought to myself. This couldn't be happening, not after all I had been through already.

There in the bathroom I gripped both sides of the vanity sink and looked at myself in the mirror. I started talking to myself softly. I spoke to my reflection then and told it, "You will remember all that you are." I visualized a copy of my thoughts and feelings being coded into a thin beam of white light and I buried that light deep inside my being, as far in as I could sense, and I hoped with all my heart that I could retrieve this copy should I ever get a chance to escape the prison that the chemicals would create for my mind.

The dosing was so high that when I woke up the next day I was lethargic and no longer thinking clearly or quickly. Within days I experienced a whole host of alarming and debilitating side effects I was utterly unprepared for. Dry mouth, blurry vision, retarded gait, (the notorious "Thorazine shuffle") slurred speech, muscular weakness and constant uncontrollable drooling from the right corner of my mouth, so severe that I carried a small towel on my shoulder to catch some of it.

As if that was not bad enough, I developed all manner of muscle tics and involuntary twitching, especially along the right side of my face. I couldn't tell you which part was worse. Trying to move as though my bones were filled with lead and my muscles had been removed or thinking through the impenetrable fog that pervaded my mind. The medication prevented me from thinking about very much of anything for very long. Even my memory was beginning to fail me.

What I did not find out until years later was that, when antipsychotics were first used on agitated and schizophrenic patients in the 1950s, psychiatrists hailed this class of chemical as a "wonder drug" which performed an effective chemical lobotomy over time. It effectively sedated patients, making them compliant, docile, and easy to handle. They were mind wiping me and I was completely helpless to do anything about it.

There was no more deep thoughts, high speed cogitating or free associating. It was like my brain's wheels were stuck in the snow or in mud. I was now intellectually ineffective and it felt like my internal battery was never fully charged.

Making my bed tired me out. Trying to think in class tired me out. I could not summon the energy to do anything during recreational therapy or exercise time. The combination of being made mentally and physically enfeebled made me more vulnerable and more helpless than I had ever been in my life before or since.

At first they saw my dull-eyed sedation as a vast improvement over the intense and threatening personality I had had before. Things got worse when I confessed to my psychiatrist that being so incapacitated was extremely depressing and that if I could think through this fog I would probably be suicidal. "You have to be patient." Dr. Wasser assured me. "The side effects are tough, but that's the medicine working. In time, some of the effects will even out as your body adjusts."

But I didn't want my body to adjust to this. I wanted that chemical out of me.

That evening they put me on another med. Next to the usual plastic cup of Trilafon was now a paper cup containing the maximum dose of lithium carbonate considered safe for an adult.

Reluctant to take more drugs, I inquired dully in my slurred voice, "What is this for?"

"Lithium is a mood stabilizer." one of the psych nurses told me. "Because you are bipolar, your moods cycle uncontrollably from one extreme pole to another (demonstrating the highs and lows with her level palm). Since your body doesn't produce enough lithium to balance your emotions on its own, this drug is to help you stabilize at the 'equator'," she explained (and again with her palm flattened for emphasis).

Too befuddled and fogged to think critically or to protest, I meekly swallowed the lithium with the Trilafon.

Obviously, psychiatrists don't really believe that manic depression is caused by a lack of lithium. The real truth is that still, after decades of using lithium to treat manic depressive patients, nobody has any idea whatsoever why lithium seems to quell mania or suicidal ideation in some patients. No doubt, the psych nurse who gave me that disingenuous answer to my question thought that lying to a fourteen-year-old patient to get them to be medication compliant was preferable to simply telling me the truth, which was: A couple of apparent "experts" had written a modern book on the treatment of manic depression and lithium was part of that protocol.

The lithium came with another slew of side effects, most of which were never explained to me. All I was told was that there might be some occasional dry mouth and maybe some slight gain in weight. What actually happened was that the side effects were multiplied incredibly. At 500mg three times a day of lithium and 8mg of Trilafon twice a day, my suffering vastly increased while my ability to do anything about it or communicate my distress was exceedingly limited.

A new side effect, constant hand tremors and even some slight tremor in my jaw, soon became an ongoing inescapable torment. Reading and comprehension became nearly impossible. My memory began to gap constantly. The muscle tics became more noticeable. The whole body fatigue got more and more pronounced. I was tired all the time and nodded off in class, in groups or during TV hour.

I was now on two drugs which both shared the same side effects of dry mouth, lethargy, weight gain, libido reduction and akathisia. The combination only magnified my suffering. My voice did not even seem to be part of me anymore. It took a deliberate exertion of will to formulate accurate speech. It was altogether too much effort to do or think much of anything of my own initiative. I had now become a human vegetable.

They never informed me about the central nervous system ataxia (lack of coordination of muscle movements) caused by both drugs. They never mentioned that lithium made my blood toxic. Nor did they tell me that excess lithium interfered with my thyroid and hormones and could lead to hypertension and hypothyroidism as well as renal failure, which would eventually necessitate regular dialysis. Altogether, when it came to being informed about short and long term side effects of polypharmacy, I was treated like a mushroom.

The dry mouth was bad. My tongue felt thick and swollen and tasted like desert sand. No matter how much water I drank, it didn't seem to help for long. To deal with this side effect they gave me another drug (can't remember the name) which left me incredibly constipated nearly every day.

Lithium seriously interfered with my bladder function. It's a salt, it dries your body out, prompting you to drink excessive amounts of water and thereby increasing your bathroom attendance. But whenever I tried to urinate, it would take a minute to find my pee reflex. I had to push to let it go. Once the stream started, it burned so fiercely that it brought tears to my eyes. It caused my toes to clench and my legs to shake. I could never seem to completely evacuate my bladder. I would stand up, thinking I was done and then, feeling the pressure again, I'd sit back down and force myself to squirt out another halting jet of liquid agony.

Simply peeing, a normal process that can bring relief along with release for most people, became an ordeal for me. Something I had to psyche myself up for. If I tried to avoid water for a few hours, my mouth dried up so completely that I couldn't get any saliva to speak. It was awful.

Not one of those drugs actually cured anything, instead, they only made me feel worse and worse. They took from me everything that I valued. They stole my physical agility and blunted my intellectual ability. I lost control over my own bodily functions. I was stripped of my mental and physical defense. I moved like a palsied senior citizen with early onset Parkinson's disease. For all I knew, that was what the experience of dying in old age with dementia was like.

They violated me in both mind and body, poisoning me with their chemicals and making my life worse than it had ever been before. I lost my fitness and radiant physical health. I lost my whipcord thin body, my strength and flexibility, as I became fatter and fatter with every week spent inert while inpatient. I watched all my abilities waste away, day by day. The loss of pride in my mental and physical prowess and the loss of dignity utterly destroyed my remaining self-esteem and will to live.

A swift, brutal corporal punishment would have been infinitely preferable to this slow death of personality as sentence for my crime of mental illness. At least it would be quick. A beating I could get over physically and mentally. I would not get over what they did to me in that place for a long, long time.

While things were awfully foggy in the weeks after starting perphenazine, once I was on lithium too, my sense of time became warped. I had no memory from one day to the next. Trying to recollect what inpatient life was like after the drugs were started, I find there are huge gaps. I was unable to contemplate my situation or my surroundings. I was unable to contemplate escape, suicide or anything else for that matter. It was just one long interminable limbo. What little I do remember comes in small spurts and the chronological order is certainly suspect.

Shortly after my psychotic break and the subsequent diagnosis of manic depressive illness with schizoid tendencies, my grandparents relinquished their legal rights as my guardians. They had obtained custody of me soon after I had been kicked out of my house by Tim's mother, Nana. Now that it was certain that I was mentally ill, it seemed that they wanted nothing more to do with me.

To be fair, after much consideration and many years later I appreciate and accept that I was an incredibly unstable, unpredictable, high intensity agent of chaos. As an adult in my thirties now, I can't imagine allowing someone like I was within a thousand feet of me. In retrospect, I am surprised that neither of them had a heart attack while I was living with them. Both of them were old and the stress of dealing with me on a confrontational basis was just way too much.

But at the time it was just more family who had given up on me. That rejection hardened my heart even more while adding to a sense of being up against the world, alone, by myself. I refused to let myself cry about it.

No one on my mother's side of the family would have anything to do with me. None of my other relatives wanted to deal with me. My father Andrew believed that if he took me in, sooner or later I would cost him his visa, which would cost him his job as managing director of a semiconductor group in Hong Kong. I was much too psychologically disturbed to move permanently to a foreign country.

When they asked me the whereabouts of my mother, I could not speak for long moments. The words "your mother" had triggered a phantom black rope that was constricting my throat. Finally answering, I said that I did not know, but that she had skipped out while I was on vacation with other relatives the year before. I didn't know why she left or where she was living now or how to contact her.

The unit social worker filed what is called a state CHINS (*Child In Need Of Services*) petition. This is filed with the birth county Child and Family Services division, and generally followed up by a state social worker, who opens a case file and begins an investigation.

Then one day, Sarah was on the ward. I was forced to sit in the same room with her and a few counselors. I had put her out my mind, and without warning she was here, of all places and now, of all times. I was terrified because I was completely helpless, mere feet away from one of the prime abusers I had grown up with. I had no idea what she was doing here.

She was capable of lashing out in the blink of an eye to smack you in the ear or mouth without warning, for the tone of your voice, your posture, because you gave her a "look," or contradicted her or interrupted her in conversation. She could go from calm to violent to calm in less than a minute, like a freak storm.

The staff had no idea that she was one of the people responsible for my anger and depression. I hated and feared her. She would smash us in the head when we lied, yet she told more lies than anyone I knew. In a discussion or argument she made up facts and trivia to hurl at you but punished us for doing the same thing. When I had slammed the wall near the sharps closet in anger I was modeling her.

She had ritually kicked me out of the family almost two years earlier, banishing me to my room until further notice. She wanted nothing more to do with me.

Here I was, sitting like a vegetative slug. Slumped in a chair, hands trembling, face and mouth twitching, drooling a constant stream on my shoulder. I could barely think or move. If she started screeching arguments at me or slapped at me, I could neither mentally or physically do anything about it.

I barely remember our exchange but one of the things she said was "it" was all for the best and, "I hope you are getting here the help you need." I remember breaking composure as I complained, "You have no idea about the misery inside me right now." I slurred and drooled some more as I tried to summon the effort to make my speech intelligible. I pointed out, "I can't even move straight or stop myself from drooling." I told her, "Don't see me like this!" and added, "Never visit me again."

The next thing I remember is a visit from my father. First thing out of his mouth was to observe sarcastically that I was fat.

"So," he inquired. "Are you getting better?"

"Not yet," I answered. And I added flippantly, "I think I am worse."

Andrew got infuriated with me in a quietly contained burst of irritation right there on the unit. Low-voiced he advised me, "Well you had just better reconsider your attitude immediately. You are receiving top notch state-of-the-art psychiatric care, and do you know who is paying for it?" It was costing his insurance $800 dollars a day and it was not inexhaustible. When it ran out, there was no way he could or would pay for it out of pocket.

I briefly remember him signing me out for a few hours to meet up with my brother. We went to lunch and he brought me back to the hospital afterward. Then the fog comes back and there's a long blackness where one day passed exactly like the rest, save for the ebb and flow of new patients and the never ending series of restraints.

CHAPTER 5

BEHIND THE WALL OF SLEEP

For weeks no one would say anything about who was responsible for me or who I would live with when I was discharged. When I asked, "Could someone please tell me if I am ever getting out of here?" they stonewalled. "You really should not be thinking about leaving right now," one of the nurses at the triage center apprised me, "You need to concentrate on getting better."

Discharge day, when it came, was a total surprise. I was so sedated and out of it that I hadn't noticed the changing seasons. When I had been admitted it was green and warm outside. Now there was snow on the ground. Thanksgiving Day was right around the corner. I had spent almost eighty days of my life in that place.

My father's insurance had run out. In the interim I had been placed into State's custody. The State had taken over responsibility for the astronomical cost of my stay in the clinic and was not willing to foot the bill for that place unless I was in critical need of that level of care. According to the findings of my multi-disciplinary treatment team, I did not appear to be psychotic or in imminent danger of hurting myself.

On the outside I presented as a meek and appropriately contrite mental patient. But no one seemed genuinely interested in how I was really feeling on the inside. Hell, I did not even know myself. I was so cut off from cognitive reflection and so emotionally vacant because of the psych drugs that there was not much danger of me harming myself or showing initiative at all. Which in their institutional myopia meant that I was making progress, getting better. Neuroleptics are not called "chemical restraints" for nothing. Four point restraints for your brain, your personality goes down the drain.

They claimed to have done all that they could do for me and recommended that I continue to receive intensive supervision, special needs schooling and ongoing monitoring to ensure that I remained medication "compliant."

Because I was now a ward of the State, it was up to the local government to find a placement for me. The state Department of Health and Human Services had a facility that would meet the "needs" of a juvenile psychiatric patient with emotional dysfunction and sub-acute symptoms. I had no input or say in the matter of my placement.

I don't remember exactly the time or day I was discharged, nor who came and got me. I think it was my grandmother, but I can't be sure anymore. She seemed quite upset that the State couldn't (or wouldn't) handle the transport themselves. She took me to the New Hampshire State Hospital and I remember the ride down narrow roads that meandered all throughout the grounds.

In 1838, N.H. Legislature laid down the charter for The New Hampshire State Asylum for the insane. Upon its establishment it became the seventeenth such hospital in the United States and the seventh in New England. The parcel of land that was later renamed the N.H. Hospital is vast and estate-like. Over the course of 150 years, through various grants, donations and trusts, the main hospital expanded into a sprawling complex as during that time thirteen additional buildings were laid down. At its peak, in the 1950s, the State hospital housed over twenty-five hundred people.

The entire institution of the N.H.H. is living history. There are noticeable architectural differences in both the interior and exterior of the various buildings. Many of those differences reflect changing attitudes towards the mentally ill over the decades.

Some of the earliest buildings, constructed in the mid to late 1800s, had been deliberately softened in an attempt to comfort the insane while they lived out their lives there. Some of them had extensive porches and balconies, panoramic views of gardens and tree lined paths. There had obviously been an era when people favored a more compassionate, hospice like approach towards caring for the mentally ill.

The Tobey building had been erected during the 1930s. A time when the ranks of the mentally ill overwhelmed institutional capacity and psychiatric treatment reflected the aims of the eugenics movement. Named after a late New Hampshire governor, the Tobey building was the very model of a new era institution.

A stark and imposing, three storied, red brick building on a slight rise greeted us as we got out of the car. Steel mesh screens covered the multi-pained windows on every floor. Sparsely placed trees weakly thrust their naked branches into the chill air as we walked towards the entrance.

Once inside, I felt immediately as though I had stepped into an old hospital like the ones depicted in movies. Overhead fluorescent lighting reflected off of glossy white tile floors as you walked down the white corridors. Gone were the soft carpets, private bathrooms and hotel quality furniture of the private psychiatric hospital. The rooms here were all painted institutional green, yellow or blue.

The waxy white floor stayed underfoot as I was escorted to my assigned room. My bed was a thin mattress over a metal frame, covered with white sheets printed with the logo of the N. H. State Hospital. A narrow steel closet, paired with a decrepit chest of drawers, completed the furnishings. When those items had been installed in these rooms, back in the 1960s, it was considered a new standard of care for the inhabitants. This was to be my new home indefinitely.

When the Tobey building was completed, it housed over a hundred adult males. When I was there, in the late-80s, the building was used as a coed residential treatment facility. A state funded and operated private school, designed to meet the needs of emotionally or behaviorally challenged children and teenagers.

Some of the students went home at night after the school classes, which were held on the first floor. But most of the students lived in lockdown on the second floor. The third floor was an adolescent detention center. The Tobey School was a structured living program that was less restrictive then a psychiatric hospital or juvenile detention, but it featured similar elements.

You were told what to do and when to do it. Everything was a group activity. Staff in casual clothes shepherded the residents from one activity to the next.

We had about five hours of classes during the day.

Then there was recreation hour and TV hour at night.

We had group therapy and art therapy.

We received three meals a day according to a prepared menu.

You learned to look forward to some meals more than others.

Every day was largely the same and the weeks mirrored each other. The only real motivation to progress through the level system was to gain the privilege level needed to go outside on group walks around the state hospital grounds and to go home every other weekend or on holidays.

The three things that I remember most from that period were: kids still got restrained and put in a quiet room (although less frequently), the population turnovers were also less frequent (so a new resident was a big deal), and that there were unannounced fire drills in the middle of the night.

Within weeks, I met my new parents.

My new "mom" waddled slowly onto the dorm one afternoon. My head snapped a double-take because I thought it was Tangina Barrons from the 1982 movie *Poltergeist*. She was a diminutive but immensely obese woman, complete with a flowery tablecloth for a dress, cheap plastic bangles and the beaded necklaces.

This lady literally huffed and puffed as she stood, walked or sat. Her face, under its greasy corona of curly grey hair, was so plump that it made her eyes appear beady and recessed. The round, over-sized eyeglasses on her dimpled face just enhanced the impression that for her simply looking at things was just as big an effort as moving was.

Earlene was a social worker for the state's Division of Child and Family Service and also the one who decided on placements for me. She handled all transports and welfare related issues and had to organize for my dental care, clothing or eyeglass vouchers.

My new "dad" had a quiet, composed air about him. He was a narrowly built older man, balding, bespectacled and dapperly dressed. The kind of man who smiled at you with his eyes. Gavin was my court appointed guardian ad litem. His responsibility was to legally represent me and my best interests in the court system.

Gavin told me that he knew my social worker from dealing with her in court and that he hated her. He said with a wink and a nod, "If you ever have any problems with Earlene, call me and I will deal with her." I would have hugged him if I could stand embracing anyone. I gave him a broad smile along with my thanks as I accepted his business card.

Around the same period that I met my new state-issue parents there was also a family court hearing. Gavin informed me, "It's a custody hearing and your mother will be there." He told me gently, "It's okay if you don't want to go, and you're not required to do so, but it is your right to go if you want." And I did.

It's against the law to just abandon your children whenever you feel like it. The State had caught up with my mother Sarah. She had to have her day in court.

My mother and her public defender sat on one side of the courtroom. I sat on the opposite side with my social worker and my appointed guardian. This was my first time in a court and it would not be the last.

My mother's counsel did most of the talking on her behalf. She plead no contest to charges of child neglect and abandonment. No, Sarah did not want me back. It was her wish that I be remanded into state's custody until I turned eighteen. The judge turned to my mother and asked for confirmation that this was in fact her wish and she answered with one word, "Yes."

I should have been shaking or crying, angry or laughing. Instead I was so divorced from my emotions because of the lithium that I felt very little at all. I knew it was wrong that I should feel nothing, but on the neuroleptic I couldn't contemplate why that was so. Instead I thought to myself: *Good! I don't need you anyway*.

Back at the residential facility, I continued to serve my sentence. Mental health care consisted of a once a week session with a psychotherapist. For awhile I only ever left the unit to see an off site psychiatrist or to get my blood lithium levels checked at a nearby clinic.

Tobey School's program was geared to teens with learning disabilities, and so it could not address my needs. At some point they began letting me out to walk three blocks to a nearby high school. I attended a handful of mainstream and special needs classes.

I moved up the level system after awhile and gained the privilege of leaving the dormitory lockdown on weekends. Eventually my grandparents assented to allowing me an occasional visit, but only so long as I was medication "compliant." Late in December that year, some of my friends from my hometown had contacted my family to invite me to a New Year's party. My father was back from overseas for the holidays and drove me to my friend Ann's house.

My memory is full of long gaps from the psych drugs back then and the only thing I remember is being woken up in the wee hours of the night by my friend Ann's mom. I was quite embarrassed and completely surprised to find that I had come downstairs in my sleep and was seated at a chair by the table, clad only in my underwear. The lady told me, her husband did the same thing on the meds he got from the Veteran's hospital. I went back to Tobey School the next day and then there is more fog and limbo for awhile. My fifteenth birthday came and went and I have no memory of it.

My grades at school gradually declined. My mainstream courses were math and social studies or maybe chemistry or something. Under the influence of neuroleptics and lithium I had no cognitive or calculative ability. I had to take a powerful dose of both these drugs before breakfast and school. By the time I finished the walk to school, I was so tired that I basically slept through first class and part of the second class. I missed an entire semester on ionic bonding and covalencies.

During the course of a routine education assessment, it was I who suggested to my teachers and counselors that my academic performance decline might have something to do with how stupid I had become. Soon after, I was taken off the liquid form of perphenazine and put on the pill form at a slightly lower dose. After awhile, a few dim bulbs in the mental attic came on. I gained some mental ability back, albeit only a little, enough at least to begin to add up everything going on around me.

When they changed the delivery and dose of Trilafon, I began sleepwalking a couple times a week. I would wake up, sometimes in the bathroom, under the flickering fluorescent lights, standing there talking to myself in the mirror. It was as though late at night, when my system and bodily functions were at their lowest ebb, some part of my real self struggled behind the wall of sleep to break free of the drugs and possess me.

Sleepwalking in a residential lockdown was one of the many scary things that happened to me while being treated with those poisons. These episodes were just another egregious reminder of how little control over my life, or even my body, I had left.

When on one day a schoolmate, passing me by, remarked, "Watch where you're going, fatty!" I was shocked. I felt as though I had been slapped. I was *not* fat! Then the doubts crept in. I went into the teacher's restroom and locked the door. With morbid anxiety I partially disrobed and stared at myself in the enormous mirror over the sink under the bright lights.

When I saw myself half naked, I was painfully shaken back into reality. From my swinging double chin to my flabby arms and bloated tummy: I *was* fat. I had stretch marks all along my hips and thighs. My once smooth skin now was pickled with cottage cheese dimples, sunken in, blue and purple. I was a corpulent mass of water fat and cellulite. Before entering psychiatric care I fluctuated around the upper 120 lower 130 pound range. Now I weighed in at over 200 pounds, a more than a seventy pound gain in just the past six months.

My once beautiful, athletic and wiry body was gone. Take someone, put them on steep doses of two different drugs that cause lethargy and sedation. Add to that the water fat from losing the battle against perpetual dry mouth. Plus the lack of outdoors activities because of the winter, and you have a surefire recipe for expedient weight gain and loss of physical fitness.

Every day we had TV hour. Anyone not on privilege restrictions spent an hour or two in a room watching either TV or movies. At that time, the staff had rented the '80s-era Steven Spielberg movie *E.T. - The Extra Terrestrial*.

The plot of the movie, in short summary: An adorable little green alien is accidentally abandoned on Earth by the others on his ship. With the help of some local children he builds a transmitter out of old toys and junk and sends a distress signal into space. Towards the end of the movie there is a race to free and save ET, who had fallen into the clutches of the scientists and is dying. At the last moment ET is saved and brought to the alien-landing site and he escapes in their spaceship. He had phoned home and his people came and saved him.

As the climactic ending scene played out, a great quaking began to come loose from deep inside my guts. Into my head came a cold realization that I had no ship that would ever come to rescue me. My entire family seemed to have washed their hands of me. My mother would not come onto the ward, wielding sorcery and save me. My father would never come bursting through the windows in the dead of night, dressed head-to-toe in assault and tactical gear. No one was ever coming to rescue me and take me home to a place where I was wanted.

After a half a year undergoing a chemical lobotomy, the reality of my situation finally gelled. I was supposed to live in this place until I was an adult. In the '70s and '80s there was another red brick institution a short ways down the road on the State Hospital grounds, called the Brown Building, where many mentally disabled adults spent their lives. No doubt, that is where everyone expected I would end up in a few years. It seemed there was little or no hope for a free and normal life.

Most everyone who knew me at the time had thought that the pathetic and befuddled version of me was preferable to the agitated and intimidating person that I had been before. I suppose this was a just punishment for inconveniencing people with my problems. Tears of fear, abandonment, aloneness, helplessness, hopelessness and desperation finally broke free and poured down my face.

That night I tried to figure out how best to kill myself. One possibility was hanging. I could string a twisted sheet over the exposed fire extinguisher pipes, then step off the clothes dresser into open space. But the fixing of the sheet might be noticed by the occupants on the other side of the wall (because the rooms were built like stalls, without a separate ceiling). What if they did? Would they keep silent or sound an alarm? How much noise would the deed itself make? And what if my fall ripped the pipe out of the ceiling? Or if the staff would come and find me still alive (although I already had started timing the bed checks)?

Since hanging myself from the overhead pipes had too much potential for failure, I looked around for alternatives. There was the small, metal stand-alone closet. I thought, maybe I could try partial suspension by using belts to hang myself from the cross bar.

I took everything from my closet, and with the contents I made a rough attempt at creating a human form under the blankets. Then I stooped into it, hung the belt and tried to slide down the wall to the floor as quietly as I could. As I sat there, curled up in a ball at the bottom of the closet, I tried to adjust the belt to put pressure on my carotids, similar to a blood choke in martial arts.

Why did I have to go through this when everyone else I knew got to have a normal life? I thought of my grandparents, snoring in their recliner chairs with the Home Shopping Network droning in the background on television. I thought of my friends, going to an Iron Maiden, Ozzy Osbourne or Judas Priest concert without me. I thought of my brother, alone in his room back at the Hell House, probably reading a book.

This was the only thing left that I could control.

The choice to continue this existence or not.

My body was now useless and disgusting.

My intelligence, imagination and artistic inspiration were gone.

My vision was slowly turning black at the edges and red in front of me.

It took this much despair to feel sadness again, in spite of the drugs.

Then a small voice starting talking in my head and told me, *You can not go out like this. Not on these drugs, in this closet, in this place. If you are going to kill yourself, it should be your way, on your terms, and not here.* I wanted to taste physical and mental freedom one more time.

As fast as I could I sat up to get some slack. My fingers worked furiously on the knots on the hanger bar, all the while I was thinking that this would be the worst time to get caught. With the belts off, I crept out at last, careful to not cause the steel closet panels to pop as I shifted around. I threw myself onto the clothes on my bed and got under the covers, panting with exertion while listening for the sounds that would indicate discovery.

A few minutes passed. Then my door opened, an arm appeared and panned a flashlight over me. I waited until the sounds of footsteps and doors closing settled down. Then I stuffed all my clothes back into the closet and went back to bed. I was smiling as I drifted off. I had a plan.

The next day I took all the money I had concealed in my belongings, altogether about thirty dollars, and put it in my schoolbag. Having built up months long trust with med compliance, I was no longer closely watched at med time anymore. It was easy to pull off the old tilt-the-head back, under-the-tongue, paper cup-into-the-trash maneuver and I fought to keep my body language from giving anything away.

As I walked back to the day room to line up for roll call and breakfast, it was nothing to make a random gesture which concealed the transfer of the meds from mouth to hand to pocket. After breakfast and community meeting it was off to school with me.

As I passed the little duck pond on the hospital grounds, I remembered the pills in my pocket and I laughed as I threw them far out over the water. I continued to walk casually as though there were nothing out of the ordinary and I hummed a little ditty in my head to keep myself from thinking of mental images of the means of my escape plan, just in case.

The next step in my plan was to get on a bus. I made it to the bus terminal and bought a one way ticket. While waiting for the bus, I hid behind a stand of short pine trees that bordered the parking lot. I boarded with no problems, and as long as there was no one waiting for me when I arrived at my destination, I was off to a good start.

The bus arrived in my home town and I got off uneventfully. I walked for miles until finally I ended up on the grounds of Alvirne High School. This was the school that I would have gone to for my freshman year had I continued living in the Hell House.

I hid out here and there until I caught some of my friends in a hallway at the lunch bell, heading to the cafeteria. Some of them hadn't seen me in almost a year and they were surprised when I showed up completely unexpectedly, seemingly out of nowhere. I spent a half day successfully pretending I was a student there, I even attended my friends classes and sat in the back.

Tyler was introducing me to some of his older companions, one of whom asked me, "So why were you in a psych ward?" I told him honestly, "I tried to kill myself." And without warning, he instantly hit me in the face, spinning me around as I fell to the ground. His excuse for the attack on me was that years earlier his dad had shot himself in the head and died.

I was completely helpless to defend myself. I had so little control over my muscles or my fat and out of shape body. My reflexes and situational awareness of critical things like a person's intensity, threat potential and body language were gone.

Had I had my wiry old body from a year ago and my nervous hypervigilance, he would've never come close to hitting me in the face. I had become good at blocking and dodging blows to the head from much practice with my parents. His posture would've given it away and I would have already been moving out of the way as his hand came up. But on that day, I never even saw it coming, and now there was blood in my mouth. Six months of "treatment" and "help" had turned me into a big, slow moving target.

That evening, out of nowhere, I began to have a sick sense of anxiety in my guts. A sure sign that some of my abilities were coming back, as the clamps of the neuroleptic were starting to slip off my mind. I should have trusted my intuition then and there, instead I made the mistake of asking my friend to make me a sand-wich to run with.

That's when the cops knocked on the door. It took a short while for me to connect the dots. There was only one person who could have possibly given the police the location of my friend's house. The only person who had it written down in an address book somewhere. I raged inside when I realized who it was. My grandmother had betrayed me. It was like a stab in the back from yet another person who claimed that they loved me. Grandma now took her place with the rest of Them.

They handcuffed my wrists and shackled them to a thick brass ring on a wide leather belt they put around my waist. Then the county sheriffs transported me back to Tobey School. *This isn't supposed to be how it goes*, I thought to myself. I expected to stay free for at least a couple of days. Long enough for me to feel my real self again. And then I would hang myself out of a tree, some-where in the woods, so I would not have to live as a fugitive from the state hospital.

I had never been body searched so many times in one day. First by the local cops, as I was put in the patrol car. Then by the sheriffs, before I went into their car, and then again by several staff counselors upon arrival at Tobey Building. I was put on twenty-four hour suicide watch, stripped of my sneakers and belt and put into the isolation room. This was standard punishment procedure for anyone that "eloped" (ward-speak for an escape).

The next evening they came to escort me to the administrative office on the unit and told me the penalties. All my "privileges" were removed until further notice. The next two days I would have to spend in seclusion and only at night would I be allowed to sleep in my own room. Staff would offer me the chance to use the toilet twice a day, escorting me there and back.

After forty-eight hours, I was to stay in my room and be fed there for two weeks. If I dared to make a scene or spoke to any of the residents, I would have to spend more time in the isolation room. My sentence would be reset and I would have to start it all over again.

I had made up my mind that I would protest my existence in this place. I refused to answer any questions when the staff interrogated me, "What did you do while AWOL?" They really wanted to know how I made it so far from the hospital grounds in so short a time.

The last word I spoke for a week was, "Yes," when they asked me, "Do you understand the penalties?" I went on a hunger strike and I took a vow of silence. I refused to cry or show any emotion at all. I refused to speak to anyone or acknowledge anything other than to obediently march back and forth from room to room whenever I was told.

For days I ignored all food and the meds in the paper cup that came with the plastic tray. I would have refused forever. I spent all day trying to use meditation to stop my heart. Supposedly yogis could make their heart stop. How hard could it be if you spent every waking moment trying? But no matter how intensely I concentrated on my heartbeat, to slow, slow down and stop, it didn't work. My heart kept on beating its own rhythm, strong and steady.

The nurse started to visit me after the second day and asked me to come to the exam room. I obliged her requests to get on the scale. She almost got a weak smile out of me when she announced cheerfully, "You are losing weight!" *There is now physically less of me imprisoned in this place*, I thought to myself wryly.

That particular nurse, Susan, was one of three people I really liked there. My assigned counselor, Dr. Pritchett, one of the overnight staff by the name of Drew, and this nurse were the only people I could tolerate. It was their personalities, they didn't seem to look down on us. Those three staff were naturally optimistic, cheerful people who always had a kind word for us residents.

They acted more than just "professional." They enjoyed working with troubled kids and tried to make our lives better while we lived there. I really looked forward to when they were on shift. I felt that their presence protected us residents somewhat. I didn't get bad vibes off them the way I did from many of the other staff, who seemed to enjoy flexing the power that they had over us.

On the third day of my starvation protest Susan came to my room and begged me to eat. I ignored her. "Starvation is a painful way to die," she warned me as she left.

On the fourth day she came to my room to tell me, "It's clear you are trying to hurt yourself." She was the facility nurse and she could not allow it.

"If you keep it up," she began concernedly, "I'll be forced to have people from the main hospital come and get you. Since you are just wasting away, they will probably force feed you, which is most unpleasant," she advised me. "If you continue to withdraw like you are, they may be forced to use alternative treatments on you."

My own imagination filled in the blanks. She was alluding to electroshock "therapy." If I did not start communicating and stop refusing nourishment, they could strap me down and fry my brain with far more electricity than it normally made on its own. It's considered a "last resort intervention" for treatment resistant depression. It's a total crap shoot whether ECT works and it often leaves lasting memory loss and cognitive deficits.

The voltage disrupts brain cells, literally cooking them, in an attempt to induce cascading cortical seizures in order to "jolt" you out of your frame of mind. The shocks far exceed the normal seizure threshold in humans and leaves people susceptible to seizure events afterwards. This is a medical procedure that is less sophisticated than trepanning. And from what I've read about it, the disorientation and amnesia that can result from a single session resembles the effects of head trauma one might endure in a car accident or assault. Regardless of whether or not it was successful in alleviating depression, many ECT patients still end up on meds after it, so I didn't understand the appeal.

She never openly threatened me with ECT, but I believed that the procedure was done in one of the buildings there. (The state did not have a ban against forcing teens to undergo ECT until the late 1990s.) Besides, what other emergency alternative treatments were there? Maybe they could just hit me in the head with a club repeatedly, thereby inducing amnesia and call it kinetic impact therapy. As I imagined the technicians pushing a gurney into my room, I decided that this could simply not be allowed.

On the morning of the fifth day she came into my room, cautioning me, "If you don't eat today, I can't be held responsible for what happens to you." And added, "It will be out of my hands."

An inner voice told me to lull them and start all over again. *Work your way back to the privilege level needed to leave the building unsupervised and try again, though it might take a year or more.* If they refused to let me die passively then I had no choice but to escape again. Patience I have in spades and I would have to continue to cultivate even more. It took some moments to find my voice to make myself heard coherently.

"Alright," I croaked out weakly, "I'll eat."

I broke my fast with a special meal they made for me and I felt refreshed, energized and alive. All of the sudden, as if by magic, I realized that I was thinking, calculating, analyzing once more. My mind had returned. I was situationally aware again and truly recognized my surroundings for the first time in a half a year. Instantly I decided that I had better conceal my abilities and continue to pretend as though I was still sedated.

My favorite nurse gave me a concerned speech about how lucky I was that I didn't have serious neurological side effects from coming off prolonged high doses of lithium and neuroleptics. Up until then no one had ever taken the time to tell me that it was dangerous to go off lithium or antipsychotics cold turkey. The staff at Brookside had told me I was supposed to take psychiatric drugs for the rest of my life and I was sent to Tobey School to learn to live with my disability.

I still had another week of restricted movement to serve and that was fine with me. In a lot of ways I was going to miss isolation. It was similar to when I was banished at home. Being in my room all the time kept me out of contact with the daily hassle. I got fed in my room instead of sitting at the table with the freak show and the staff.

After my two week isolation was over, I was now at the bottom of the structured privilege level system. Since I was no longer a level two or three, I couldn't leave the unit for off site activities. I could not even go downstairs with the other residents and use the basement gym at recreation time.

Most of the staff went with the main body of kids wherever they went. On the unit there was only one residential counselor left to answer the phones. I was completely bored out of my mind with nothing to do. I asked for and received permission to go into the games room.

The games room was largely unused because it was unheated. Since it was near the end of a typical New England winter, my breath was visible in puffs as I walked in. I found incomplete sets of board games, a variety of books on shelves and a table soccer rig in the corner.

As I wandered around my questing eyes fixated on a poster on the wall. It was the patient's Mental Health Bill of Rights. Out of sheer boredom I wandered over and let my eyes scan it. As I was doing so, I realized with an internal shout of exultation that I was reading fast, with full comprehension.

Portions of my mind were multitasking and one of those circuits was analyzing the meaning of what I was reading. As I realized that I was reading effortlessly, I could not stop from gloating over my newfound mental processes again. My powers were back and I had no intention of losing them again.

CHAPTER 6

NONCOMPLIANCE

A new plan was coalescing in my mind. Assuming the system operated like it read in the fine print on the Mental Health Bill of Rights poster, it might just work too. Hope began to surge through my breast. And with that surge of hope came an elevation of mood which swept aside all depression and gave me a reason to smile in that freezing room.

To implement my idea I had to begin cooperating with everyone in order to lull them into believing that I was submissive again. When I was offered the chance to resume going to school off site, I had to agree on paper not to run away again. I signed the contract in all honesty. If all went according to plan then I would be walking out.

My psychologist, Dr. Pritchett, agreed to my request to borrow some of his psychology books and his *DSM III*. Every day now I studied psychology and started tackling the formidable diagnostic manual. I made a formal request to see my files and I was allowed to read some of them. I read clinical observations and summary reports with notations and learned what exactly it was that they had diagnosed me with.

I studied the entries on manic depression and schizophrenia repeatedly. I began to understand my mistakes and how to correct them. There were three strategies I developed. The first, was not to talk about how I honestly felt with anyone in the mental health field. Never again. There could be no more talking about hearing voices. Not ever.

The second strategy involved total cooperation with staff. Remembering to act as though everything was blue skies and roses every single day, convincingly. Except I couldn't appear too happy because expansive moods indicate manic episodes in someone diagnosed with bipolar disorder.

The third and hardest part was to gain an understanding of the mania aspect of manic depression. Much of it made no sense to my fifteen-year-old mind. It's symptoms had first become apparent to my grandparents and my aunt Myra, during the time I had lived with them. I remembered that they used to ask me questions like:

"Is there a reason as to why you can't seem to sit still?"

"Do you ever let another person start or finish a sentence?" And similarly, "Is it possible for you to ever not dominate a conversation, from beginning to end?"

"Are you aware that you have just been carrying on a ten minute monologue?"

"How did we go from talking about subjects A, B and C to subjects X, Y and Z in two minutes?"

"Stop, slow down, take a deep breath, back up. Now, what did you just say?"

According to the *DSM III*, the elements of my speech that caused my family to respond to me in conversation the way they did, were classic symptoms of mania. In psychiatric parlance those symptoms included, (in no particular order):

Irritability or psychomotor agitation.
Verbal incoherency.
Pressurized speech and thought derailment.
Flight of ideas.
Grandiose thinking or inflated self-esteem.
Distractibility.

As I read the definitions for the condition of mania, of being "high" (euphoric and intense), of having a manic episode, it dawned on me that my own behavior, seen from an observer's perspective, matched these manic symptoms. To me, those behaviors were quintessentially who I was as a person, it was how I was born and meant to be. Everyone, from my friends and family to teachers and clinicians, described me as an intense person.

From early on I realized that not everyone was gifted with my kind of intensity or the ability to understand my transmissions. My brother could understand me just fine because we are synced to similar frequencies. But he was about the only other person I had met in my life who also had the same kind of mental pressure. In the secrecy of my thoughts I decided, not to view my brain as abnormal, but possessed of a special advantage, a useful mutation. An unexpected benefit of the crossing of my parents genes.

As I read the entry on treating manic depressives, I encountered a section which stated something like:

> *Manic depressive patients do not always present symptoms that easily identify the patient as being in a manic or depressive phase. The patient may feel that their illness has spontaneously remitted. During those times, patients are most likely to discontinue their medications. It is imperative that patients be made to understand that their illness will always be there, and that it is necessary to take medications at all times in order to avoid future episodes.*

My gut feeling screamed an alarm, "Danger!" as I read this in the DSM, and I thought to myself: *This is bullshit*. If they had their way, they would take away my ideas and imagination, my psychic abilities and inspiration, and turn me into a drone. I was terrified as I read the DSM. Psychiatrists wanted to take my powers away from me before I had a chance to learn how to control them.

As I was reading and rereading the entry on symptoms of mania, I became self-conscious that my mind was racing right along as per usual. That was one symptom. Another symptom was fidgeting and inability to sit still. As I viewed the symptoms in print, I glanced at my hand and realized, that while my eyes were speedily devouring the text, my fingers had been drumming along the cover of the book, marching to the rhythm of my inner state of energy the entire time.

According to their definitions, I had shifted manic (which for me was normal) within days, if not hours, after coming off psychiatric drugs. I felt exposed. There was nothing that could be done about "being manic" but to learn to conceal it by any means possible. In the event that they figured out I was manic, I would need to flee or fight. In either case I would need to have my body back.

With my newly learned mania-symptom awareness at my disposal, I realized that just sitting in my room, DSM on my lap, fingers tapping, getting agitated about what I was reading and making these "grandiose" plans to hide my symptoms from staff counselors and clinicians, that this too was, according to the text, part of my so-called illness. The third part of my plan, controlling mania, was going to be harder than I thought. To succeed here was very important, it was life or death serious.

My juvenile safety-net was gone and I had to face this hard reality on my own. Failure meant that the chemical lobotomy could be reinstated and I'd never get out of this place. With my plan in mind, I got to work rebuilding my body's strength and conditioning.

The summer before, thanks to karate training, I could briskly perform fifty military style push ups and over one hundred sit ups. I was appalled to find myself barely able to perform one push up and two sit ups. It was like straining against the gravity of Jupiter. Emotions no longer suppressed by lithium, I wept. My fat, out of shape body was disgustingly feeble. As soon as the lethargy and fatigue had passed, I rolled over on the floor and tried for two more push ups.

Bit by bit, my brain became stronger and faster as I spent time pouring over college level psychology books. Gradually, I could do more sit ups and exercise longer. I kept losing weight steadily. I started stretching and doing my martial arts punch and kick drills several times a day in the privacy of my room, before roll call or during Quiet Hour.

At some point during that time the Tobey staff tried to coax me to get back on meds. I had been so compliant, so cheerful and agreeable that the sole nurse at the med closet did not watch me closely. She handed me the tiny paper med cup. I accepted it while simultaneously glancing pointedly past her shoulder at a medical chart on the wall behind her and asked an innocent-seeming question about medical terminology.

As she turned her head to see what I was referring to, I made a gesture that raised the cup to my lips, and followed it with the expected tilting of the head while tossing the cup into the garbage. I took a sip from a cup of water, and as she turned her head back to me, I stepped forward and obligingly opened my mouth, raised my tongue and made an "Ahhg" sound to satisfy her that I had taken my meds like a good patient. That was the most delicate and exciting part.

Suffice it to say that this maneuver requires an ability to achieve a rapport with a person and the ability to create expected body language cues in order to set up a deception. I was quite good at it and able to effectively use sleight-of-hand and misdirection against all the med nurses.

After a couple of weeks I finally got caught, not because I was sloppy, but because the nurse, Susan, who was checking my weight records, became skeptical.

Prior to my escape I had steadily gained somewhere between 10 and 20 pounds a month. After my escape I had been steadily losing weight every week. The weight loss continued, despite discontinuing my starvation protest and my apparent med compliance.

She turned and stared at me and would not be distracted while I had the med cup in my hand. I could tell by the searching look in her eyes that I was busted. Long, uncomfortable moments passed as we stared at each other. Finally I smiled, and without breaking our staring contest casually tossed the cup, pills and all, into the trash.

"How long?" she inquired.

"I never restarted," I answered with a grin.

"How do you feel?" She asked.

"Better than I have in a long time," I replied insouciantly.

"You know I have to inform staff about this."

"I know."

That evening I was summoned to the offices of the director for the Tobey residential lockdown (a different administrator oversaw the Tobey School itself). We talked and I took the offensive immediately. I demanded to know why I was here, at this placement.

As for my "medications," I told the director that I was now fifteen years old and had the legal right to reject medical treatments and to refuse consent to any medical procedure unless I was incapacitated, suicidal or psychotic. I was in none of those conditions and therefore I did not have to be treated for anything.

"I have the right to live in the least restrictive setting for my needs. Since I am no longer manic or depressed, nor have I received treatment for any mental health conditions in several weeks, Tobey School is an inappropriate placement for me, and as of now, I want to petition for a writ of habeas corpus. In accordance with the law, the director of the program is required to review my request and start the process by informing the people who are my court appointed legal guardians," I stated.

The program director's mouth hung open slightly and he just kept looking at me for few moments.

"Where, how did you learn all that?" he inquired skeptically.

"It is right there, in plain English, on a poster in the other room," I replied matter-of-factly.

"You intend on continuing to refuse medications?" (Learning to accept my mental illness and maintaining medication "compliance" was one of the stated goals of my Individual Education Plan.)

"Yes I do." I replied stoically.

"Then there is no reason for you to stay in this program. Unfortunately, the only one who can take you out is your social worker, whom, as you've pointed out, I am now required to inform," he answered.

"The sooner the better," I answered.

The next day I got a call from my social worker.

"What's this about not being on meds?" she demanded.

"Get me out of here," I demanded right back.

Earlene was irate. She practically yelled at me, telling me in no uncertain terms, "You are in noncompliance."

"Oh well," I replied sardonically.

"You are sick and you have to be on meds," she insisted.

"Actually, no, I don't." I continued, "I am feeling fine, and furthermore, I now have the legal right to refuse drugs."

"You will never get out of there unless you start showing compliance right away," and she hung up on me.

I called Gavin, my guardian ad litem, and left a message for him. Eventually he returned my call and I told him what went down, that my social worker refused to let me out. I explained how I learned about writ of habeas corpus, informed consent, and the right to refuse treatment, and then I asked him to petition for me. He told me he was impressed that I knew all that stuff and speculated, "Maybe you have a career as a lawyer. I'll get to work on it," he added. And he did.

During that time I had had one more visit with my off-site psychiatrist, a dark haired, long-limbed man named Dr. Imhof. It was like my first visit. I had been so out of it during all the previous appointments that I didn't know who he was or what we had discussed before. When I asked him what his responsibility was, he told me it was to talk about and prescribe meds. Dr. Imhof was the person who reviewed my lithium lab results and had authorized the switch from liquid Trilafon to pills because I had been sliding so far down educationally.

Well, now I was off the "meds."

"I hear you are no longer taking your medications. Care to explain what that's all about?" he inquired when I sat down.

My medications? thought I. I never wanted or asked for them.

"Your drugs poisoned me," I said heatedly. "They have done nothing to help me."

"We can try you on something else," Imhoff offered solicitously, crossing his legs.

"No," I grated angrily.

"You know you are only hurting yourself," he said reprovingly over his Freddie Mercury mustache. "Do you really want another relapse?"

"You can go fuck yourself," I seethed as I glared at him. "And you are fired. For hurting, not helping me."

I stood up abruptly, terminating our session, and stalked out of his office to sit on the steps outside for the rest of the hour until my ride back to Tobey showed up. I was more than a little incensed over the malfunction I had been forced to suffer through while on those so-called "meds." By taking over my medication review, Dr. Imhoff was partly responsible for my misery. He was the easiest target to blame and the obvious person to lash out at. I was satisfied that our confrontation had ended the way I had envisioned.

Later in the community room, waiting for roll call, I got bored as usual and my knee went up, down, up, down and my fingers would start to dance on my thighs. As I became aware of this, I sent a command to all my limbs to freeze and be still while at the same time I glanced around to see if any staff had witnessed my "ants-in-my-pants," a symptom of psychomotor agitation associated with mania.

Eventually, after much practice, I could successfully feel the impulse to move a limb and override it before it even fired. Over and over again I would do this: Sit still, breathe calmly and interrupt the movement signals that my fidgeting mind sent to my limbs. This was easier than trying to stop my heart.

In conversation I learned to be succinct. When I was growing up, my stepfather had frequently criticized me for using ten words when two would do. It had become clear to me during my forays into the DSM that verbosity would be considered a sign of mania.

Now, I metered the words and took the time to spell out sentences in my mind before saying them. Pre-caching my thoughts also had the advantage of increasing the time it took me to respond in conversation and to impose a sentence limit.

Although my mind-body discipline was limited, I was nevertheless able to successfully conceal the external signs of bipolar mania. I refused to show anger or annoyance, but they were always just under the surface. My mind still churned and blazed, but this new self-discipline gave me a workable means to hold a conversation without betraying the myriad thought processes and constant rapid cerebration.

The slower speech, absence of fidgeting and my now amicable attitude put everyone at ease, much the same way it had been when I was sedated. I learned to keep my problems to myself and not draw attention to my behavior, no matter what was going on inside. Isn't that normal and expected behavior of adults?

My court date came and I had rehearsed for days what I would say to the judge. My case worker, Earlene, had the job of transporting me. An aura of tension filled the car, along with her effluvia, commingled with the rancid miasma emanating from the landfill of Styrofoam containers and fast-food wrappers which completely obscured the floor of her Toyota. The drive was short. This was it. This was the moment I had imagined when I had read and reread the full text of the patient's Bill of Rights.

The courtroom was tiny and cozy, only a few people present. The judge, the advocate and the social worker took turns talking. After a minute or two the judge asked me if I had anything to say on my own behalf. I nodded my head and he beckoned for me to step forward and speak.

He asked me, "What do you want?"

"I want to live my life like a normal teenager," I answered.

"What do you have to say about your mental health problems?" he queried.

"Your Honor, a certain amount of depression is normal for any teenager," I said. "I come from an abusive family. I've had some problems, yes. More than some but less than others." I added, "But I'm fine now. I've learned more ways to cope then I knew when I tried to hurt myself."

I stated my case, "I have been fine for months, there is no reason I need this level of supervision."

He gave me a kindly smile and told me, "You are quite articulate." He was impressed that I had asserted myself so well.

"Thank you," I replied, as I smiled back gratefully in return.

The judge thought that mine was a perfectly reasonable request. He turned to my social worker and told her, "Make it happen."

I could see Gavin, my advocate, smiling too. In fact, the only one who was not smiling right then was Earlene. I had to spend another two or three weeks there as she dragged her heels, but by the middle of May I finally left the Tobey School residential facility and was on my way to my first foster home.

CHAPTER 7

PARALLEL UNIVERSE

M y new home was a considerable distance out in the boonies, a house bordered by Douglas pines, country roads and barbed wire fence. My foster parents, Roland and Hope, were in their mid-forties and they were professional caregivers. They had taken some kind of training program and had certificates that allowed them to take in kids with emotional, behavioral or learning problems. They received subsidy for each foster kid that they had.

Roland worked some distance away. Hope was a full-time housewife and parent. They owned a couple of horses, dogs and other pets. I was given an allowance and saddled with taking care of the horses' food, water and manure. They were pretty straight forward about how everything worked and what the expectations were.

Hope took me aside to talk to me about my foster siblings. The youngest, David, was in second grade. He had been sexually abused by his older sister since he was a baby. They were adopting him as their own child and they spoiled him.

Next came Kevin and his sister Shannon, both younger than I by a year and two respectively. They had been extracted from an abusive family where the father was an alcoholic and the mother a drug addict. Like David, Kevin and Shannon had both experienced some amount of sexual abuse at some point.

Although they were teenagers, they acted barely older than the younger boy. Both were slightly retarded and mildly speech impeded. The brother much more so than his sister. Regardless, deep conversation would not be coming from any of them, so I felt alone.

What I would not have given for five minutes of high speed transmissions with my brother back then. I contemplated the irony of coming out of an institution only to become the eldest of four psychologically damaged siblings in a family with a mom who stayed home all day and a father that spent all day working.

In less than two weeks things started going wrong. The first time Shannon tried to wake me up, she put her hand on me and started shaking me. Like a bomb I exploded, thrashing and kicking my blankets aside as I erupted off the bed, out of a sound sleep. I raged at her, "Never touch me again!" She immediately ran screaming to our foster mother who in turn yelled at me to come out of my room at once.

When Hope confronted me she was pissed-off. She was controlling it at first, but as she continued speaking, her voice began to rise with each sentence until it became shrieking hysteria. I had not seen this kind of display in a long time but I recognized it all too well. Once she had triggered my anger and hypervigilance, I was just acting out scripted behavior patterns and survival mechanisms.

She started threatening me, "You had better do something about that dirty look on your face if you know what is good for you." My so-called "dirty look" was the look I had learned to give everyone that threatened me. My eyes were narrowed as I paid careful attention to your body language in preparation to move when the inevitable assault came. My mouth was a tight slit. I kept my face devoid of expression so as to prevent you from reading my emotions accurately.

Like all escalating confrontations, ours became more explosive and tense with every second. Hope was standing now and telling me to avert my eyes to the ground, and I was hearing it but not registering her words. I continued to stare intensely at her, just waiting for the slap to my face or a hand to come grasping my hair or ear.

My brain was in combat mode, my knees were shaking from the adrenaline. Time slowed down and her voice was distant and out of sync with her angry gesturing as my mental defense grid offered up targeting solutions and range estimates of her body to mine. Parry, block, dodge and riposte was all I could think of as I altered my body angle and began to crouch and bend my knees ever so slightly.

I was so angry that I was seeing red. Finally I walked past her and stepped outside for a small demonstration so she could get an idea of what was in store for her if she kept pushing me. Fueled by rage, I began methodically punching the wall of the house like an industrial piston. Boom! Boom! Boom! Each blow split my knuckles until the blood spattered on the wall and my hands were swollen.

The machine-like percussion only scared her into greater histrionics. She came out and ordered me to stop and come inside before she called the cops. When I came in, Hope told me I was not allowed to talk or interact with the other kids anymore without permission. She commanded me to get on my knees and stay there with my hands laced over my head until further notice. But I refused.

Then came the final ultimatum. "If you have any desire to stay in this house and remain a part of this family," she glared at me, trying to keep the quaver out of her voice, "You had better obey right now." That's it, go ahead," she threatened, "keep ignoring me. I've had it with you. I am calling CFS." She went to the phone, picked it up and asked me, "Which is it going to be?"

She would not tell me again. Either I got on my knees right now or it was back to the hated institution I would go. It was no idle threat. Earlene, my case worker, had insisted that I needed structured living programs, and being kicked out of my first foster home in less than fourteen days would prove to everyone that she was right.

A terrible, cynical and desperate battle played out in my mind. I could not, would not go back to the Tobey building on the state hospital grounds. I quickly analyzed the pros and cons. I realized I could take punishment better than I could take restricted, structured and supervised living. I had already faced both crazy family living and living with crazy people at facilities. In the foster home there was at least a chance of semi-normalcy.

We had home cooked meals. There was no sharps closets and no group therapy meetings. There were no staff with their thick brass rings jangling against their hips from all the keys on them needed to open all the locked metal doors. There would be no unannounced fire drills at two o'clock in the morning. I could go outside by myself and smell the woods, which was preferable to escorted walks on hospital grounds. The house had curtains instead of steel mesh over the windows. Table lamps and light stands illuminated the place instead of overhead fluorescent lighting. I had dealt with my mother. I could deal with this woman too. There really was no choice at all.

I refused to bow my head or look down. I kept my head high and stared at the ceiling instead. I was forced to kneel down on the floor for hours, until my foster father showed up. Roland would be the final arbiter of judgment as to whether or not I would be allowed to stay, and any further punishments as well. As the other foster kids came into the room at various times, Hope warned them not to look at or speak to me. That little detail was straight out of Sarah's playbook.

Hours passed as I continued to kneel on the painfully hard wooden floor of the living room. I did not even know if my submission would be worth it since my fate was still an unknown. But Roland was considerably more rational than his wife. When he finally came home from work he actually asked me what had happened and listened to my explanation thoughtfully.

"Well, alright then," Roland mused as he rocked in his chair. "We'll give you two more chances before you're out. Sound fair?"

"Yes," I nodded respectfully. Like I was going to say anything else.

The next day was Sunday and the entire family drove nearly an hour to get to their church. I had lied and told them I grew up atheist, so I was allowed to stay home. After so many years of unrequited filial piety, coupled with all my unanswered prayers, I was more sure than ever that the all-knowing god-king who lived in the sky was almost certainly nonexistent.

As I explored the house and grounds, I found they kept a caged rabbit on the porch. I opened its cage and slowly advanced my fingers towards it. It came forward to assess the offering and promptly bit me on the tip of my finger. It bit me so hard and so deep that blood from the wound dripped in a steady patter on the cage, the floor of the porch and my clothing.

I rushed to bandage myself up, but the blood flow was too continuous for a bandage yet. I had to tie my finger up in a towel and elevate my hand over my head to stop the bleeding. As soon as I had it under control I went scavenging around the house for some items. I procured a clear plastic bag from the kitchen and a padded leather work glove from the porch. Then I went to deal with the offender.

Seeing my own blood splotches all over the floor only nourished the notion in my head. I restrained the creature that had injured me so. I forced the plastic bag over its head and held it there with my gloved hand. I put my face close so I could look it in the eye and I spoke to it.

"I'll bet, when you woke up this morning you didn't know you were going to end up dead today, did you? Was biting me worth dying for?"

Its struggles just made me angrier, fueling my grip on it. It didn't take long until it stopped moving. I watched its eyes glaze over. It was an amazing feeling to kill this thing and it vented some of the pressure in my head.

Immediately I felt stupid and cheated. This thing was just a dumb animal. It didn't know any better. I picked it up and evaluated its state of death. *Why did I just do that?* my mind screamed. There was nothing to it anymore, only an inanimate warm bag of soft fur. *What have I done?*

I remembered reading somewhere that serial killers often had a history of violence and cruelty towards pets and animals, and like me, many psychopaths had a history of being bullied and humiliated at school or at home. All those thoughts came and went in a heartbeat of time. With the next beat came a cold, clear voice which calmly informed me: *You too are now a psychopath, you do realize that, right?*

I shook with fear and sudden remorse. Not so much for the pet but for me. *What the hell is wrong with you?* My mind raced along trying to formulate an excuse. I would come forward with it. I had at best two hours to plan how to cover it up. I panicked and screamed at myself for being so stupid. *You are going to end up in a padded cell for the rest of your life because you couldn't control your anger.* I told myself silently.

Maybe twenty seconds had passed since it had died and all those thoughts had come and gone in a short moment. None of the cover up options were really all that workable. No matter what happened, the facts were that one of the house pets would be dead or missing the first time I was left alone, and I doubted they would let me stay once they had time to think about it. For a few more seconds I was frozen by indecision and fear.

Then, out of nowhere, I remembered that I had taken a CPR course almost three years earlier as part of health class at school. I cupped my hand into a tube over the animal's nose and mouth and blew into it. Like a fur covered hot water bottle its sides expanded as it inflated. I let the weight of its body cause the exhale and I performed it two more times. I counted to five, then slapped its rib cage smartly with two fingers and looked at its eyes for a moment before I blew into nose and mouth again.

On the third breath of the second set of repetitions it moved. It stretched itself and panted for a few moments before rolling off its side onto all four feet and hunched into a ball. I must have said "Oh my god, thank you," a thousand times as I sat there and petted it for half an hour without taking my eyes off it.

The rabbit was fine. It remained healthy and unaffected by neurological issues. It outlasted me too because it was still living there over a year later. I could not believe how lucky I was that day.

That I had anger issues relating to institutional life and the things that had happened to me over the years was apparent. That those anger issues and my traumatic stress reactions had been triggered by my new family was just too much to bear. I had come within an inch of being kicked out of here and put back in lockdown. The pressure never seemed to let up.

The next day I asked Roland, "Why do you smoke?" Wondering if his reason would be any different from, say, my friends or family members' who also had the habit.

He took a gratuitously large drag off his cigarette and pondered my question as he exhaled slowly.

"Stress," he said, nodding to himself, "helps deal with stress."

That's what I had thought but I didn't say so aloud. I was suddenly awash in memories of childhood promises I had made to my mother, to her glowing approval. I would never cuss, smoke, do drugs, steal, lie or have sex before I was married. What good were my promises to her now? This was my life, not hers. She obviously wouldn't know, so how could she care? Besides, Sarah wasn't my mother anymore. She had made that clear in court.

"Do you mind if I have a cigarette?" I asked Roland.

"I thought you said you didn't smoke when you got here?" he quizzed as he passed two of them to me.

"I do now," I answered him, with just a hint of irony in my voice.

Only he could smoke inside. I had to go outside. Which was fine. I missed being outside anyway.

It was raining slightly as I found a dry patch under a dense pine tree on the side of the house. I smoked my cigarettes and was glad to find something I could do to cope. My allowance for my chores would cover a pack of smokes a week, and every time I wanted one I could just go outside and sit under the tree and be by myself for a few minutes, undisturbed. I was guaranteed two to three cigarette timeouts a day. I would take my sweet time smoking them to make my out-of-sight breaks last while enjoying the brief solitude.

Things leveled out for awhile. Life with them was not always bad all the time. In fact I would go so far as to say that most of the time we functioned more or less like a family. The hardest person to deal with was my foster mother. It was impossible to forget what she had done to me soon after I arrived.

Hope was always prone to over-reacting to things. I palpably sensed that she looked down at us as being inferior. She'd become used to dealing with educationally and intellectually challenged kids and didn't like dealing with me. I was under the distinct impression that she preferred the learning disabled children because they were simple, and aside from adopting David, they were really in it for the money they collected from the state for each child placed with them.

With Hope, every little thing mushroomed into a debate. I was one of those teenagers that always had an answer for everything, and, like my birth mother, Hope didn't appreciate being told she was wrong, even when I could prove it. (*Especially* when I could prove it.) Whenever I could best her in an argument she would complain to Roland, who would tell me to knock it off and stop giving her grief.

That summer I got a chance to go to my grandparents house and retrieve my belongings. My grandmother had terminated my occasional weekend visits when she found out that I had discontinued the psychiatric drugs. That meant that until my discharge, I had to spend every day and night in the Tobey facility. No weekend reprieve for good behavior.

She relinquished the guardian rights she had won in court once I received my official inpatient diagnosis. She had volunteered information about my friends, which had expedited my capture when I made my escape from the Tobey Building. She had recommended that I stay at the residential school program. My grandmother was a traitor to me and I hated her, along with every one of Them that had ever harmed or opposed me.

A heavy tension hovered over the household when I arrived. My grandparents no doubt were waiting with baited breath to see if I would come unglued in front of their very eyes. Instead, I kept my words minimal and left as soon as I had what I came for.

What I had wanted most at that time was my snorkeling gear. When I had been in Hong Kong my father had bought me a top notch mask, snorkel and fins for diving the South China Sea. In the humid heat of a typical New England summer day, the best place to be was in a cold river or lake. New Hampshire is dotted with small, clear lakes and streams, all created from the glacial activity of the last Ice Age. It was at one of these summer watering spots where I quite possibly saved my foster sister's life.

While Roland commuted to work many miles away, Hope would pack the five of us into the back of the station wagon and we would go to local ponds and rivers to cool off. That particular day we were at the side of a river.

An observer would have been greeted by an idyllic scene of children at play. Kids swung off a rope that had been suspended from a tree overhanging an embankment. There were kids on the beach with toys. One father stood hip deep in the water and continuously tossed his kids over his shoulder into the river to their shrieking delight. Most of the adults on the beach were mothers and most of them were enjoying the sun in reclining beach chairs.

I had already enjoyed an extensive swim and snorkeling session. As one of the oldest teens there and a complete stranger too, I simply kept to myself and swam far and deep in the refreshingly cold water.

I was lying on my beach towel beside Hope, resting, when I heard Shannon cry out in alarm. Amidst the background of laughter and high spirited carrying on, the sound and tone of her cry instantly yanked me into a sitting position and riveted my attention on her.

She had been lounging on an inflated inner tube. Gradually the inner tube had floated further out into the river, where the inner tube had casually sped up until she had realized that the scenery was moving by way too fast. Shannon didn't know how to swim and when she saw how far and fast she was moving from the shore, she cried for help.

Instantly I assessed her situation and my options. My swim fins lay next to me and could have been a powerful aid in getting to her and pulling her back. Unfortunately, it takes long, awkward moments to put them on, and she was moving further away every second.

She screamed again, even more desperate this time. I could not chance a delay for the fins. I ran at top speed across the beach and turf. I hurled myself into the water at an angle designed to make maximum use of my momentum and the river current. I swam as fast as I could, and aided by the river itself I caught up to her languid inner tube.

With one arm around the tube I began to reverse my direction and at first we went nowhere. The current was powerful and I swam vigorously just to overcome our combined inertia. Then, gradually, I pulled us out of the middle towards the sides and, once there, was able to swim against the current until we could get out at the edge.

As we came back towards the main area, I was cheered with applause by several people. Others asked us if we were okay. It was kind of embarrassing to be the focus of attention by strangers. On one level I felt good about it, but it was really no big deal.

Reviewing what just happened, I couldn't believe that no one else had noticed the difference between her scream and all the screaming going on by the other kids. Granted, only my foster family knew that she could not swim. A few mothers had sat upright, shielding their eyes with one hand and looking in her general direction, but no one moved. Most of them had not even interpreted the danger or taken notice.

I was a hero for a short while, I guess. No one was more surprised than me that I was still capable of selfless action.

Shannon thanked me over and over.

Roland congratulated me upon finding out.

Hope was actually nice to me for awhile.

I could do no wrong for a time and it was great to be in favor with both of my foster parents. At least while it lasted.

That summer we moved a few miles down the road and away from the rural highway. Now we lived in an old farm house, complete with meandering stone walls along the property border. Vast green fields butted up against new birch forests. Two old and sway-backed grey barns stood empty and unused by the side of the house, having shrugged off their original coat of paint long ago. Deep ruts gouged the earth on both sides of the dirt roads, owing to snow runoff in springtime. Only the main rural road was paved.

New stalls were built for the two Appaloosas in the more structurally intact of the two barns. Unfortunately, I still performed chores in my usual rushed manner using a minimal amount of attention and effort in order to get back to whatever I was doing previously. My foster mother would come out to look after all the animals and inevitably come scream at me for not doing my work properly or thoroughly.

One of those incidents involved the giant water bucket that I had to fill for the horses every day. On that day, Hope confronted me in an image of Sarah. She screamed at me to come down from reading in my room to the barn.

Red-faced and livid beneath the frame of her golden hair, she pointed out the green algae that had built up on the sides of the dark brown bucket. I never even noticed them until she showed me. "You will wash and rewash the bucket," she commanded. "Until I am satisfied you've done it right." I had been through this kind of thing before with my stepfather Tim. I was terrified the entire time that the bucket incident would be considered one of my remaining strikes.

What I didn't realize until a few years later was that my foster parents expected I would do chores diligently, and in the course of filling the bucket, I was supposed to notice the algae building up, then take the initiative by cleaning it before Hope or Roland ever had a chance to see it. That was beyond my ability because I lived inside my head to the point of distraction. Besides, nobody ever took the time back then to demonstrate in exquisite detail exactly what they wanted of me, so I tended to do the bare minimum.

I learned a lot of manual labor activities that year. I got comfortable being around farm animals. I shoveled up and carted off goose dung and horse manure. I tossed bales of hay and learned how to string an electric fence. There was always plenty of work that could be done around that place.

One upshot to the time spent in foster care was the continual weight loss. Between the physical nature of farm chores, the stress from living with my hysterical foster mother, and my new smoking habit I lost a lot of weight. I continued to practice the exercises, forms training and striking drills from karate whenever I wasn't depressed.

All I really needed to motivate myself to train and lose weight was my memory of how I got fat in the first place. I would work up a good angry and it would overtake me. I would get so enraged dwelling over what had been done to me that I would start running.

The property was big enough that I could run long circuits, endlessly. I would cut across the grass, jump on the stone wall and run over occasionally unstable surfaces as fast as I could. I would run until I dropped, breathless. Then I screamed at myself for being so weak and forced myself to get up and start doing jump kicks.

The net result was that in less than a year I actually weighed less than I did when I went inpatient the year before. The only visible scars of the damage that the psychiatric drugs had done to me was a soft tummy that no amount of sit ups could tighten. It was loose skin and I could pull it away from my body in one hand. The loose skin and the purple stretch marks on my hips and thighs took a long time before they finally went away.

By the years end I was tough, flexible and lean once again. It was a personal victory. For the second time I had won both form and fitness on my own volition based on how I wanted my body to be. When I achieved it the first time, in my early teens, I had been grossly uncoordinated, sensitive to the cold and somewhat frail. I had changed my body by hammering coordination and endurance into my nervous system because my survival demanded it.

With my rebuilt body to go along with my unchained mental faculties I was now feeling better than I ever had while I had been institutionalized. Aside from the smoking, I was in phenomenally great shape. The me that I knew was finally and completely back.

CHAPTER 8

RAMIFICATIONS

The person that I knew to be "me," that is, my overall character, was prone to reactive behaviors, disregard for authority and an inability to consider all avenues of a personal course of action. As a result, it was only a matter of time before I got in trouble again. For most American teenagers, the trouble I got into was fairly low key. Because I was in a foster home for emotionally troubled kids and I was also a ward of the State, it mushroomed into a big deal very quickly.

Autumn in New Hampshire was in full swing as the trees abandoned the summer's green for red, orange, and golden coloration. It took a series of long car and bus rides for me to go visit my friends in the southern region of the state. I had agreed to be back from my friend's house by a certain time. But I was really absorbed in a marathon role-playing game session and out of reluctance to leave I deliberately missed a bus connection to stay longer, figuring I would just get another.

My foster mother called me up at my friend Ann's house. Hope was incensed that I hadn't followed the plan that we had agreed to and demanded that I return home immediately. Unfortunately, there were very few buses remaining that evening and no easy way to get to the bus station. I couldn't get a ride from my friends simply because, being teenagers without jobs, they didn't have the gas money and neither did I.

As it turned out, Roland worked in the area, only some ten miles away. So I agreed that I would try to get a ride to his place of employment and sit in his truck until he got out of work the next day. I was already in trouble for not being back on time. But I couldn't get a ride and things got a lot worse.

In order to be at Roland's work place, I needed to walk at night through several small towns to get there. I was walking through one such town around midnight, when I noticed a sole car driving slowly, coming from the opposite direction. It was a police car and the cops inside had pulled over to the side of the road to question a hitchhiker.

I knew that the cops would see me, turn around and come ask me what I was doing, out walking around this late at night. They would then realize I was a minor and that I lived fifty miles away. It was one thing to get into trouble for doing house chores poorly. It was another thing entirely to be in police custody. There would be no avoiding the notification of my social worker, which automatically endangered my placement at the foster home.

Sure enough, the cops drove by in the opposite lane, turned promptly around and came up behind me to talk with me. The instant they called me over to the car I made my decision and ran for it. If I could lose them in the woods, I would double back and take a different road into the next town.

I turned and bolted through an overgrown field dotted with small trees and shrubs. The ground was exceedingly treacherous to navigate in the dark and my face was lashed by branches repeatedly as I dodged and feinted to elude capture. Even though I was carrying my overnight bag, the cops were no match for my foot speed.

They called for backup, and soon, everywhere I looked, I saw approaching blue lights strobing in the dark. I ran through backyards and across front lawns, trying to ration my energy, constantly searching for a potential hiding place, when I spotted a series of fuel trucks in a parking lot.

As I was looking for the best candidate and trying to figure out how to scale up one, several police cars overran the parking lot and there were many officers with flashlights, talking urgently with each other. I was breathless from running so hard and I needed to rest and there were far too many policemen closing in from every direction to escape. Cops burst into view and I heard them behind me as well. The officer closest to me blinded me with his flashlight and I couldn't tell whether he had a gun trained on me or not. I have watched enough movies to know what not to do if you don't want to be shot by the police, and before he even started yelling at me, I dropped my bag and raised my arms up over my head slowly.

I surrendered peacefully and without issue, but that was not enough for the adrenaline-charged young rookie coming up behind me. He kicked the back of my knee, put me in a choke hold and slammed my face into the dirt before they cuffed me. They didn't warn me to watch my head, but threw me bodily into the back of the cruiser, causing my left temple to smash into the roof of the police car.

All the cops were mad as hell. I had probably interrupted their philosophical chats at the nearest 24-hour a day Dunkin Donuts when the call came in to apprehend a fleeing suspect. They were even more upset that I didn't have any firearms, a pound of cocaine or stolen diamonds in my overnight bag. I was just some scared teenage kid that had bolted from the police and, up until that point, my record was clean of criminal offenses. Not an impressive midnight catch for all that effort. And so they were not pleasant with me.

I spent the rest of the night and part of the next day in jail until I was delivered in handcuffs to the nearest court that oversaw juvenile cases. Since my social worker was my legal guardian, she had had to drive the fifty miles down here and that was not a good sign. Earlene informed me that my foster parents hadn't yet decided whether or not to have me back. Luckily for me, the police in their magnanimity had decided to drop their charges of violating curfew, disobeying a peace officer and "resisting" arrest.

My foster parents did allow me back, but I was no longer allowed to go and visit my friends again. I was to come home from school and go to my room every single day. I was only allowed out for the bathroom, dinner, or chores. I was permitted to have a cigarette outdoors after I had fed the horses and done my other chores. If I complained or showed any more bad attitude, that was it. I would be kicked out. This was my last chance.

For weeks I endured the intensity of that threat hanging over me. At first, I was so depressed that I nearly killed myself again. I was so scared of failing that I didn't know what to do. I had one more chance and it had to last for more than two years, until I was eighteen. I knew from past experience that I couldn't last that long. It was inevitable that I would screw up sooner or later.

Hope's definition of discipline-worthy offenses was whimsical and unpredictable. There was no way of knowing what would set her off. I was genuinely too scared to want to interact with her. I was happy to be confined in my room and spend my time lost in my books. I was overwhelmed with the certainty that I would do something within the next two years and it would be game over, and I would be institutionalized again.

I became so distraught at the idea of living in a lockdown again, that I fashioned a noose from my karate belts and tried to hang myself in my room that night. My bedroom was the attic and you had to stoop to walk around in it. It was not ideal for a hanging. I used my own body weight to cause a blood choke, similar to what I tried to do in my closet back at Tobey.

As before, when the red-out came over my vision, I heard this voice in my head cry out for me to stop. It didn't have to end this way. Tobey School had not been my death, and these people were not going to be the death of me either. I was almost sixteen now, which meant I could drive legally. If I got a license and a car, perhaps I could simply flee the state if they kicked me out. Now I had a new plan and a glimmer of hope as I untied the belts knotted around my neck.

After that last, my third suicide attempt, things stabilized for a time. A few months later I got a part-time job at a Dunkin Donuts coffee shop. With the money from that job I was able to save up for my first car. I passed my driver's education exams flawlessly and had my license. Because I was a minor, I could not register my vehicle without my foster father's co-signature.

Around that time, my real dad, Andrew, was back from overseas again and he visited me at this foster home. When he found out that I had a car and a driver's license, he actively tried to persuade Roland not to sign the vehicle registration (which would allow me to put plates on it).

When I found out about this, I was incensed. Any person that tried to help me I gave my loyalty to. Anyone that opposed my plans or recommended confinement and structure for me was my enemy. Accordingly, I transferred my loyalty from my biological father to my foster father. Roland thought that owning and driving a car would be a great maturity building responsibility. The sooner I mastered it, the better for me. Finally, someone was on my side, for a change. Someone who was trying to enable me and not retard me from what I wanted.

My foster father was a complex man. For him alone I tried to be good. Not for anyone else. I didn't care for my foster siblings and I hated my foster mother, but Roland inspired me and taught me many things.

He was a survivor. He had grown up in an ethnically dense and racially charged urban neighborhood in Massachusetts. He had been in several knife fights in his teens. A talent scout spotted him in a local YMCA where he would box and he was ferocious. He was a Golden Gloves boxer in the '60s or '70s and was known for knocking out his opponents with his left hand.

One night, on the way to a fight, he was struck by a drunk driver and hit so hard that he flew through the windshield onto the street. He died three times that night, once in the ambulance and twice in the emergency room. He had had to lie flat on his back for months. He had metal pins installed throughout his entire body, and a steel plate held his jaw together. A set of false upper teeth replaced the ones that had been knocked out and scattered onto the road. He had a steel bar for a tibia. When they replaced his tibia with the bar, they told him, that in all likelihood the bone would never grow back. But it did grow back and eventually there were two bones competing to occupy the same space.

I asked him why they didn't take the implant out. He told me that they would have to break his leg again to remove it, and that he couldn't afford the down time. Indeed, even though they received a subsidy from the state for each of us foster kids, he needed to work full-time to get ahead financially. No longer able to earn money from boxing, he had fallen back on other work. At one time he had become an alcoholic.

When I first met him, he had recovered from alcoholism and was a scratch baker who got up at four o'clock in the morning to drive to work. He is one of the few former alcoholics I've ever seen drink. He was able to have a beer or glass of wine every now and then with no problem.

After getting up in the morning he would be heavily limping and contrary as all hell, he wouldn't speak to anyone unless he had to. He'd stalk out onto the breezeway and sit in a rocking chair. There he would stare out into the woods and smoke one or two cigarettes while drinking coffee. When he got up ten or fifteen minutes later, his limp was barely noticeable and he was less forbidding and more approachable.

Throughout the day he smoked almost two packs of Winston brand cigarettes and drank two liters of Coca Cola. He carried his bottle with him everywhere. He had an enormous action movie collection, consisting mostly of Clint Eastwood and Charles Bronson films, and would watch them frequently after dinner.

I once watched him work a small boxing bag (called a peanut bag) in the barn. He always told me not to smoke in the barn, but he didn't follow any such rule. I had heard a repetitive drumming impact coming through the walls and when I investigated, I saw him standing in the hay, head tilted to the side with a cigarette in his mouth, his hands were a blur as he punished the peanut bag. I'd never seen anyone move their hands so fast in my life. I asked him one day why he was so tough. (Because he really was a little guy, five foot seven or eight maybe, with narrow shoulders. He didn't look all that strong.)

"How can you stand the constant pain of having your tibia fuse to a metal bar, every single day?" I inquired skeptically.

Pointing to his head he said, "The mind is infinitely more powerful than the body."

Roland had learned martial arts and some kind of meditation when he was growing up. "I learned meditation a couple years earlier myself," I told him eagerly, "and I practice karate." Roland was the kind of father that I had often fantasized of having back then.

We got along much better after our one-on-one talk. Roland later taught me how to work a swivel bag with boxing drills. He also taught me some military combat techniques he had picked up in the Army. Altogether, he had a major influence on me and I learned a lot from him. I looked up to him.

Certainly none of the other parents I had had caused me to model myself after them deliberately. My stepfather and my biological father had both threatened me with harm. Both had tried to limit the reach of my grasp with some song and dance about how I was not old enough or mature enough yet.

My natal mother Sarah and foster mother Hope were ineffective parents, prone to over-reacting and hysteria. My grandmother was a traitor to me. Roland was the only parent that actually had traits that I wanted. And he believed in me. So it was unfortunate that it was with him that I destroyed my last chance to remain there.

I had been more or less perfectly behaved for quite some time. The perpetual grounding had been removed months earlier, once I got a part-time job. I owe those months of good behavior to keeping to myself as much as possible. Until I brought someone home after school with whom I had been dating for awhile. We were hot and bothered for each other and did what most any unsupervised teenagers in lust with each other would do. We had sex up in the hay loft of the barn.

Roland suddenly walked into the barn, through the breezeway that connected it to the house, to have a cigarette, and caught us in *flagrante delicto*. I had long forgotten about the ban my foster parents had imposed on anything sex related a year earlier when I had first moved in with them. My three foster siblings had all suffered sexual abuse. Sex was not approved for a topic of discussion in our house, ever.

The very next day, during my martial arts workout, David came outside and we played at fighting a bit. As I put my foster brother into a gentle arm lock, I saw, out of the corner of my eye, my foster father coming in our direction, fast and purposefully.

Roland ordered David to the house. Then he picked me up by my throat and stated, "If you ever touch my son again, I will kill you." Releasing his grip, he stalked back into the house.

I will kill you. I will kill you. I will kill you.

His words echoed in my mind as I watched him walk away. Conflicting emotions crashed inside me. On the one hand, I despaired that I made him angry at me. I didn't mean to. On the other hand, my combat radar was online again, and my whole body was shaking with outrage at this treachery as well as out of fear, from having just been assaulted and so powerfully threatened from someone I had begun to trust.

I am positive that in my youth I frequently overestimated my fighting abilities. But I knew that, unlike my stepfather, Roland was not an unskilled bully. I recognized that, as a former professional boxer, he would have put the smack-down on me if I had been able to overcome my reluctance to strike him. And I was angry at myself because I was not strong enough to fight him, and so, deep down, I became still more obsessed with learning the martial arts and self-defense.

The next day, Hope smugly informed me that I had used up my last chance, and that Roland had become terminally infuriated with me. She allowed me to pack one bag before driving me an hour into the city and dropping me off in the front office of the Child and Family Services building.

I had spent just a little over a year at that foster home. I had been mistreated, even mildly abused occasionally by both of my foster parents. Hope had been by far the worst of the two. Her repeated use of my fear of being institutionalized to guarantee my good behavior was very hard to bear. I never knew, from one day to the next, if that was the day I was going back into the madhouse and the oppression of its structured living programs.

That lack of predictability and safety meant that I never really engaged with my foster family, or even the local school. I knew that my stay there was temporary and I always felt like I was just visiting.

Far worse things happen to other kids in other foster homes than what I went through there. There were plenty of good times interspersed with some occasional awful times. Times, when we were just like any other family, I suppose. I very much regretted having pissed-off Roland. I had hoped that we could get along indefinitely.

I loved and now missed the property we lived at. There were deer, bobcats, opossums and all manner of woodland creatures dwelling in the surrounding forests. I used to stealthily climb out of my attic window onto the steeply pitched roof of the pantry annex, on those nights when manic energy kept me wide awake. I would smoke cigarettes and let my mind wander while staring at the incredibly clear, star-filled sky that permitted me a view of the edge of the Milky Way.

My social worker was considerably peeved that I had been kicked out. "At the age of sixteen it will be hard to find you another foster home." Earlene told me, "Consider yourself lucky if you don't end up in a residential facility."

The first new placement that my social worker found me wasn't bad at all. It was deep in the heart of the city of Manchester. I would live by myself in a small, subdivided apartment downstairs. I had my own kitchen, bathroom, bedroom and living room. I couldn't believe my good fortune.

Doug, the guy who ran the transitional program, gave me a set of rules to follow. I never really paid him any attention. Doug didn't look "authoritative" to me and so I couldn't take him seriously. He was adopting a young male teen and there was something between them I could not quite put my finger on at the time. I basically tuned him out and was all too eager to restore some semblance of independence and autonomy to my own life.

On the first weekend I broke every rule. I invited a friend over to spend the night. We had smoked cigarettes inside the house. I went back to my friend's house in a town over an hour's drive away without telling anyone. Because of a setback in finding a ride I failed to make it back before curfew.

Doug had gone out of town before we had had a chance to connect. He in turn had left a message with Earlene, telling her to find another placement for me, because he could not find me and did not know where I was.

I had returned early that morning and prepared myself for going back to school. I walked to Manchester Central High to register myself as a junior and get into classes on the first day back. When the admissions counselor asked for my records, I told her to call my social worker to get them. When the counselor connected with her, the first thing Earlene asked was to speak to me.

"You're in a lot of trouble" she started.

Surprised and annoyed I inquired, "What are you talking about?"

Earlene advised me, "There is a bench warrant for your arrest and detention in several nearby towns," and then added, "The police are looking for you right now."

Apparently, Doug had kicked me out the night before, but only my social worker knew that. She in turn, didn't know where I was and arbitrarily concluded that I had run away. I was flabbergasted at the series of gross overreactions.

"I simply failed to catch the last bus back the night before, " I explained. "It was beyond my control." (A repeat of the same mistake I had made with Roland and Hope months earlier.) It seemed I was the only one calm and collected about this.

I had attended my new school for barely an hour before I was picked up and relocated again. For awhile I spent my evenings at a variety of halfway houses and overnight shelters. During the day, we were often driving for hours just in one direction to various group homes and residential programs.

When the weekend came, she dropped me off, this time at a foster home in the middle of rural nowhere. It was Labor Day weekend and these people could take me for a couple of days. Their home was pastoral. Geographically speaking, they didn't live all that far from the last foster placement I was at. They had a barn too, but no horses and geese. Instead they had a cow and chickens.

By sheer luck, the old couple that lived there, Carol and Max, took a liking to me. The other foster kids varied widely in age. I was again the oldest at sixteen. An eleven-year-old girl and a two-year-old boy lived there as well.

The foster couple asked me what I wanted. I stated, "I just need a place to spend less than a year and a half until I turn eighteen."

"If you think you like it here," they told me, "and if you think you could get along with everyone, then you are welcome to spend that remaining time with us." For my part, I was exceedingly grateful for the chance to resume a semi-normal, mainstream teenage life again.

I did the best I could to keep that placement. I was resolved to apply myself and make good grades. I got involved with vocational technical training. I reconnected with old friends and started making new friends locally. I caught up with my childhood friend Julian again, who was attending a college nearby.

All in all, it was a good home. My new foster parents were in their late fifties and fairly laid back. They never set off my psycho radar. They were agnostic on the subject of religion. They seemed genuine and generous. I figured, my life would now be on easy-mode until I was a legal adult.

For about twelve weeks, everything went well. I attended Merrimack Valley High School as a junior. I came home and did chores and homework. Once the newness wore off, I had no interest in getting to know these people long term. I was just visiting. Most of the time I kept to myself at home.

I took pottery classes that year and I had created an incense holder with a black and white yin-yang patterned glaze. It was designed to hold several sticks of incense vertically and flammable liquid in a small bowl in the center, which functioned as a brazier. As I was a practicing Wiccan at the time it was to be used as part of magical ceremony and ritual.

When I finally brought it home I couldn't wait to test it. Ideally, I would use something like rubbing alcohol but I couldn't find any in the kitchen or bathroom. So fixated was I on seeing this brazier at work that I cast about for any combustible substance. I just needed a short, quick test, so any flammable liquid would do. I went outside to the barn and appropriated a tiny amount of gasoline. After taking special care with the setup, I poured the gas into the brazier and fired it up in my bedroom.

The test was a success. The gasoline burned hotter, faster and brighter than alcohol and consumed itself in seconds. The brazier worked perfectly and for a moment I had a nice little fire going on. Unfortunately, the one thing I had not factored in, having never ignited gasoline before, was the fumes. The vapors from the gasoline overpowered the room. I opened my windows enough to get some air flowing and kept my bedroom door shut to make sure the smell did not make it out.

It wasn't enough. Late that night, my new foster father Max, having wakened to use the toilet, smelled the gas and found that it was emanating from my room. Alarmed, he knocked rapidly and opened my door a crack to investigate.

At the time I was quite asleep, but wakened the instant Max opened my door. I gave him a sleepy rundown on why my room smelled like gas, "There is no more gas in my room, I'm not planning on burning it again, everything is fine," I mumbled. "Sorry about the smell." He closed my door and went back to bed, and I thought that was the end of it.

The next morning Max and Carol acted as though there was nothing wrong or out of place. I told them I wouldn't be home until late. I had a date immediately after school and then a job interview in the early evening at a local supermarket. I left for school, assuming everything was status quo. I had lived for about three months in their home and had no idea that I would never lay eyes on them again.

CHAPTER 9

IMPULSE

Halfway through my second period class, I was summoned to the guidance office. I was not in any kind of behavioral or scholastic trouble in this school, so I was surprised since I had no idea at all why anyone would have me summoned to their office. I didn't particularly like surprises or the unexpected because they typically did not bode well for me.

As I walked down the halls, my curiosity and trepidation were replaced with anxiety and dread. Suddenly, I didn't want to know what was waiting for me in guidance. When I turned one hallway and started down another, my anxiety and dread suddenly tripled in intensity. My intuitive danger sense flared. Intrusive voices in my head all came alive at once and started commanding me:

Run! Now! You are in danger! Run away! Do it now! Do not go to guidance! Run! Run you fool! Run!

My adrenal glands fired, tunnel vision came over me and my legs started shaking. I knew not what awaited me a few doors down, but I knew that if I escaped it by running away right then and there, my current life would change immediately for the worse. At the same time I sensed that if I kept going, my life was going to be altered anyway. And from the overwhelming gut feeling of danger I knew that whatever I was about to walk into was bad news.

I reminded myself that I had done nothing illegal or wrong and therefore was probably not going to jail or juvenile detention. Running away would only forestall whatever was waiting for me and would serve to demonstrate my capacity for impulsiveness and delinquency at a time when I was trying to avoid coming across that way to the adults in my life.

I decided to marshal my inner forces to deal with what was waiting for me in guidance. I started counting my breathing. I slowed down even more and made each step I took cause a wave of superficial calm to come over my demeanor.

When I walked into the office, the appearance of Earlene, my social worker, seated at the guidance counselor's desk, was unexpected yet somehow not surprising. The actual guidance counselor was not present. Earlene bid me to sit down in the chair by the desk. As I did, I angled myself to present the shortest distance between me and the door. I could feel and hear the blood pulsing in my ears, face and neck.

"So how are you doing these days?" she inquired.

"I am doing just fine," I replied coolly. "Why do you ask?"

"Well, we have some reason to believe that you are not feeling fine," she said (as though I hadn't just told her how I was doing a moment ago). "We thinks it's time for you to go for a reassessment."

Impatient and growing suspicious I tersely inquired, "Well, how long is this going to take? While I don't mind missing a few classes, I do have a date and a job interview taking place shortly after school and I have no intention of missing either."

"Well, I am afraid you are going to miss your date," Earlene replied.

"You are about to seriously inconvenience me," I said, this time without trying to conceal my righteous anger. "And this had better be for a damn good reason."

"Your foster parents think you tried to kill yourself in your bedroom with gasoline fumes last night," she charged.

"I am not depressed or suicidal," I shot back indignantly. "That's ridiculous."

"They say you keep to yourself and hardly ever leave your room when you are home," she accused.

"I don't even know those people," I parried. "I have nothing to say to them most of the time."

I thought to myself, *I am certainly not going to hang out or play at being family with a bunch of people I don't intend to be with when I turn eighteen.* There was no reason to socialize with my foster family beyond the bare minimum required for congeniality's sake. But my foster parents had access to my records and they knew I had been suicidal in the past.

At this point, I had a good idea of what was coming.

"This is not necessary," I stated as I continued to defend myself, "Let me call them and talk to them and explain myself."

Earlene countered, "If you're not depressed, then what were you thinking, igniting gasoline in your room? That was an impulsive thing to do and showed a lack of good judgment. You must be manic," she indicted.

"It was just a simple TEST. That's all! And my speech is not pressured. My body is calm. I am not twitching with ants in my pants. My thoughts are not racing or grandiose, I am not manic." I protested.

"Well, maybe you just don't realize whether or not you're manic or depressed," she remarked.

"We don't know what's going on with you and we want to find out. That is why we think it's best that you be in a hospital, right now."

Fear-terror of that environment, along with flashbacks of what had happened to me when I was there, overwhelmed my sanity.

Kill her! Run! You are in danger! Run away now! Get up! Move! Move! Run! Now!

As a plan for a violent and desperate escape shaped itself in my mind, my nerves remained ready while my rational brain waged an inner battle with the impulses coming from my survivor-self. I knew not where I could go and be sheltered if I ran away, because I lived in a small town that was slowly coming into the grip of winter. My options were extremely limited, for I was ill equipped to spend my days and nights outdoors in hiding.

Some part of my mind informed me that if I took flight, offered resistance, or assaulted them, that it would only serve to affirm their belief that I needed acute care and constant supervision. The one remaining voice of sanity struggled mightily to overcome the violent clamor from the others.

Meanwhile, Earlene was having trouble getting me a bed at the nearest general hospital. There were complications because they didn't have a bed in the children's ward and that I could not take an adult bed unless a doctor had pronounced me a clear and present danger to myself.

Inwardly, I cheered at whoever was on the phone on the other end because Earlene's tone of voice alternated between petulance, insistence, and frustration. As that conversation ended, she put the phone down, unable to get me admitted to the adult psych unit. She went through her wire-bound notebook of contacts and resources and made other phone calls. After several possible placements didn't pan out for one reason or another, she found a private psychiatric hospital with several available beds in the adolescent unit that would take a ward of the State based solely on her recommendation.

As my social worker readied to leave, I reminded her that I was not prepared for an indefinite stay anywhere since all I had with me was my school bag and a few textbooks. We needed to return to the foster home so I could get some clothing.

At that statement Earlene finally revealed the truth she had known from the moment I had walked into the office. She had already picked up a bag with a few random clothing items selected by my now former foster mother Carol. Earlene informed me that I would never return to that placement again. It had been *fait accompli* within the first hour that I had left the house for school.

All the plotting and phone calls had been done behind my back. I had kind of hoped I could somehow manipulate the situation to get a few minutes of face time with Max or Carol so I could use my wiles on them, explain myself and my actions, and hopefully, get a second chance. I nodded my head as I appreciated how thoroughly checkmated I had been right then.

I was informed that the rest of my possessions would be boxed, picked up by other social workers and stored at the offices of Child and Family Services. The privacy of my personal space and effects was nonexistent. My desires and interests were deemed irrelevant and it was off to a psychiatric institution for the second time. I seethed with hatred and anger over my lack of control over my situation.

The entire ride to the mental hospital was a constant battle of will inside my mind. I was so angry I could barely speak. Constantly I had to fight against the impulse to harm myself or her. A new plan of escape spawned in my imagination and the voices urged me to act before it was too late.

The inner war persisted. Minutes and miles ticked by, and my admission into mental health lockdown was fast approaching. I buckled my seatbelt and continued to mentally rehearse the process of causing the car accident that would allow me to escape.

A wiser voice inside me kept telling me to breath deeply, be calm and endure. *Lull them*, the voice urged me. *You can do it. You know how the system works and you can beat it. You've done it before. Prove that your social worker is wrong. It's that, or let yourself go off and make the situation worse.*

Ultimately, we arrived safely, and I was duly admitted inpatient. The first time I entered a psychiatric facility I had really wanted help. I was genuinely suicidal and truly depressed. This time things were different, because now I neither wanted nor needed any help. I hadn't been suicidal since I was being repeatedly threatened with being sent back into institutionalized living by my first foster mother, Hope.

If you've seen one of these modern psychiatric facilities, you've probably seen them all. Lake Shore Hospital was for all intents and purposes Brookside II. It occupied a sprawling one storied building nestled at the back of an industrial park. The individual patient rooms, hallways and common areas were reminiscent of some college dormitories, but the nurses station, seclusion rooms and magnetically locked doors served to continuously remind you that you were in fact in a mental hospital.

I was admitted in the middle of a holiday week and there was nothing I could do to effect my release until next Monday. The potential physical violence that could happen here lay like a dark aura over the place, that was tangible to me. I was bored, irritated, and agitated, but there was no way that I could reveal those feelings for even a second because of their association with bipolar disorder.

It was exactly the kind of environment where any active teenager who had better and more interesting things to do, might pace or fidget. Any such activity would not be seen for what it was. Instead it would be misconstrued as mania, a symptom of mental illness. My behavioral performance, in terms of not manifesting possible symptoms, had to be near-perfect at all times.

Thanksgiving Day I spent on suicide watch, hanging out at the triage center, chatting with the psychiatric nurses. My dinner was wheeled in on a cart. I sat at a folding table in my socks and sweatpants, eating runny mashed potatoes, slices of rubber turkey, and tasteless squash out of a Styrofoam tray, with a spork. Someday, there had to be a reckoning with my social worker for this, I thought to myself as I ate.

The phone rang at the nurses station and they called me over. I was baffled. I had no idea who might want to call me. I was not even sure anyone other than my social worker and a friend I had called from the payphone on the ward, knew where I was and why. It turned out, everyone in my family knew I had been hospitalized for a suicide attempt again. The person on the other end of the line was my mother.

Sarah started talking and I couldn't speak. My thoughts and emotions crashed like two separate tidal waves and my throat closed up. Hatred, mixed with sadness, paralyzed me. Every time I would try to say something it came out like a harsh croak.

I kept thinking to myself, *how dare she think she can come and go into my life as she sees fit*? That she could call me up with a voice of concern after giving me up. Didn't she remember family court? I didn't understand back then that, despite our distance and situation, even self-centered mothers like mine can occasionally feel pain when they know that their children are hurting, and want to reach out to them.

"I hear that you are having a little trouble again," she began.

"Don't believe what you've heard," I defended. "I am not remotely depressed."

"Listen to me for a minute, because I have something to tell you that I've wanted to tell you for a long time." she pleaded.

Curious, I listened to what she had to say next.

"I just wanted you to know that, like you, I have suffered from depression my entire life." She told me sincerely, "I too have thought about killing myself, many times."

I started to shake my head in rejection of what she was telling me. I did not need to hear this right now.

"Look . . ." I interrupted.

She asked me again to just listen.

Sarah went on to tell me, that every time she felt like hurting herself, she would start praying to Jesus. That had helped her through the dark times and she thought that perhaps if I would just allow Jesus to come back into my heart that . . .

"I have to go, right now," I said, "Don't call me again." Then I hung up on her before she could say anything else. I turned to the nearest psych nurse and instructed her, "If she calls again, I refuse to speak to her."

I went back to the common area and sat down. Certain memories intruded and I began connecting all the dots. In my own depression and youth I had seen it, had known Mama was often sad for some reason. But I had not entirely understood that it was depression with a capitol "D." She certainly had the irritability that comes with persistent clinical depression. Sarah was not known for her patience. She routinely exploded on us over the slightest thing we did to annoy her.

In that old-fashioned house we had grown up in, Sarah had slowly lost her mind. Burdened by repeated bouts of postpartum depression and seasonal affective disorder, my naturally mercurial mother idled apathetically, watching soap operas like *General Hospital* and *Days of Our Lives* for hours and took long naps every day. A smoker since her teens, she was taken to brooding in the darkness with her cigarettes or occasionally writing poetry that she would never show anyone. Alternately, she would spend time praying over her rosary, a devotional candle, and a picture of the Sacred Heart of Jesus.

Her depression gnawed away at her, sapping her passion for life and her interests. It left her too fatigued to do the never-ending laundry, clean the kitchen or perform all the housewife duties she wanted so much to have. While depressed, those responsibilities proved to be too stressful and overwhelming and that's usually when we would get neglected. She would shut down and not be available to us, functionally, emotionally or otherwise.

Over time, it became apparent that she had depression cycles. I recognized her cycles, because I developed them too. The psychiatrist back at Brookside, Dr. Wasser, had said that my chemical imbalance was genetic. Now I knew that in addition to positive traits, like musical and artistic ability, I had inherited her negative ones too.

Her revelation was hard for me to take. I refused to believe and accept that my existential depression was just some series of genetic switches. There was more to it than that.

My depressions meant something. I sensed that there were complex, multi-layered reasons for them at the edges of my awareness. Back then there was no one specific thing I could put my finger on. It was more like existence itself was depressing. Periodically, the futility of it just sort of hit me all at once and stayed for awhile, causing me to brood on little else. That Sarah's confession was coming out now, when I was not the least bit depressed, was just more evidence that there was far too much irony loose in the universe.

When I got off suicide watch and was allowed to be left alone in my room, I did a lot thinking. I sat in the dark at a desk with my feet up on the window sill. I stared out through the narrow, mesh-infused windows at the tiny drifts of weak snow billowing around the sodium vapor lights outside.

How the hell did I end up in a mental institution again? I wanted to scream or hit something so badly out of frustration, yet knowing the entire time that doing so would "prove" that I was agitated because of mania. They would be looking at my behavior with a bias and try to match it with the symptoms of the conditions I had been diagnosed with two years earlier. I was desperate to avoid forced drugging at any cost. As long as I had my undrugged wits about me I could survive and plot and plan.

From moment to moment it was a struggle to remind myself to keep my focus on breathing. *Keep intercepting and denying those impulses to go off. Breathe. Relax. Don't go off. Don't show any emotion other than congenial optimism and you will get out of here.* At last I turned my mind inward, using the only thing I knew. I began to take deep, slow breaths and practiced meditation.

After awhile I came into contact with that wiser, internal self. One voice began to converse with me, back and forth.

What do I really want? *To be left alone.*

Why couldn't people just leave me alone? *Maybe because you are doing something that chronically begs for attention.*

Why wouldn't anyone believe me when I claimed I wasn't depressed? *Maybe it had something to do with how much time you spend by yourself. Nobody knows the real you.*

So why can't I socialize with people? *Because you hate people. You're scared of people and the things that they do to each other.*

All my life I'd been absorbed with my own agendas and internal fixations. I could focus all my attention on certain things to a fault. It caused a kind of tunnel vision in which the only solution is to simply satisfy the present impulse by any means. I had never really taken the time to wonder how other people might interpret the results of my actions. I had never really considered other people's perspectives.

Suddenly, as if by thinking about the possibility of it, I gained a new function. The ability to put myself in someone else's shoes. A rudimentary and beginner level facility to look at myself objectively from outside myself. My brain seemed to suddenly expand with capacity the longer I thought about it. A new strategy would have to be deliberately hardwired to my interface with the world.

I saw myself as Max, my former foster father: I see myself walking downstairs to use the bathroom. I smell the gasoline fumes, and, following my nose, I find the smell coming from the bedroom of a person with a history of suicide. Once I saw myself from an outside point of view, I understood exactly how I had found myself here.

That insight was profound. I shook all through my spine with the wonder of it. I had always been so caught up in the moment. I remembered my studies of the DSM back at Tobey, specifically the part about obsessions and poor impulse control. I finally glimpsed how someone could easily interpret those as a signs of mania.

As the ramifications of that realization settled in, I mentally cursed and flagellated myself for my stupidity. I felt the last vestige of whatever child I had left in me fade. I had reached a new level of awareness which came with a greater responsibility. I saw now that I couldn't just do whatever I wanted the instant I felt like it. I had to pay attention and plot people's possible reactions. Through gross oversight I had done exactly the opposite of what I wanted.

The way out of this mess would be to create a perfect illusion of compliance. But to even think of obedience and appeasing authority was de facto submission. It was a crushing blow to my pride to consider this when what I really wanted to do was fight. One part of my mind immediately began calculating how long I would have to suffer this distasteful submission strategy.

One year and three months. Less than five hundred days. I knew I could endure it that long. The reward would be total freedom. Once there, I could go have a massive party and kill myself if I still felt like it, but I could do so freely. I began to think of it in terms of, "if you can't beat them, join them."

Upon asking the nurses how I could get released, I was told that my discharge was entirely up to my assigned psychiatrist. Because of the holidays and the long weekend, about seven days went by before I could talk to any specialist about my case.

When I finally got to see the psychiatrist, Dr. Allen, my whole position was:

There has been a serious mistake. I was involuntarily committed here. I was not in the least bit suicidal. I was not even depressed.

I took a deep breath, relaxed, became mindful of my body language and sent commands to my hands and feet to remain completely still. I mentally counted out time, one-Mississippi, two-Mississippi, deliberately metering each of my statements, so as to ensure that my speech did not come across as racing or pressured, which are symptoms of a manic episode in progress.

I told him that, until I had been delivered here, life for me had been going great. I was moving on, putting my past behind me and preparing for the real world. I tried to express what an inconvenience this whole thing has been to me.

"I have been forced to stand up my first date at my new school, (*one . . . two . . .*) I have been forced to skip a job interview without even a phone call to tell them I couldn't make the appointment I had scheduled. (*one . . . two . . .*) With regards to my incense holder and the gasoline, well (*one . . . two . . .*), I had made a huge, dumb mistake. (*one . . . two . . .*) When can I get out of here and back to my life?"

As Dr. Allen perused my intake forms, he asked me about how my experience on lithium and Trilafon had been and I told him bluntly, "Those drugs made me worse in more ways than I care to remember."

As though he had just received an invisible cue, he went on to tell me that things had changed since the last time I was inpatient. These days, they had a new "wonder drug" called Prozac. "You could try that, if you wanted to," he offered me congenially.

Incredulous at his gall to try to pimp the latest drug on me after I had just told him I was fine, with a touch of derision in my voice, I said, "Pay attention doctor, that I have no alcohol or substance abuse problems in my file. (*one . . . two . . .*) Drugs are used to escape from the hard reality of life. Only losers and weak-minded people depend on drugs to get by, so: No, I don't want to try your Prozac."

Sarah and Tim would've been proud to hear me preach it.

Dr. Allen shrugged his shoulders to indicate his ambivalence towards my convictions once I had concluded my self-righteous rant. My psychiatrist's conclusion? I did not appear to be depressed, psychotic or manic. He thought perhaps there was some mild narcissism there, but nothing clinical. He asked me if I would be willing to help him get me discharged by taking all their psych battery exams, and I nodded my head to indicate my compliance.

"Basically, getting you certified 'sane' involves seeing a different psychologist and getting another opinion. Tell her everything you just told me," Dr. Allen said of my impending second assessment. "Assuming there are no issues with any of the psychiatric testing batteries and a favorable report from your psychologist, there is no reason you could not walk out of here by the end of next week," he assured me.

Woot! I was ecstatic. Unfortunately, I couldn't see my assigned psychologist until she rotated back to this hospital. As the days passed, I took all their tests. This time I answered "No" or "Never" to all those questions on the *MMPI* (Minnesota Multiphasic Personality Inventory) that I had checked "Yes" or "All-the-time" a few years ago.

I finally did see my shrink, Dr. Holden, and we had a wonderful chat. Dr. Holden was clearly exceptionally intelligent and I got good vibes from her the moment I walked into her office. She really listened carefully to me when I explained how I had accidentally set myself up to be perceived as either manic or depressed by not thinking carefully about the ramifications of what I was doing.

It had been quite a wake-up call for me to see how a stupid mistake led to a grossly out of proportion response. She concurred with me and with my psychiatrist that I was in fact fine. I was to be discharged, with a clean bill of health, no less, as soon as possible.

I was never diagnosed with or treated for anything while I was at Lake Shore Hospital. By the time I was discharged, my personal liberty and daily routine had been suspended for almost five holiday-season weeks. I languished in that psychiatric facility at the cost of roughly seven hundred to a thousand dollars a day. Perhaps they gave the State a bulk inpatient discount. I don't know how much it cost exactly, but it was all paid for by the N.H. taxpayers.

Earlene was really irritated to hear Dr. Allen's and Dr. Holden's professional opinion when she came for a visit on the ward to see me for herself. It was in her voice, her face and her walk, that she had better things to do than deal with me. She was completely unapologetic about this whole hospitalization thing. She told me there were no foster homes that would take me and that I would have to be in a group home until I was eighteen.

She took her sweet time. Every few days she'd pick me up and I was driven out to various facilities, like Chase Home in Portsmouth and Dover Children's Home, where I'd be interviewed by the admissions staff to see if I might be a good fit for the program. I visited placements from Maine to Massachusetts before we finally found one in Vermont, called "Bennington School," that seemed appropriate for my situation.

Chapter 10

Hemlock Punch

Earlene drove me out of state, this time to attend the Bennington School in Bennington, Vermont. A low-security coed therapeutic group home for emotionally and behaviorally "challenged" teens.

The enormous brown building with it's faded yellow trim and entryway columns resembles a historic plantation estate or manor home and at the time it housed about thirty residents. In addition to the main administration building and the dorms, there is the on-site private school, a full-fledged outdoor basketball court and a lot of open space. The entire property sits on the flattened top of a grassy hill, overlooking vast deciduous and evergreen forests.

It was one of the better placements I had seen. Life there was not ideal, but it was not always intolerable. There were many aspects of it that were similar to private boarding schools. The primary difference was apparent in the kinds of residents and staff that lived or worked there.

Bennington School was another structured program with a level system. A level system in a place like this actually meant something. It was what you lived for.

There were three levels and everyone started out at level one by default. Each level was automatically earned after a certain amount of time. Level one lasted for the first thirty days. Level two lasted for sixty days. On level three you stayed until you left or got demoted. The only thing that prevented you from attaining a level was being penalized "checks." The majority of residents were at level two.

Checks were given based on a set of rules. Failure to make your bed and clean your room or shower received a check. Failure to perform assigned chores or bring your linens down once a week earned a check. Failure to comply with direction or arguing with staff earned a check, as did cursing or threatening a resident or staff. Disrupting group therapy and community meetings earned a check and so on. If you got too many checks in one week, you had to start over.

Most of the perks of attaining a level were related to bed time and lights out. Some perks included being eligible for leaving on holidays to be with family. Other incentives included an increase in allowance for chores, approval to leave the building and go on field trips.

Level three was the real prize. A resident on level three could leave the facility and go into town unsupervised. You were allowed to have a job and attend local schools. You made more money than other residents for the same chores. You could be in the TV room and watch what you wanted long after the level ones and twos were in beds with lights out.

We did some cool things while I was there. We went on field trips once a month or so. We went on fishing, caving, and wilderness expeditions. I learned how to climb a rock wall and rappel down it at a "confidence building" life-skills course. When I reached level two, I was able to go on the Friday night roller skating trips we had during the wintertime.

Evening recreation time at a typical psychiatric hospital or residential facility might have meant a group walk around the grounds or use of the indoor basketball courts. At Bennington however, if you were at the right privilege level, then evening recreation consisted of van trips to the local YMCA to go swimming and lift weights.

What made Bennington School awful, besides being forced to live under and obey the rules of its structured program, were the other residents, their behavioral issues, and the resulting consequences upon violating the rules of a level system. Nearly ever day someone would act out, sooner or later. Frequently, these disruptions ended up escalating until whatever the bulk of the residents were doing was interrupted.

One resident swore at another resident and got a check. Then that resident would cuss out the staff that gave them the check resulting in another check. Then the resident would suddenly curse the staff with a slew of verbal abuse, resulting in a half dozen checks and a time-out. Then the resident would kick or punch the wall out of anger at the staff. Shortly thereafter, the kid would get manually restrained and dragged off to sit in a hallway, secluded from others.

This place essentially warehoused difficult, abandoned and unwanted teenagers like me. For some, this was a conditional diversion from serving a sentence in juvenile detention back in their home state.

The residents of Bennington School had psychiatric labels, criminal records, drug and alcohol addictions. Many of these teens had come from homes rife with child abuse, substance abuse and sexual abuse. Some of the kids didn't even know where their real parents were. Other kids were chronic runaways, felons, gang members. It seemed nearly every female resident there had had unwanted sexual contact with family members or relatives before they even hit puberty.

Mario was a rugged young man with French-Canadian ancestry, originally from Maine, who had moved to Florida with and eventually run away from his drug addicted and abusive parents. He ended up in a street gang that would rob tourists. Mario had a mile-long rap sheet at the age of sixteen. This placement was his last chance. If he messed up, he was going into juvenile prison until the age of twenty-one.

The residents here were teenagers that no foster home would take. They were too disturbed for an unrestricted living program, but not troubled enough to warrant being inpatient or under a more restricted lockdown. The diagnoses of the various residents ranged from depression and attention deficit disorder to borderline personality disorder.

I once watched a resident fall out of his chair and go into seizures at breakfast time. In the days before Big Pharma scientists better understood the interactions between SSRIs and MAOIs it was not uncommon to see petit mal and even grand mal seizures in people going from drug to drug, if they were not allowed to taper completely off of one med before starting another.

That particular resident, Jaime, was being put on the brand new "wonder drug" Prozac. After seeing these med-related seizures, and kids walking around twitching and spasming, it only reinforced my opinion born from past experience, that psychiatric drugs were a dangerous and unhealthy "medicine," best not used at all.

Fighting, while not always a daily occurrence, did happen frequently. Normal adolescents act out, get moody and irritable. They will test boundaries, rules, and be aggressive. Average teenagers can lose their temper and get into fights. Teens with emotional and behavioral issues take all that to a whole new level.

Accusations of wrongdoing or offense, both real and imagined, would be enough to start an escalating confrontation with one resident and another. Sometimes several students were involved. I had stood up to my abusive stepfather and I practiced martial arts, so it was their peril if they put their hands on me.

I was involved in several fights while I was there and witnessed dozens more. These fights could come at any time. You could never really be sure what would set any particular resident off. The only thing predictable about assault and battery in that place was the sure knowledge that it would happen again, sooner or later.

Sexual assault was not entirely unheard of either. I once witnessed Mario stand up, walk over to a male resident he hated and in a blink of an eye, he pulled his phenomenally long and thick penis out of his pants and slapped this younger boy in the face with it. This was a completely primitive domination move which put the slapped kid at the bottom of the social pack, instantly. About half of us laughed, the other half stared at the TV, pretending they hadn't just witnessed it too.

One day, Jaime, a sensitive-looking, trench coat wearing sixteen year old, who wore his dirty blond hair unkempt and shaggy in imitation of his alternative music idol at the time, Kurt Cobain, admitted in group therapy that he was bisexual and shortly after had a "blanket party" thrown for him in the middle of the night. He was tied to his bed with his own sheets and blankets and then sodomized with a broom handle by his roommates.

Runaways were not uncommon. Kids would bolt in the middle of the night, mostly alone, but sometimes there were conspiracies for entire groups to elope together. Almost all of them were finally caught and brought back. Their shoes were confiscated and they had to wear bright yellow tracksuits and white socks for the next few days. They would not be allowed to speak to the other residents for the duration of their "punishment." If they had not already blown all their remaining chances, they would be allowed to stay, but were busted down to level one.

One morning, fifteen-year-old Helen sauntered down the stairs to the common room and calmly announced to us all, "I just drank down an entire bottle of hairspray and I am going to die." Of course, we gave her an applause. She leisurely walked back upstairs, followed shortly by the pounding footsteps of the youth counselors. Helen wanted attention and these kinds of suicide gestures were what she did to get it.

Occasionally a student would bring contraband onto the dorms, a cigarette for example. That student would tell a few others and then three or four residents would smoke it in the bathroom. Invariably, a staff would notice the smell, and when no one owned up to it, the entire place would get locked down for a contraband search.

I had become used to room searches and seizures. I hated this recurring invasion of privacy. My parents had openly done it to me whenever they had felt like it, whereas my grandparents, my brothers and sister had done it behind my back. I experienced room searches at every single placement I was at. I kept my space and belongings in an almost military-style perfection at all times. This ensured that my room search lasted merely a minute or two.

It wasn't like I had many possessions anymore. My belongings were supposed to be picked up from my last foster home and sent after me to the school. But thanks to social worker negligence, all my stuff was misplaced at the CFS offices. I eventually got less than half of it back almost a year later.

Of course, then there was the random and unannounced fire drills in the middle of the night. A feature common to both Bennington and the Tobey School. Take an entire facility filled with emotionally and behaviorally challenged boys and girls, set off alarms and strobing lights while they are sleeping, then watch the chaos.

After ninety days I was up for a review to confirm that I had earned level three. It was an interesting meeting. In the days preceding it I had rehearsed over and over in my mind how I would act and what I would say. I tried thinking of something I had overlooked, in case I had to defend myself, but there was nothing. This meeting was really the fruition of the plan I had set in motion back at Lake Shore hospital, when I was brooding in my room about my impulse and lack of foresight.

My performance had not gone unnoticed by the other teens there. For some it was very galling to watch someone that had been in the program for far less time than they to pass them in the level system.

In recent weeks, there had been a tremendous amount of peer pressure to act out and be like the others. I had been provoked and antagonized without let up by many of the other students. They would walk by me, call me a traitor for "sucking up" to the staff by behaving obediently, then bump into me deliberately, or spit in my face, in the hopes of getting a reaction from me.

All it would take would be a threat or a curse from me that was overheard by a staff and I would get a check. Then the resident would win. Those that harassed me were mostly level one residents, some twos, and they had nothing to lose or didn't care. With level three I could get the hell out of there and not have to deal with it.

When I walked into their office there was three heavyweight group home administrators present. They sat in large chairs placed side by side. I had a seat opposite them. It reminded me of an impromptu court proceeding.

They told me that "There is some extra significance to this meeting." It was exceedingly rare for any resident to make it to level three in their first ninety days. I had not even earned one "check" during the last three months. They looked at each other in unspoken conversation for a moment.

"We get the impression that you are waiting for something," stated one.

"I am waiting to leave," I replied.

Continuing adroitly, I said "You are waiting for something too. You are waiting for me to crack. From what I've seen so far, the girls usually crack after about four weeks. The boys after one or two. They forget themselves and where they are. They exhibit their frustration with this place and with living in a life of structure. As soon as the newness wears off, most of them dispense with their best behavior and go war against the program. It becomes residents versus the evil staff. I don't have any interest in that nonsense. I have plans for my future and they do not involve being here."

I made a calculated guess then, knowing they wouldn't give me a check for it and said, "It's not all that hard to not say the word *shit* in daily conversation. If you think I am going to snap, you will be disappointed."

I paused, took a breath and continued.

"If you let me have level three then I am going to use it. I'll get a job, go to public school, go to the town library and the recreation facilities. I am not here to rebel against anyone. I am just trying to prepare myself for being on my own."

They asked me why I thought I was there in their program. With my files right in front of them, they certainly knew that almost two months before my arrival I had been involuntarily hospitalized for an apparent suicide attempt and that I had been released with a clean bill of health.

I answered, "I am here for several reasons. In part because I made a huge mistake in judgment and scared several people into believing I wanted to hurt myself. I am here because my social worker couldn't leave well enough alone and was too incompetent to find a more appropriate placement for me."

The school staff granted me level three, and life did improve. I got my own wake-up time which I used to get up an hour before the other residents. That allowed me to jog a few laps around the Bennington war memorial and back. It also gave me the chance to use the shower before the other residents were up.

That was a real luxury perk. For months, I had had to shower with the rest of the plebes. When all the residents were hitting showers at once, the water pressure and temperature went down significantly. Now I could bask in hot, full pressure showers.

Being level three was a rarefied atmosphere. There were only three or four of us at any time. Often residents lost their level as soon as it was awarded to them. For some level threes, it was their second or third time being there. The real test once you had some latitude was what you would do with it.

I got a job in the fast-food sector in downtown Bennington. I did janitorial work around the building for extra cash. I finally learned to focus on what I was doing and how to clean something thoroughly. I even found a sense of pride that came with knowing a job was well done.

My money went into martial arts instruction, uniforms and equipment. I studied at two different schools, learning both the Korean system of taekwando and the Okinawan karate tradition of Uechi-ryu. I took absolutely every advantage that I could wrest out of that level.

During my whole time at Bennington I got into trouble only once. Not for fighting or acting out but for having oral sex with a resident that I was really hot for. That resident had bragged about it, and because the scandal involved me, the always obedient level three resident, it spread like wildfire. When the staff brought me in, I could tell they believed the rumors were true. I was busted down to level two for a couple of days and had to maintain a distance called "the five-foot rule" from the person in question. However, I still got to go to work and school on the outside.

I had no problems with that. The staff really had no idea what I was doing behind the scenes. The resident that I was involved with had AA meetings in town approximately the same times I had one of my martial arts classes. The AA meetings took place in the rectory of a church and about once a week we would rendezvous and have sex in the stairwell inside the church. In spite of the loose lips of my lover, no one ever found out how often we broke the rules regarding sexual contact. It was our secret and I imagined that we enjoyed far more sex than all the other residents.

The school also had strict rules about smoking. If you got caught, you instantly lost a level and everybody's room would be searched. But I was smart enough to keep my cigarettes hidden off premises. I only smoked at work, during my breaks behind a garbage dumpster. It was my own little private act of rebellion. It gave me a chance to have few unsupervised minutes alone and it helped me deal with stress. I never once bragged about it to the other residents and so I got away with it, the entire time I was there. It was actually a great lesson in learning to be discreet.

I got along with most of the staff. There were certainly a few there that I hated, like at any other placement I had lived at. Generally speaking, I felt I had more in common with the adults than with the residents. After awhile I was almost untouchable and I got away with stuff others might not have. I was able to make the best of the Bennington School and I really prospered there.

Still, towards the end of the school year, when it came time for all the residents to submit something for the yearbook, I wanted nothing to do with it. This was not my home. I had no pride in this school nor was living here something I cared to boast about to my out-of-state friends. I had held myself aloof from almost everyone the entire time I was there. I looked down on the other residents for being unable to understand the circumstances they were in. They could not see the big picture, which was why the bulk of the other students failed to ascend past level one or two.

Finally, after much encouragement and cajoling from the youth counselors to contribute something to the yearbook, I decided to play along.

By *contribute*, they were asking me to draw a picture or pen a short essay or provide some kind of creative or artistic expression of my experience as a student, and that's exactly what they were going to get. I used the opportunity to exact a kind of subtle revenge against the structured program, the residents and the staff alike.

With premeditated sarcasm, I wrote a satirical and seditious little poem, describing one day of life in their group home.

Sometimes I wake up in my bed
Wishing I was really dead
Knowing that I will very soon
Be eating from a dirty spoon
Then I'll have to clean my room
Wish that I could sleep till noon
Now we have to do roll call
Isn't this fun, let's have a ball
Now why don't we all
Go bash our heads against the wall
But no, I think its time for school
So I'll sit and sit and sit and drool
Oh gee, it's finally time for lunch
Nuclear pork or hemlock punch
The program twists the essence
Of personal responsibility
To not get checked for little things
Is a test of mental agility
How quick the day becomes a bore
Dodge this check and do this chore
The program is just a silly game
Every day the rules the same
Today is so intense to get nothing done
Tomorrow those memories will be all but gone
To join this program is to play the fool
But I guess that is just the Bennington School

Eventually I got sick of life in that placement. Summer had passed, and as autumn arrived I took advantage of my level three privilege to attend Mount Anthony Union High School for my senior year. But unlike most of the other students, I went home to the surreal closed-off world of the group home.

As the months inexorably dragged on, I was getting closer and closer to adult age and I was basically just doing time there for no good reason and I had had enough. So finally, one morning before school started, I called up my social worker and presented this argument to her:

"I have less than six months to go before I turn eighteen. I want to be enrolled and employed locally where I intend to live when I become a legal adult. I want to be closer to resources and support I will need. I don't want to have to leave Vermont for New Hampshire in the final hour and have to build everything from scratch."

"Forget about it," Earlene replied brusquely. "There is no way you are leaving Bennington School before you turn eighteen."

That was all I needed to hear, and I hung up on her, taking care not to slam down the phone. I had accepted in advance that she would say something like that, almost verbatim. Besides, you have to ask first, before you can get denied.

Alright, I thought to myself. *Time to use my ace in the hole.* A resource I hadn't used in awhile, but kept in reserve the last few years for just such a problem. I contacted my guardian ad litem, Gavin. Gavin had been assigned by the family court system to be my legal advocate.

"She's doing it again," I said, as I told him about her recalcitrance. I gave him my sales pitch about moving to my home state. He thought it seemed like a sensible idea and told me, "Your social worker could arrange it if she wanted to, but is refusing because she simply doesn't want to get off her ass and handle it." And he went to work on my behalf, telling me, "Sit tight, I'll deal with her."

The way Gavin described it to me later was that he called Earlene up and asked her, "Are you ready to lose in court again?" She wasn't, so she submitted to arbitration instead.

Staff from Bennington (the assistant program director and my clinical therapist) had to drive for hours to come to the meeting at my social worker's office. My advocate was there too.

It was the general consensus of everyone present, except my social worker, that I didn't need to be in the Bennington School. Earlene insisted there was nothing she could do. The school staff for their part agreed that the program did not meet my needs and they would have no problem simply discharging me if it came to that. It was a waste of their resources and inappropriate to boot.

In the end, my reluctant case worker found an adolescent-to-adult transitional living program, and a very discriminating one at that. She didn't even know if they had a room for me there. A placement like this often had a waiting list, and as such, she couldn't simply drop me off on a moment's notice.

I did interview there and I got accepted. I signed a contract with the program director, stating that I either had to get a job and my GED or go to school instead. I told him that I'd do both: go to school and work as soon as possible. I just needed a place to cool my heels for a few months before I was on my own.

Almost another month had gone by before everything was finalized. I spent the remainder of the year in the Blue Heron Independent Living Program, a division of Odyssey House in Hampton, New Hampshire. I transferred from my job at a popular fast food restaurant franchise in Bennington to one in Seabrook, and attended Winnacunnet Regional High School.

The Blue Heron was an ordinary and unassuming, three-storied white house that blended in with the other homes on the tree-lined street. It did not look like a facility for teens, deliberately so.

The good news was that this house was located near a boat launch that led out to the Atlantic and so it scored points for being near the ocean. The bad news was, the launch was built near a channel flowing through the midst of a vast salt marsh. Until the marsh froze during the winter, the air was overwhelmed with the smell of rotten eggs whenever it was low tide. A consequence of the sulfur that is released from the organic decay (which is quite healthy for the marsh ecosystem).

At the Blue Heron program, we had a ten o'clock evening curfew and were allowed unmonitored use of the phone which was a welcome change. We could eat what and when we wanted to. We could watch whatever we wanted on TV. And were allowed to smoke outside on the porch. We could hang out with our friends after school. We were expected to. It was a sweet deal, like a retirement program for group home veterans. I was able to coast through more or less uneventfully, all the way until my eighteenth birthday.

I did watch several residents lose this coveted placement over stupid stuff. One girl, who came and went during my stay there, couldn't obey the curfew. Sixteen-year-old Venus was given the same number of chances to behave that we all had, and when she came home late one too many times and reeking of marijuana, she was kicked out. I was sitting on the front porch, smoking a cigarette, when the sheriffs came and took her bodily off the property in handcuffs while she was screaming to the program director, "I'm sorry! Please! Give me another chance! I'm sorry! Please! Don't do this to me! I'm sorry!" all the way to the patrol car. She was headed back to a lockdown.

Another resident, a short and spike-haired girl named Tina, also relapsed into drugs once she had the latitude to do so. Cocaine, it turned out, was Tina's substance of choice, and it made her angry and combative. One morning I got in a short but brutal physical confrontation with her up over something ridiculous and petty. I was forced to restrain her, using a shoulder lock that I had learned in self-defense, to prevent her from ripping out a fistful of my hair. Paranoid that she would get kicked out and dragged away in shackles like Venus had, Tina fled the program shortly before she turned eighteen.

My social worker made one last visit during the final week before I turned of age. Earlene informed me that I was not required to leave Blue Heron upon becoming an adult. They could extend services up to the age of twenty before you had to go into adult programs.

"I have no desire to remain under the thumb of the State one second longer than is required," I answered. The last thing I wanted to do was live in a structured program as an adult. Infusing my voice with anger, I sought her shifty eyes with my own and stated, "You have been a thorn in my side for four years."

The only reason I had never requested a change in social worker was that Gavin, my legal advocate, informed me that he knew her tactics and what to expect from her. He eventually proved on two separate occasions that he could checkmate her when I needed it.

Over the course of many long hours of driving around with her in search of placements, I learned that she suffered from lupus and that her husband had worked with depleted uranium munitions while serving with the US Army during Operation Desert Storm and had come down with Gulf War Syndrome.

"I know we don't get along. But I have always tried to do what's in your best interests," Earlene informed me.

As my social worker, she wasn't required to treat me as an equal. Her ineptitude when it came to handling my case, her negligence with respect to my belongings, combined with her steadfast refusal to look me in the eye and listen to me, like one human being to another, made it hard to stir even one iota of compassion for her.

"You have no idea what my best interests are because you never asked me," I returned coldly.

I took a puff off of my cigarette, exhaled the smoke to the side, and grimacing I said to her, "I despise you. Your presence offends me and I sincerely hope you go to hell."

Earlene waddled off to her car, huffing and wheezing, and I never saw her again.

At promptly two minutes past midnight on my eighteenth birthday I moved out. I had surreptitiously prepackaged my belongings. Mike, the full-time residential counselor, who dwelt upstairs, came down to see what the disturbance was and found me arranging things in my car.

He stood on the porch in his bathrobe, with a flashlight in one hand and asked, "What are you doing?"

"Leaving," I stated.

"It's the middle of the night. Why don't you go back inside, we can talk about it tomorrow."

"I am a legal adult!" I nearly shouted at him. "You will never, ever, tell me what to do, again. I told you weeks ago, that I was moving out on my birthday and I meant it."

I stood straighter and faced him, "Go back to bed Mike, and leave me alone."

Resigning, he asked me to turn in the house key when I left, and he went back inside. I lit a cigarette and continued packing my stuff.

Up to this moment I had received therapy and counseling from over two dozen individuals. At least half of them had a PhD or otherwise specialized in mental health. Prolonged hospitalization, coercive drugging and dehumanization had stemmed from my attempt to get help for my problems. Then came residential schools, group homes and foster care. None of it had done me any therapeutic good and had arguably made me more depressed, more resentful and more bitter than I had been before I was institutionalized.

In all that time I never felt safe enough to talk openly about my issues. No one had ever gained sufficient trust with me to coax out my innermost feelings and fears. Not one person in over a decade of on and off again counseling had ever given me the keys to unlocking, understanding or mastering my mind.

As I inventoried my memories, I recalled that I'd been to eight different public high schools and two private special needs schools over a four year period. I couldn't begin to remember how many times I'd been threatened or assaulted by other people. My family was sundered. I'd lost my dogs and most of my possessions. Everything I owned fit in my 1983 Subaru wagon, with plenty of room to spare.

A heavy, wet snow was falling. The sound of the car tires was muted as they crunched over the snow-covered driveway. I drove the half mile to Hampton Beach and parked my car. It was almost one o'clock in the morning. Roiling white foam outlined the dark waves of the Atlantic as they crashed and thundered into the seawall. I sat there in my car, wearing a black turtleneck sweater and my army field jacket, smoking one cigarette after another while staring out at the furious ocean, its violence a perfect counterpart to my inner world.

I had somehow survived growing up and was, at long last, finally on my own.

- PART TWO -

CHAPTER 11

LIVE FREE OR DIE

I was eighteen years old and I was free. For the last four years that I had been a ward of the State, I had had no choice but to do whatever anyone ordered me to do. And no choice but to take disrespect or grief from any adult who wanted to give it to me.

I moved into a small apartment with a middle-aged woman named Petra whom I'd met in the course of my martial arts classes. She allowed me to sleep on her couch and I gave her a ride to work whenever I was around the house. Petra was happy to have the company, and this arrangement allowed me to save up for a security deposit for my own place.

After I got up in the morning, I would drive to the nearest Dunkin Donuts to get a "Big One," a medium coffee with three creams and three sugars and then I'd head to school. Once there, I'd park my car, and smoke a few Marlboro cigarettes until my first class started.

It wasn't unusual to find a teacher nosing around the student parking lot in the morning, looking for illicit or inappropriate activities. On this particular day the teacher on patrol saw me smoking in my car and started walking over to me. As he approached, he motioned for me to roll down my window, which I did. Then he ordered me, "Put it out and come with me." I looked him in the eye for a long moment. I took a long, dramatic drag off my cigarette, breathed the cloud of smoke at him and said, "No."

His face began turning various shades of red and purple and he started yelling at me, "It's against the rules to smoke on school property!"

"I am not technically on school property," I explained to him. "I am sitting in my car, which is my property."

"Stop arguing with me!" he raged. "Put out your cigarette, get out of your car and come with me right now!" And he came even closer to me.

"If you so much as lay a finger on me or my car," I warned him, "I will stab you." My right hand was reaching casually for a knife handle, peeking out from its sheath where it was lodged, under the plastic lip of the transmission case.

He paused, started looking over my car, probably searching for a parking permit number to identify me. When he couldn't find my permit (I didn't have one), he demanded angrily, "You will give me your name!"

"No," I replied sarcastically, shaking my head without breaking eye contact. "I will not."

This confrontation was going nowhere, so I started my engine and prepared to leave. I put my Subaru in gear and eased out of the parking spot. As I did, I heard him yell standard-issue angry-adult rhetoric after me: "You are finished! You will pay for this! You are in Big Trouble!"

I looked him in the eye again and said, "Shut the fuck up." and flicked my cigarette at him. I aimed for his forehead but it struck his gut, bouncing off and spraying orange sparks every which way. I gave him the middle finger salute and drove away. I liked the idea that I would be a complete mystery to that obnoxious, self-important, and petty little man. No one knew who I was, my name, or where I lived. He would just have to get over it.

That outburst had been some years in the making and I felt quite satisfied that I had stood my ground and told him off. I was an adult now and he had no business talking down to me like I was some delinquent teen. He had triggered my combat mode and he had no idea that there was a target reticle superimposed on his face, projected on a virtual head's-up display in my mind. If he forced another confrontation with me, outside or in the school hallways, I would attack him.

I was "in trouble." Within minutes I had managed to violate half a dozen school rules by refusing staff direction, smoking on school grounds, threatening and assaulting a teacher and parking on premises without a permit. Attending school under the circumstances didn't seem like an auspicious way to start my new life, and besides, as an adult, attending classes was now optional. So I quit my senior year of high school just four months before graduation, preempting a suspension or other disciplinary action. I could always get my GED later on if it mattered.

I didn't have any idea what to do with all my free time, but long ago I had promised myself that if I survived to make it to eighteen, I would go and indulge and have some fun. In order to do that, I would need more money. In fact, I needed more money than ever before just to support myself. I had to buy my own clothes, pay for my car's running expenses and the liability insurance. In addition to my grill cook job at Papa Gino's, I procured employment delivering subs and sandwiches at a competing franchise, D'Angelo's.

There was plenty of non-work hours during the day, now that I didn't have school. I would fill up the gas tank, pick a road at random and try to get lost. On one of those long drives through back woods I discovered a short cut from the coast to my hometown. I began looking up old friends. Some of them had moved to out-of-state colleges, but I did find my childhood friend Julian.

Julian is a sandy haired, spindle-shanked scarecrow of a man. He had taken me into his eclectic group of friends when I was thirteen, and, along with several others in the group, showed me how to fight. Julian also had taught me several different forms of meditation and helped foster my passion for the occult and mysticism.

We started hanging out again. I didn't feel inclined to talk about where I had been the last four years and he didn't ask me about it. At some point, when we had caught up with each other after work, the marijuana came out.

Julian's stepfather spent weeks away from home on business trips and his mother was a late shift ER nurse who slept in all morning. One evening Julian and I were sitting on the floor of their basement lounge and he was getting me up to speed about what our mutual friends were doing, when he started packing a pipe with weed and asked me if I had picked up the vice during the intervening years.

I had smoked the stuff before, but I never allowed myself to really try it. I had taken a token puff off a joint or a pipe that was being passed around on three separate, widely spaced occasions. More to make the other people smoking it comfortable than to get high myself. My folks had raised me to believe that all drugs were bad and users of drugs were weak. My own experience with psychiatric medications had done the rest and turned me off drugs forever, or so I thought.

In the '80s there was a television commercial that had aired for years as part of a widespread effort to scare people off of starting drugs. It showed you a preheated frying pan: *This is drugs*. An egg is cracked open and dropped into the pan. Within seconds, the egg white was bubbling and changing colors and you could hear the sound of it cooking. Then: *This is your brain on drugs. Any questions?*

I valued my intelligence and didn't want to be turned into an idiot. I shared my misgivings about smoking marijuana with Julian. "Bullshit," he told me, warming up to the topic. "That was government anti-drug propaganda. You remember my uncle Eddie?" I nodded my head to indicate that I did. "Well, he started smoking pot in his teens and he passed the Mensa exam in his late thirties."

Amazed, I thought to myself, *I am an adult now and I can do what I want. I can use my own judgment and come to my own conclusions.* If a person could smoke pot for twenty-five years and still pass the Mensa exam, then obviously his brain was not "cooked" and those commercials had indeed been disinformation. I smiled and told him to pass me that pipe.

We smoked his herb and took hits from a bong. Until that evening, I had never been really high. When you are manic, psychiatrists like to say you are "up," "high" and "euphoric." Manic behavior, with rambling, uninterruptible speech, grandiose ideas and the intense excitability that leads to staying up all night, strongly resembles the effects of a dose of methamphetamine. Mania is not remotely the same kind of euphoria or "high" as being stoned. This was a totally new experience. I lowered my shields and inhibitions, opened myself to feel the effects.

Julian rolled a joint and we smoked that too. As I dived into a sea of relaxation, I got a good glimpse of how much tension I had in my body. I had been locked-up into defensive mode, ready for fight or flight for so long that I had grown used to being on guard all the time. Now the voices in my head spontaneously abated. The experience of being relaxed, feeling good and the growing quiet in my mind, all at the same time, was just profound. I never wanted to come down. Life could actually be good and not so raw when you were stoned.

Julian had another bag of weed when this one was done. Neither of us had to work next morning.. When we were done with the last bag, I was sprawled out on the floor barely able to speak or move.

"Thank you so much," I said to him. "I had no idea how badly I needed that."

Amused, he grinned and said, "You are very welcome."

It was time to pass out. Julian helped me onto the couch and tossed a blanket on me. As he turned off the lights, leaving on only the feeble glow from his aquarium, I called out and asked him, "How is it that we both smoked the same amount and you are walking around, and I can barely move?"

He chuckled softly in the dark and said, "That was your first time getting properly stoned. I smoke like that all the time." Low-voiced he added, "You'll develop a tolerance."

He went upstairs to bed and shortly thereafter I curled into a ball on the couch, smiling and crying tears of joy. I went on an internal voyage of peace and contentedness. I had a whole-body orgasm without touching myself in any way. Years of physical, emotional and mental tension released all at once, spontaneously. It was easily one of the best experiences that I ever had in my life until that point.

It only took a few more nights like that, before I wished to smoke marijuana on my own terms whenever I felt like it. I bought my first piece of paraphernalia at a local head shop and Julian introduced me to his dealer. I especially liked getting high in the morning to start off my day, and before I went to work. That allowed me to deal with people better. I was able to take grief from customers or supervisors without taking it personally.

It was true, after awhile I no longer became incapacitated when I smoked it. Even so, marijuana quieted the noise in my head. I didn't relish the idea of having the voices come back at full volume, and that necessitated learning to live under the influence. I liked being relaxed. I was easier to be with and people were easier to be around. How serendipitous to have stumbled upon nature's own remedy for anger, anxiety and depression.

With the grill cook and delivery job and my constantly changing schedule, I made about $150 to $250 a week. What I needed, in terms of employment, was stability and predictability. And there it was, in the classified section of the local newspaper, in bold letters:

Make $400 a week. No experience necessary. Mandatory overtime. Start immediately.

My shift started at seven in the evening, and ended twelve hours later. I had to bag and bale nylon pile fibers to be used in the velour interiors of automobiles. In this hot and noisy environment I wore ear plugs and a protective mask over my nose and mouth. This was my first factory job and it was an eighty mile commute just to get there.

It was hard work in near sweatshop conditions, but it did pay well. I was excited to see my first paycheck. My friends would joke about the soft white nylon fibers that I brought home with me. They were quickly named "fuzzies" and they ended up everywhere, in my hair, in my car, on the laces of my steel-toed boots and on the couch at my friend Julian's house.

For awhile, things were stable again. I could more or less afford to pay for my weed, my rent and other expenses. Several months later, the engine of my beloved but well-used Volkswagen Scirocco (which had replaced my Subaru wagon awhile back), died on the way to work. This was back before the age of cell phones. I was stranded and had to walk for miles in the emergency lane of an expressway until I found an exit which led to a gas station with a pay phone. At $400 a week I could afford to stay afloat, but I couldn't afford to buy, and have professionally installed, a new engine. Consequently, I lost my factory job the same day that my car died.

Around that same time two of my best friends, Julian and Kurt, decided they had had enough of New England and moved to California. Friends of ours who had already moved there, including Julian's uncle Eddie, described a place where the people were generally cheerful, instead of dour. Possession and smoking of marijuana was decriminalized, and it never snowed.

They packed all the stuff they didn't sell into Julian's truck, and together rode off into the night. It was a sad time for me, not knowing if I would see my friends again. Most of the other people I knew were nowhere near as intelligent as those two and life would not be same with them gone. Although they were leaving, I did get a needed job and car out of the wake of their departure.

Kurt had worked at a used auto dealership and was in possession of several old trade-ins that were barely running. My friends were not going to be around to help fix my car and so he gave me one of his junkers and warned me that it was on its last legs and could die at anytime. I was quite grateful. Another thing I inherited was Julian's job at a Citgo gas station.

I worked there for a time, but it was my penchant for being high which was my undoing. I accidentally put unleaded gas in a Mercedes Benz that ran on diesel and my boss, an honorably discharged Navy man in his fifties, correctly guessed that I was stoned.

I commuted via a back country road from home to work, but despite my caution, a passing policeman in the opposite lane spotted my outdated inspection sticker on my windshield, turned his patrol car around, lights flashing, and pulled me over.

The traffic officer ran my driver's license, discovered that in addition to the outdated inspection sticker I was uninsured and unregistered, and he arrested me. Once my car was towed and I had been brought to and cited at the nearest police station, I was released. I didn't show up for work that day, and that was the last straw for my boss, who promptly fired me.

The towing fee plus storage charges plus what I would need to pay to get my car out of impound, amounted to over two hundred dollars. Add that to the hundred dollar fine I had just incurred by driving without registration. I also had a thirty-day eviction notice on my apartment and those thirty days were almost up. All I had was $300 and no idea what to do.

To get around my predicament I bought yet another nickel and dime car. I paid $100 up front for it, but I knew I'd have to renege on the other $400 I had agreed to in writing. Now I had a big, hulking, black Chevy Camaro that had languished unattended in someone's backyard for years. It was running on seven of its eight cylinders. One of the T-Top windows flapped at highway speeds and the car came with a nest of carpenter ants in the back trunk. I lived in this car during my search for work.

I had a brand new temporary plate and ten days grace before this car also needed to be registered and inspected. When that time was up, I parked my Camaro at the back of a sprawling parking lot that was part of an enormous shopping mall complex in the city of Manchester. I was too paranoid that I would lose my Chevy like I had the other cars, through mechanical breakdown or for moving violations.

At this point, I had less than twenty dollars to my name and just a few cigarettes left. I was all out of my head "meds," and out of luck. With trepidation and shame, I called up my grandparents to plead for help. My grandfather was kind enough to drive the thirty miles at night and he picked me up.

I took whatever work I could get. A distant relative had recently died and my grandparents had inherited a nearly-new compact car. They loaned it to me. Since I now had a street legal car again, I could pursue those industrial jobs that usually turned out to be in the middle of nowhere, along some rural route, miles away from any town.

Some jobs were temporary and after two weeks I had to take another assignment. I got lucky at a respected local company and was trained and certified as a forklift operator. My job was unloading steel from tractor trailers and putting it on racks inside the warehouse.

The management decided to take me on as a full-time, permanent employee. But there was a catch. I needed to take a preemployment drug screen. Which I had to refuse. When you turn down a piss test, they just assume you are a hard-core druggie. Their corporate insurance policy won't cover the liability.

Not only did I not get the permanent position, but I lost my temp assignment there as well. Ironically, you can come to work on three or four psychotropic medications with Black Box warnings about homicidal and suicidal ideation attached to them, and no one would think to have a drug screen for that or even consider it as a deciding issue for a job position. But smoke a joint to relax after work and you are unemployable? So much for parity in treatment options.

For awhile I just kept bouncing from one temp job to another. I had intense pressure from my grandparents to get stabilized and get out on my own as soon as possible. My father called me at their house when he heard I was living with them again.

"My parents have not forgotten what happened the last time that you lived with them. They have grave misgivings regarding your mental health," Andrew informed me. "Please, do my folks a big favor, and move out as soon as you can."

They kind of expected that I would have another breakdown sooner or later. After all, I was a diagnosed manic depressive and my psychiatrist had explained to them that I would always be subject to bipolar mood cycling and my grandparents didn't want it to happen in their home. And understandably so. They were just too old to deal with that sort of thing anymore.

As luck would have it, I found the perfect job and started as a rural newspaper delivery contractor. I would get up at two a.m. and be at the loading docks of the local newspaper distribution center by three a.m. Then I had to have a few hundred newspapers delivered out in the middle of nowhere by six-thirty a.m., seven days a week.

The compensation for this job was unbelievably good to an eighteen-year-old with no job skills. I would be paid about $600 dollars, plus tips, every two weeks. With that amount of money I was quickly able to get myself back on my feet.

CHAPTER 12

DOWNWARD SPIRAL

For awhile I prospered. I had the ideal job for my temperament. I didn't have to deal with anyone that I didn't want to. I used to get gas, cigarettes and coffee from an all-night fuel station and truck stop on a rural highway that I traveled along. The cashier on the late shift had a great hash connection, and together we'd go out back and smoke some while listening to the Skinny Puppy or Nine Inch Nails tracks coming from my car. Then I'd finish up the rest of my paper-route and hopefully I would see nothing but skunks, porcupines, deer and other wildlife on the quiet dirt roads that ran through the woods.

As I was rebuilding my financial life I started dating again and I fell in love with Gene. Gene has the most seductive pair of come-hither eyes I'd ever seen on a guy, and at 5ft. 10in. he stood but one inch taller than me and as an aside, let me say that structural symmetry makes easier just about any intimate physical activity you care to think about. With a spacious intellect to match his sensitive looks, Gene seemed quite the catch.

Gene and I met at a local Dunkin Donuts one evening and soon became inseparable. Once he got out of work at his job as a shift manager at a retail store, we would rendezvous, drink coffee and smoke cigarettes together, and talk about life until coffee shops closed down and kicked us out. Then we would get high together and take a drive through the woods in one of our cars while just holding hands and listening to music.

The late summer and autumn of '93 was one of the best in my life. An adult now for more than half a year, I had really been enjoying the freedoms that came with it. I worked the best job I'd ever had. I had a good car that ran well, and access to a reliable source of decent weed. I had money in the bank and would soon be moving out into my own place again. I was in love and believed I had found my soulmate. Things had never been better.

I had never known such a good time and such good feeling in my whole life, so it may sound strange when I say that I thought seriously about killing myself. I knew from past experience that good things in my life would not last. I didn't relish losing what I had.

This would be a great time to check out from life, now that I was on top of things, instead of at the bottom. I contemplated suicide, not because I was depressed, but because I was happy. I had been subtly or overtly depressed for so long and for so many years, that I didn't know what to do with such bliss. I wanted to die because I could die happily and at peace. At the same time I was addicted to this experience of loving and being loved by Gene, and so I chose to stay alive.

I left my grandparents house when I had saved enough money for a security deposit. Gene and I decided to cohabit, and together we rented and moved into a cozy little cottage on a lake. My life was perfect. We really had some amazing chemistry, like near-telepathy from the moment we met. There was both a mystery and a familiarity about him. We were like two old souls meeting up again across many lifetimes. I was even imagining having a family with Gene some day. I never had thoughts like that before in my life. I wanted it to go on forever, but of course it didn't.

It all began with a broken tail light on my car. A state trooper who had pulled me over to cite me for a defective signal violation discovered that I didn't have required insurance. My car was towed to my grandparent's home. They put me on their insurance. But three hundred people didn't get their paper that day.

Then, only a month later, my car's engine quit and needed to be replaced. My grandparents covered that expense too and they got me a rental car to carry me over for my job. This one lasted only a few days, as the left front wheel fell off while traveling a rugged and generously pitted dirt road.

The last straw came with the winter. There were certain steep hills on my route. As my car didn't have four-wheel drive, when snow and ice came, I couldn't get up the hills and deliver to my customers on that stretch.

I was summoned to the corporate headquarters to be asked why my deliveries were late and the director for distribution asked me if I could get an SUV or other 4WD vehicle, immediately. I told him, "That's impossible." Then he let me go, telling me that they had someone on the waiting list who had a jeep.

I sat in my car, smoking a cigarette, infuriated at my misfortune at losing this one of a kind job. I was so angry with the unfairness of it that in a burst of rage I punched the windshield and instantly cracked it from one side to the other. This was the same car whose engine had just been replaced a month earlier.

Everything was going down the drain in the dead of winter. I owed my grandparents thousands of dollars that went into repairing two cars, a new engine, and now adding a windshield too. Then there was a state hearing pending about the future of my driver's license. I had rebuilt my life, made plans and invested in my future with Gene and now I couldn't pay my share of the bills. All I had as a buffer was almost a thousand dollars in my bank account. This would keep us afloat for about a month or so.

It was all my fault. This was too much stress and served to push me into suicidal depression swing. I was a loser. There was no way around it.

"I am a total fuck-up," I told my beloved later that day, "I have had enough of this life." I said, as I launched into an explanation of my latest series of mishaps. Coincidentally, Gene had battled depression throughout his life and had been near-suicidal for a time, not too long before we'd met. He even had an outfit picked to do it in. Consequently, Gene totally and completely understood how I felt. Which is very seductive in its own right. To find someone who knows exactly how you feel.

"I am not going to lose you so soon after I found you." Gene breathed. "If you are going to go," so passionate, "then I am coming with you." Heartrendingly serious.

We proposed to each other on the spot. I tried to get my aunt Myra, who was a minister at the time, to marry us that evening. She knew something was up, but what exactly, she couldn't fathom. We wanted to get married "too much" too suddenly, and she refused us, sagely advising us to live with each other for awhile first, before deciding on marriage.

Dismayed at that setback, but undeterred from our plan to go through some kind of marriage-like ceremony, we improvised some of the more traditional marriage vows and pledged ourselves to each other in my car. Then we went back to our tiny cottage on Lake Todd to make love again and again.

The next day we got up and had coffee and cigarettes together while listening to the ice cracking and settling on the lake. We wrote a suicide note and considered how to kill ourselves gracefully. It was my idea to use carbon monoxide poisoning. We didn't have a garage, so we fitted what we had at hand, a garden hose, to the exhaust and ran it into the hatchback.

With the car turned on and heat blasting, we cuddled up together in the back seat and waited to die. After some time we realized that the smell of the exhaust had lessened, and we were not noticeably sleepy. Upon investigation, we found that the hose had melted. An unforeseen consequence of attempting this method.

Still undeterred, we drove into town and bought bottles of Benadryl and Jack Daniels. Once back home, we got into bed and drank down our cocktails. We snuggled up next to each other and waited to fall asleep.

After we both woke up the next day, alive and a tad lethargic, we decided that perhaps this was a sign of sorts that it wasn't time to go yet, for either of us. We tore up our suicide note and started doing Tarot readings together, trying to understand what our fate's held.

That was the end of our relationship. Although it took another month before it was truly over, the failed suicide attempts were the crack that ended our harmonious interactions. For my part, I had charmed someone, not only into loving me, but to the point where he was willing to die with me. Driven by my own morbid depression I nearly took two lives that day, not just my own, but also the life of a really wonderful person. For reasons that were, in retrospect, not as awful as I thought back then.

We'd spent a lot of time together in recent months and during that time my unstable personality had become increasingly more apparent. Our lack of money aggravated the gloomy atmosphere. We had had to apply for heating assistance locally, and because I couldn't afford to pay off hundreds of dollars in unpaid fines, I lost my driver's license for awhile. Nevertheless, I was genuinely surprised one morning when, after making me breakfast, Gene packed his things into his Plymouth, told me "Goodbye," got into his car and drove away, never to return.

In my pain and grief I vandalized the home we had lived in together those precious few months, with my bare hands. I walked outside and onto the snow-covered lake. For several minutes I stomped all over the ice, hoping that it would break, I'd fall into the frigid water, drown, and this awful nightmare would be over. I couldn't break through anywhere and, fatigued from the effort, I walked back into the cottage and mulled over my options.

I needed help. And I felt like a total disgrace to my family because of it. Once more my grandparents would come to my aid, and I would never ask them again.

After I gave them a call, my grandfather came down and picked me up. He drove me back to the city in his truck. I was given $500 dollars for food and a month's rent somewhere cheap. I rented a room in a giant old-fashioned house, located squarely downtown. Bathrooms had to be shared with the other residents. I was allowed to have a tiny college-dorm style refrigerator and a hot plate. I now had a month to get employment and pay the rent.

A giant abyss inside me, created in the wake of Gene's departure, left me more physically vulnerable than I'd been in quite awhile. For a long time I thought I would die from a broken heart. I became so depressed that I could think of barely anything but my loss and death and the seeming futility of my life. I took sick that winter and was ill for literally weeks.

I had to walk for miles through the snow and cold, looking for work while I was sick in body, mind, and spirit. I did have some luck and I found a job at the University of N.H. as a grill cook. I got to look in the fresh faces of inbound college students, and I hated them.

I hated them for their luck that they were getting degrees for high paying jobs and careers. I hated them for looking so damn healthy, and new, and inexperienced. I hated them because they seemed to talk amongst themselves like they knew everything about anything already, and I surmised that most of them knew nothing at all about living a hard life in the real world. I hated them because I should have been one of them, and instead I was making them fried egg sandwiches for breakfast.

Eventually, I became friends with some of the computer science majors. They were always looking to score some weed and I knew where I could get plenty. That was how I got to see college life and the dorms at the age of nineteen. I started dealing marijuana to the out of town, out of state kids. It was not a thriving business, but if I could sell enough, I could just about afford to smoke it for free.

A lot of folks don't realize that depression is not about "being bummed out." It's not merely feeling sad or gloomy. It's feeling morose, melancholic, hopeless. Depression sinks into your bones and the gravity of it wears you down and leaves you too fatigued to care about anything. Those feelings create internal dialogue along the lines of, "It's not worth this anymore." Your outlook on life changes and you become pessimistic. You don't see the good along with the bad. Your perception becomes very selective, excluding all but the negative. And if there's nothing negative to find, then you simply fabricate it.

Occasionally, at home, in school or in the workplace, you encounter people who are highly energetic, sunny and unsinkably optimistic. Those kinds of people can always tell when you are feeling down, and for some reason they seem compelled to say the dumbest, most unthinking things to you like, "Cheer up." And, "It's far too beautiful a day to be depressed." My personal favorite used to be, "Smile!"

Meanwhile you think to yourself: *Why don't you go shut up and die. No one has a right to be so cheerful. You can't be that happy and also be in touch with reality. Life is not something to smile about.* Unless they have experienced persistent clinical depression themselves, most people have no idea that you cannot simply flick a mental switch and voilà, you are no longer depressed. It doesn't work that way.

I slowly began to rebuild my broken life.

I still had major depression. I was suicidal.

No amount of sleep would fully refresh me.

I really just wanted to lay down forever and stop functioning.

I knew that if I allowed myself to indulge those impulses, eventually I could be hospitalized, and I would not allow that to happen.

Give myself over to Them? There was nothing they could do for me except drug me or shock my brain. I just wanted my life back. I wanted to rewind about two months or so, when I still had a driver's license, a car, an easy and decent job. And Gene. I had been truly happy for a little while there and barely had enough time to really get acquainted with that feeling before everything detonated.

I partitioned my mind and created a personality that could get up and move, despite my crisis. I was just a shell of basic impulses that twitched my strings, causing me to get out of bed, put on clothes, make coffee, put up my hair and walk to my job like an automaton. That's when I began to get really addicted to caffeine and sugar. I needed tons of it to have enough energy to get through the day.

I forced myself to work so hard that I had no time to think about how awful my life was. I eventually left that grill cook job and found better paying, but harder work. I worked part-time as a janitor and forklift driver at an iron worker's factory, and later became an apprentice iron worker myself. That was my morning job.

I took a job as an attendant and cashier at a gas station for the afternoons. During the evenings, I became a Service Star carpet and floor care specialist. All told, I worked about twelve to sixteen hours a day and walked, to and from every job, for months.

At one point I found myself counting the money from my various jobs on the coffee table in my room. I put all this physical energy into working for other people to collect these very few pieces of green paper, only to pass them to other people. After setting a few of those green papers aside to pay off all my fines, I had no more green paper to spend on me. That was the breadth and depth of my existence. Without Gene in my life, it seemed pointless to live like that. I wondered why I even bothered.

Clearly, becoming a legal adult was not the cure for my existential depression that I thought it would be when I was seventeen and counting the days. I had been an adult for a little over a year, and adulthood brought with it a whole new burden of obligations and interdependencies and relationships that caused no end of stress to me. My failure to be able to handle those stresses had cost me Gene and kept spilling over onto my remaining family, unfairly increasing the burden in their lives.

Depression can make you a mean and selfish-seeming person. To other people you come across as bilious and bitter. Gene, my grandparents and other relatives had all experienced my black temper and hair-trigger irritability. It's hard to endure someone who is chronically depressed because they can get abusive and appear to have no empathy for the pain that their intractable mood swings cause others. They are too caught up in their own suffering. My mother Sarah is another classic example of just such a depressive type.

In my father's family you were expected to pull yourself up by your bootstraps and handle your affairs. My grandparents were self-made and both had their own small businesses. Like my dad, my aunts and uncle had gone on to make something of themselves. "We cannot keep bailing you out," my grandmother had informed me.

Unlike my other family members, I had been a teenage mental patient. My first psychiatrist had predicted a life of intense manias, suicidal depression and schizophrenic tendencies, and so far her prophesy was coming true. No doubt my relatives wondered why I didn't just take prescribed medications to help me "get my act together." But they didn't understand that suffering off of meds was preferable to suffering on them. The drugs manipulated my thoughts and diminished my feelings while making me feel like crap. They only added to my misery.

Witnessing my struggles just trying to get by, my family probably felt like their hands were tied. They knew that I could get myself out of forced commitment to a hospital by faking it and that I would only hate them for trying to intervene, now that I was an adult. Mental illness was something I had to battle on my own. Although it took them awhile, I think they eventually realized that I truly did not want help for it.

I gave myself an ultimatum. I would rebuild the material aspects of my life. Work on getting a car again, then a better apartment, then some money saved in the bank. If I could not find a reason to live by next year, then I would kill myself, once and for all, and get it right.

After months of saving my money, I finally had enough to pay off all my fines, get my driver's license reinstated, and to put my beat up '81 Chevy Z-28 on the road. Just as I was becoming mobile again, I heard from my father that my brother was to turn eighteen shortly and would be returning to the States and would I look after him for a bit, until he was on his own?

Byron had finally been kicked out of the Hell House by our stepfather Tim and had gone on to live with Andrew, our real dad, who himself had moved from Hong Kong to the Philippines years earlier. My brother also suffered from PTSD, bouts of major depression and the various behavioral issues that had contributed to his ADD diagnosis. He and my father had not gotten along well, and Andrew had banished him to a private boarding school.

I both looked forward to, but also loathed the arrival of my brother. We kinda had unfinished business, he and I. The last time we had lived together, I nearly beat him to death for threatening to kill me in my sleep after one too many altercations.

I tried to show him a good time when he got to the States, but he rubbed me the wrong way right out of the gate. I asked him to keep a low profile, since, per my rental agreement, I was not permitted to sublet my room. I would come home from my first job in the morning and find him playing with his remote control car on the sidewalk in front of the building, where other tenants, or the landlord could encounter him.

Days later I came home to find that he had helped himself to my radio and cassette tapes and had never given me the simple courtesy of asking beforehand. I didn't know what latitude he had become accustomed to in the all-boys boarding school overseas, but his lack of respect for my things and my living situation was egregiously offensive. I needed to see a demonstration that he had changed from the insolent punk who would raid my bedroom when I was out with my friends, and steal my stuff. And there was no indication that his personality had matured, whatsoever.

His attitude was that I should just "chill out" because it was no big deal, and nothing to get so aggro about. He seemed incapable of seeing this situation from my point of view. And so, within a week or two, the niceties had worn off. We were back at each other's throats as though not a day had passed since our last conflict, almost five years earlier.

We agreed to forge a financial alliance that would allow us to rent a more suitable dwelling. This way we could live together with more space and privacy. This would allow us both to live better lives than living separately, and struggling individually. After pooling our money we got a spacious apartment with our own room for each of us and parking spots for our vehicles.

We even took work assignments together. Once I had my Chevy up and running again, I no longer was forced to be employed locally. Together, we registered for temp agencies and were sent off to warehouses and factories, making identical wages for unskilled manual labor. We were a team again, sort of. The only way we could live together "normally" was when both of us were high.

Eventually he got a job at a preform cement manufacturing company, and I got one as a paper-roll tender at a large scale printing press. Splitting the rent allowed us to afford to go in on large purchases of marijuana together. We ate reasonably well. He was a kind of distraction for a few months and helped me forget about my private suicide pact for a time. We still fought over this and that. We had a lot of bad history. His inconsiderate behavior and his lack of emotional intelligence caused much friction.

For my part, I could not have been easy to live with either. I had a volatile temper, and I would routinely hit walls and slam doors while screaming at him when we argued. Out of deeply held resentments and an inner desire to get "revenge" for his past misdeeds, I contrived to screw him over financially when the opportunity presented itself. In one instance I got him to pay three quarters of our joint security deposit, promising him I'd pay him back in order to make our split fifty-fifty, but I never did.

When I was depressed, I didn't bother him much, but kept to myself. At other times, I would come out of my room all smiles and high energy, exuberant, with all sorts of ideas that I would run by him. He had no clue, one day to the next, or even hour by hour sometimes, what kind of person would come out of my room. He even remarked upon my wheel-of-fortune-like personality one day, while we were getting high and relaxing after work.

As autumn came around, I happened to be in a Napa auto parts store, shopping for oil and antifreeze, in the ongoing maintenance project that was my muscle car. As I was scanning the labels, looking for what I wanted, I heard a voice and its accompanying laugh that I'd not heard in a long time. It sent chills down my spine, triggering me into a cold sweat. My legs began to shake from both fear and rage. There was only one person in the world with that voice.

I surreptitiously positioned myself so I could see the owner of the voice without revealing my person. Sure enough, I was right. It couldn't have been anyone else. He was a giant man, a

Mississippi native that had moved to New England years ago. I had grown somewhat since I had last seen him, but he was still massive, and much bigger than most people.

His name was Gordon and he had terrorized us kids at the state residential treatment facility and school that I had lived at after being released from my first inpatient stay in psychiatric care. He looked down at all of us for being what we were, some of the most emotionally dysfunctional, behaviorally maladaptive teenagers around. We could not live normal mainstream lives, which was why we were there.

He was a youth counselor, and along with a handful of other coed staff, he had overseen the locked down dormitories that we inhabited when we were not in school classes. When he was on shift, he made an already awful living situation even worse. He had taken a special dislike to me and I hated him.

In one memorable incident, during a routine contraband search, he planted cigarettes in my room. They were first in his front shirt pocket when he walked in, but later he was pulling them out of the space inside the ceiling over my bed. I'd made the mistake of flaunting that I had always passed these room searches, and so it was really pointless to search anyway. If I wanted to bring contraband onto the unit I certainly wouldn't hide it in my room.

He busted me for possessing his cigarettes. That meant going on restricts and losing a privilege level for a week. I cursed him roundly and told him that if I could get away with it, I would smash him in the face. For cursing out and threatening a staff member, he ordered me to go to the Quiet Room immediately.

Infuriated, I balled my fists up by my sides, as if to strike him. Gordon smiled and gave me his signature laugh and dared me to hit him, knowing full well that it meant being automatically restrained by the staff and forced bodily into the Quiet Room to spend a few hours, or even days, in seclusion.

He looked forward to restraining the residents. You could see he got off on the power trip. It brought excitement to an otherwise dull job of shepherding us around, watching us eat, do homework, play games and attend community meetings. Gordon wasn't the only staff like that. I encountered plenty of people like him, at various placements. Men and women alike. He was probably one of the worst.

I did go to the Quiet Room of my own volition. I had already suffered the ignominy of being restrained and I could not bear to fight and lose against the unfairness of such lopsided numbers again.

This was the ultimate destination for any resident that acted out. Now that I was there, I started acting out even more. I turned to him and put my back against the wall. I screamed a karate kiai, took up a fighting stance and dared him to touch me. He just laughed at me again, walked out and closed the door on me.

Furious, I started doing my karate punch, block and kick drills into the air around me. He then peered through the Plexiglas and wire mesh window and informed me, "You are just making it harder for yourself to come out. As long as you are agitated and threatening, you will never leave that room." It was all up to him. And he added. "As far as I am concerned, you can stay in seclusion forever."

I walked over to the window and looked Gordon in the eye. Making my voice as hard as steel and as cold as ice, I said to him, "You will forget this incident, but I will not. One day, when you least expect it, I will be there." I swore, "And I will make you pay for this." He laughed again from the other side of the door and said, "That's another week on restricts, right there," and he wandered off, chuckling to himself on his way to fill out the incident report.

Knowing I was defeated, and so angry that I thought I would explode, I tried to calm down. I sat down with my back to the door and faced the back wall of the Quiet Room in lotus position. I fixated my gaze on a tiny dimple in the pastel-painted cinder blocks. I then began to practice basic meditation and counting my breaths. I stayed there in meditation for hours and hours, becoming one with that spot on the wall. Slowly, I had regained my composure and my masks of control.

Flash forward in time. Standing in the aisle of the auto parts store, listening to him chat it up with the guy on the other side of the counter, I had killing urges, overriding flashbacks and those memories. I also remembered my promise to him.

Here was Gordon, practically fallen into my presence as though by providence. This was my chance to get even. Just as I'd foreseen, he wasn't expecting me. *Such arrogance*, I thought to myself, to have no fear of the consequences of his actions coming back to haunt him. If he had any intelligence, then he should have been frequently looking over his shoulder. He walked out of the auto parts store, over to his truck, oblivious to everything. He had no idea at all that he was now in serious danger.

Meanwhile, I had hung back until he left the building so he would not accidentally see me. I swiftly wrapped up my shopping and walked out the door. I began singing children's songs and doing basic math in my mind to conceal my homicidal thoughts from being telepathically broadcast, as I walked out to the parking lot.

Once in my car, I watched him tinker with his truck for a bit in the parking lot. I decided I would stalk him. I would find out what this guy did in his spare time, after a day of abusing vulnerable teens at the residential facility. I would find out where he lived, plan his demise, and take him out when I was good and ready. I was doing all those past, present, and future residents a favor, by ridding the world of that man. I was about to become a vigilante.

Eventually he left and I gave him a head start. I lit a cigarette and turned on my car, revving the engine. I pulled casually out of the parking lot and then began accelerating as I merged with the highway. I drove swiftly but cautiously, like a shark on the hunt, until I sighted him, and then I just tailed him behind several cars for a few miles.

After awhile Gordon started a left turn-signal and began slowing down and I saw a dirt road that led to a river. I passed him on the right, like the other drivers in front of me, and watched him in my rear-view mirror make the turn and vanish through the trees. I turned around a couple of miles down the road, and returned the way we had come. I signaled right and made my turn a few moments later on that same road he had taken.

My car coasted to a stop shortly after I turned off the engine so as not to alert my quarry. After waiting a suitable amount of time, I got out and closed the heavy door quietly, leaving it slightly ajar. I slipped a seven-inch fixed-blade knife up my sleeve and crept slowly down and around the bend in the road until I could see him.

He was about hip-deep in the river, fly fishing. I stood there, concealed by cover and watched him for awhile. And as I did, I was focusing intensely on certain images in my mind, like a perfectly green Granny Smith apple, the red planet Mars and a sleeping Rottweiler pup, in order to mask my thoughts and prevent my homicidal ideation from leaking out. You just never know when you might run into someone with telepathic ability, and I worried about that a lot.

Then I glanced at the road and followed it with my eyes to where it merged with the beach. There were tire and animal tracks as well as human footprints. While I was sure I could succeed in knifing him, I was growing less confident by the second that I could get away with it for long. I didn't want to go to jail for life over this guy.

Somehow, knowing I could do it if I really wanted to released the pressure in my head a tiny bit. I stared at his back another moment or two and then walked stealthily back to my car. I felt a lot better, as if both a burden had been removed and control had been returned. I had been a predator, a hunter, and he was my prey. It was enough that I had stalked him for almost thirty minutes and he never knew I was there. It was therapeutic. I got back into my car, lost in inner musings, and drove away.

For months I continued working various jobs. I had lost the job working graveyard shifts at the printing press when they instituted a drug screen policy. I did a stint working outdoors in the winter, in modular home construction.

My twentieth birthday came and went. Now I was working as a machinist, in a Swiss screw machine shop. They made all sorts of precision parts, from the tiniest screws and nuts, to valves for anti-lock break systems and the Patriot missile.

It was actually a great job and I made decent money. Enough to retire my aging Chevy. My brother drove me out to a remote corner of rural Massachusetts to pick up a used Ford Thunderbird. I bought the Ford specifically because the ad in the paper said it had roaring heat and excellent air conditioning. Which it did. The rear window defrosted rapidly, and the over-sized wipers moved with enough power to clear several inches of snow off of them. The car practically sang to me when I first turned the engine over.

Every little gadget worked, from the electric mirrors, and interior lights to the wiper fluid jets. I fell in love with it immediately. It had been waiting here for months, just for me. What a marvelous find for a used car on my budget. Best of all, it was innocuous. I could drive this car past a state trooper on the highway and he wouldn't come out of his hiding spot to follow me for a couple of exits (a not uncommon occurrence when I drove my Camaro).

I finally felt safe on the road. Even if I was pulled over, I was properly insured and everything was totally legal. Weeks passed, one after another, and I had a job, money in the bank, a decent apartment, friends and great car. I had no outstanding warrants. It looked like I was finally getting the hang of this being-an-adult thing.

Despite the recent turn of events, my depression was coming back hard. It had never really gone away, but when things were going well in my life, the downward pull of depression seemed lessened. And the year that I'd given myself to live was almost up.

Gene lived less than fifty miles away from me. I had to know if it might be possible for us to be together again. Absence makes the heart grow fonder. I realized that in the year that we were apart my love for Gene had not diminished. Not one iota. I had not accepted the breakup of our relationship and therefore had not begun the process of moving on towards other romantic pursuits. I had no real reason to go on living without my soulmate.

I stalked my ex for days, in my T-Bird. I put a picture of Gene on my dashboard and wrapped a necklace that I had received as a gift from him around my hand. Every day, after work, I got into my car and meditated before going out to search. I would close my eyes, focus my heart and mind and reach out in all directions with my feelings and awareness. Then I would queue up a Type O Negative or Queensryche CD and go for a drive. I let my intuition and impulse guide my choices of highways and off-ramps.

On the fourth day of my quest, I was sitting in a parking lot of a shopping mall in Nashua, and there was Gene, walking right by me without seeing me. I didn't know whether to laugh or cry over the serendipitous appearance of my beloved. It seemed I still had my talent: psychic ability, mixed with ritual magic. I had used our spiritual connection to guide me to him. And I knew I could spellbind him with my eyes and voice, if we got within proximity to each for longer than a minute.

I refused to force a confrontation and, through a mutual acquaintance who lived in the area, I sent Gene an emotionally charged, tear-stained, pages long love-letter, professing my undying affection for him.

In short: *Hello, remember me? I love you as much today as I did when we met. Let's start over. Here is my new number. Call me, and we'll meet up for coffee and chat away the nights again, like old times. Oh and, if I don't hear from you in seven days, I am leaving for good. Where I am going, there is no coming back from. You're the only person anchoring me to this life. Please call me. I love you.*

There was certainly no pressure or implied guilt in my desperate (*manipulative*) and heartsick (*narcissistic*) supplication. Seven long days passed and Gene never called. That was it then. There would be no second chance. I couldn't accept it. The glorious days of true love were really over, and I would be forever diminished. A shadow of our combined spirit. A half-empty shell.

There was no point to going through the motions of life anymore. I was so deep-down tired of trying to be strong and invincible every single day of my life. I was tired of my existence and the weight of my memories. I was just tired. Tired of it all. It was time for me to go.

CHAPTER 13

FINAL EXIT

I had already blown what I thought was a once-in-a-lifetime opportunity. I'd lost the best person to ever come into my life at that point. I had known the taste of oneness with another person's mind and heart, and I would never share my life and my thoughts with Gene ever again.

I quit my perfectly good job. I closed my bank account and withdrew my small savings. I packed up my belongings as though I were moving and cleaned my bedroom in the apartment I shared with my brother. Then I went to the public library, in search of a book that until now I'd only heard about.

The book was called: *Final Exit* by Derek Humphry. It is a manual of self-euthanasia, written by a right-to-die advocate. Gratitude flowed out of me that I lived in an age where information like this was available.

Some people opine that suicide is a permanent solution to a temporary problem. They believe books like *Final Exit* should be banned and their authors arrested and jailed. I say to them: Do you honestly think that being born into a lower-class economic bracket, having most of your family give up on you, suffering depression for fifteen years, and being a psychopath, is really a "temporary" problem?

I was quite fed up with my inability to complete my previous suicide attempts. Surviving them had only led to more suffering over the years. I needed to get it right this time and I had to do it the way my heart wanted to go. I had brought a notebook and a pen to take notes. It was certainly not the book itself that I intended on checking out.

Hanging myself seemed like last-second desperation. I didn't want to let my blood drain from my veins or to shoot myself in the head. Deliberate car crashes and jumping off a building were just as unpalatable. I had some idiosyncratic, occult-based notions for not wanting my blood or body parts to be spilled or strewn about. Something about the life-force of a person, inhabiting their cells and bodily fluids, staining the environment with a psychic imprint as a consequence of a traumatic demise.

The one thing I wanted now was to die peacefully, with some measure of dignity, and in control of the process. I wanted to fall asleep and never wake up again. I opted to take powerful, prescription strength sedatives and pain killers and mix them with alcohol. Only, I'd not had a physician or doctor since I had left State's care. I also had another year to go before I could legally purchase booze.

For the last two years I had been totally uninsured. There was no way for me to get a prescribing doctor on short notice. I didn't know anyone who had "pharmies" (prescription drugs) I could buy. You didn't need many if you got them at a good strength and the right combinations.

What about over-the-counter sleep aids? They tended to have the same ingredients as allergy medications. Just over a year earlier, I had drank an entire bottle of Benadryl and chased it with a small bottle of Jack Daniels (purchased by my ex) to no appreciable effect.

There were the stories you heard about so and so taking a hundred sleeping pills and dying. Sometimes they survived it. Perhaps the solution was simply numbers. Instead of one hundred sleeping pills, I decided on three hundred.

Perhaps I could find something like alcohol, only more deadly. I remembered then the warnings on the bottles of ethylene glycol. You had to be careful of spilling it on the ground because animals were attracted to it. A small amount would kill medium-sized house pets. What was a small amount and how big was medium-sized? I decided on sixteen ounces. I already had at least that much in a bottle in the trunk of my car.

What if I somehow survived both the antifreeze and the diphenhydramine? What if it took awhile to die from it? How else could I bulletproof my suicide plan? I planned to drive myself out to a somewhat remote place and not tell anyone where I was going. That would cut down on the odds of some random and unwanted rescue attempt.

Temperature might help too. It was the middle of March and it still got down below freezing at night. There was still snow on the ground in places. The earth itself was frozen and hard. I could roll down my windows and let the heat of the car bleed out. How long would it take to die from hypothermia?

Was there anything else I could do to further reduce my odds of survival? I got the idea for the plastic bag and rubber bands from the book *Final Exit*. Now the entire plan was suspended in my mind's eye.

> Drive out to a remote area, telling no one, when, where, or what I had planned.

> Roll down the windows to increase my odds of exposure to the cold.

> Eat three hundred sleeping pills an hour after popping some Dramamine (to prevent nausea). Chase the handfuls of pills with sips of fresh, syrupy green, vehicle anti-freeze.

> When I started to get sleepy, put the bag over my head and secure it with the rubber bands.

When I bought my OTC sleeping aids, I purchased only one box at a time. I smiled at everyone I met. I sang little ditties in my head to prevent my suicidal thoughts from being broadcast. I didn't want to arouse suspicion and well meaning "intervention." I experimented with a variety of plastic bags and rubber bands. I needed to know what to expect from sitting with an air tight bag on my head for long minutes.

Two days later, I had piles of boxes containing hundreds of milligrams of doxylamine and thousands of milligrams of dy-phenhydramine hydrochlorate in pills, capsules and soft gels. I had my chosen bag and bands. I had back up bags and spare elastics. My suicide kit was ready.

I had spelled out the distribution of all my earthly possessions in my handwritten Last Will, which I kept with me in the car, along with the kit. My brother would soon inherit hundreds of books and dozens of CDs and cassette tapes. Music and the printed word, my only treasures.

In the days preceding my own attempt at a final exit I gave no sign to anyone what was going on inside my mind and heart. I made no phone calls to relatives, asking them if they'd miss me if I was gone. I did nothing to attract attention to myself. I drove the speed limit. I was a model citizen. I was magnanimous. When some punk cut me off in traffic, I just smiled and waved at him, mouthing the words "It's okay." I could no longer summon my anger.

I spent the next couple of days going on long drives, trying to find more secret roads and scenic vistas. On one long coastal drive I paid my last homage to the ocean before dropping in on a few friends, just so I could see what people were up to.

My last visit was to someone I had not seen in almost two years. Tyler was one of my best friends, but we'd had a falling out shortly before my eighteenth birthday. At the time he had been constantly complaining about his overbearing father and pressures at home. His dad really was a jerk, and since I had just about no morals for a long time, I offered to try to take care of the problem, using witchcraft.

He believed I had the ability, and that occult powers were real. I had no idea he loved his father underneath his angst. He became angry with me when I suggested it to him, and cussed me out. I was surprised by his reaction, quite frankly.

It'd been ages since I had seen him last, and I wanted to make peace with him before I went away for good. I found out that he had moved out of his parent's home and was living at the house of another one of my friends, who had gone off to college.

I was not prepared for his amiable attitude. He didn't seem upset with me at all. Sometime ago he had had a car accident, slipped off an icy road and head-on into a tree. He suffered a concussion and minor amnesia. In fact, he was not only not angry with me, he had no memory of what we had argued about. His lingering depression seemed completely gone now as well.

What do you know. I smiled at my luck. We got along just like old times. We hung out for a few hours and smoked some pot in the back yard.

"It was good to see you one more time. And I'm glad to know you're happy again and in good health," I told him.

He gave me an odd look, perhaps at the way I had phrased it, but that was as close as I intended on hinting anything to anyone. I smiled to disarm him, and he wished me good luck and good night. Then we parted ways and I expected never to see him again.

Back inside my car I changed into the death outfit I had chosen. Ever since I was a teen, I had worn primarily all black, all the time. There were dozens of reasons why I dressed in that color. Funeral attire for the doomed world around me as I was growing up was just one of many such reasons. Because of my frequently recurring depression over the years, any other color seemed too loud, too inappropriate. Even profane.

For my final night I had chosen a pair of comfy jeans in a soft blue shade, about the same color as my eyes. I put on white socks and new white sneakers. A white corded sweater completed the ensemble. Then I put in my earrings and let down my hair, which cascaded down around my shoulders and back, in curls and spirals. I gave instructions, that I was to be buried in my white sweater, with my hair down.

Normally I kept my long curly hair bound tightly to the back of my head. In part, because I always worked fast-paced manual labor jobs that often required me to work with machines, but also in case I found myself in a fight with someone. I didn't want my vanity to get in my eyes or provide an opponent with something to grasp easily.

Next stop was a decent restaurant and I ate a last meal of my favorite foods by myself. One more drive along the roads and neighborhoods I had grown up in, saying good-bye to places familiar. I took the Dramamine in preparation of the overdose and drove myself to a location I doubted anyone would think of. I turned my car off the pavement onto the dirt and parked far out of sight of the street, under the cover of pine trees. I shut off the engine of my T-bird and put in the Nine Inch Nails CD that I had planned to kill myself to. I programmed the tracks "Hurt" and "A Warm Place" into the playlist and hit the *repeat* button.

How had my life come to this? I sat back in my seat and lit a cigarette, gazing out my window up at the stars. If it actually turned out that there existed a God like out of the Holy Bible, I fully intended on punching Him hard in the face for the hand He dealt to me. I could've been so much more, and done so much better than I had, if I'd had a different life.

Since the day I was born I really had been a burden to everyone. First to my family and later to the State. I owed so much money to so many people, like my grandparents. That debt was always on my mind, and I had no idea how I could ever repay it, or how long repaying that money would sabotage my already lower-class standard of living.

I partly blamed myself for destroying the family I had grown up with and I'd nearly put my Dad's parents into their graves untimely, from stress. I could barely keep a job for a few weeks or months at a time. I had a small-time, petty criminal record and the cops in few local towns knew me by name.

I truly was a colossal failure at everything I'd ever done. I could not remain undrugged for long before the rage and intrusive thoughts of violence would come back, so I was unable to stop smoking pot. My fits of wrath and vengeance were bound to get me in serious trouble with the law, sooner or later.

It seemed like, no matter what happened, I would be destined not to succeed, or to embarrass myself. I was too messed up in the head to be a member of society for long. I knew I was crazy, and I couldn't do anything about it. I was sick in mind and spirit, but there was no therapy or pill for what I had.

There was no point in procrastinating any longer. I put my Last Will and Testimony on my passenger seat. I had written a note to the cops, explaining what had happened to me. For medical personnel I candidly listed each and every chemical that

I put in my system so they wouldn't have to waste their time figuring it out. I put my driver's license inside my Will and put the folded notice to emergency responders under my windshield wiper blades. Then I began the ordeal of my overdose.

About one hundred and fifty or so pills into it, my throat began to spasm shut. I had never taken a sleeping pill of any kind before. I had no idea how fast I would fall asleep. I finally got the last of them down, aided by sips of papaya juice, but it was a foul concoction nonetheless. The ethylene glycol was sweet, but it caused the lining of my mouth to shed in small strips of flesh. My stomach gave one ominous groan and heave, but that was it. Taking the motion sickness pill first was genius for this sort of thing.

I figured I had about fifteen to thirty minutes at best before lights out. I breathed a sigh of relief. I knew that this was it. The end of suffering was at hand. I smiled to know that it was true. I visualized the faces of some friends and relatives and told them good bye and that I was sorry. Not sorry for killing myself, I was apologizing for past sins and the pain I had caused them because of my illness.

This feeling of deep dread came over me then. My body knew that something had happened to it. I looked at myself in the rear view mirror and said to my reflection, "You are dying now." A tiny part of my innermost self cried out in primal fear. I wrapped my arms around myself and rocked myself like a mother would her child, whispering, "Shhh baby, Shhh."

Then the feeling of dread was gone, and I felt completely at peace with myself. I stared out my open window with a smile on my face. I surrendered to death and there was no fear in me. In that moment my entire life flashed before my eyes.

As an observer, I could see that the onslaught of my life's circumstances and the never ending stresses had shaped me into what I had become. Everyone should get a chance to look at their life like this. It's a shame it usually only happens in crisis. It is a kind of enlightenment experience.

Minutes passed and I took long deep breaths, savoring each of them and my newfound inner peace. I was beginning to have audio hallucinations and a deep lassitude was creeping up on me. Suddenly I had the most pressing need to urinate, which disturbed my mellow groove, and I had to relieve it.

I walked no more than twenty feet from my car, took care of business, stood up and started to make my way back. I got about ten feet, when suddenly I couldn't feel my legs. I felt myself falling, but could not prevent it. I don't remember completing the fall itself. I became aware that my cheek was resting on the dirt. I fought a surge of panic. Had I passed out or had a seizure?

I lifted my head and could see the open driver's-side door of my T-Bird. I had to get that plastic bag over my head, right now. I focused on the dim glow of the interior lights, and I strained mightily, gaining another few feet. Then a sound as though being thrust into a wind tunnel roared in my ears and the shadows danced in my vision. The gravity of the earth seemed to have tripled. It took so much mental power to command my muscles, to move the way I wanted them to.

Rest. I just needed to rest a second. Then the blackness came and I stopped struggling.

I saw myself at the bottom of a lake of dark red water. Its surface was like glass. I could see from my underwater depths clearly, without distortion. My mother and all three of my siblings stood at the shore of this crimson lake. Each held the hand of the other, in a chain. I could hear my mother's thoughts and she blamed herself for everything.

Then I was standing across the street, not far from where I had gone into the woods. A rural highway that should have been teeming with cars. There was only an ambulance, facing the wrong way, parked half-on and half-off the road. Was this a dream or was it real? A body was being thrust into the back of it. My body.

"*Leave me be!*" I called out to them.

The jarring of my body as it was loaded snapped me back into myself. They were putting a mask over my face. I could tell through my eyelids that it was light outside and I thought to myself. "Too late guys, too late. One more step, and I am gone."

I had gained one final experiential insight. I was not my body but something much more profound. I let myself slip back out again, and there was nothing but an infinity of darkness.

When consciousness returned, I was in a hospital bed. I was grateful for the dim light. There were tubes and wires attached to me, coming out of various medical equipment just barely out of my sight to my left. I was not in any pain. I wondered how badly I had damaged myself. Rarely had I felt this vulnerable and weak.

My very first concrete string of thoughts and feelings was self-recrimination, disgust and despair. How had I survived? I cried then a little. How pathetic. I couldn't even kill myself. I would just have to try again, as soon as I got out of here.

Nurses came and went, checking on vital signs. None of them seemed talkative. I tried to sense their thoughts. Were they avoiding interacting with me? I fell back into darkness, exhausted from the effort of perception and awareness.

The next time I opened my eyes, my friend Tyler was seated in a plastic chair on my left. He was crying and I felt bad, having never seen him cry before. He'd had no idea at all that I wanted out of life. I reached out my hand to take his and squeezed it firmly. I asked him if I was still strong. He nodded and began cursing me gently, without rancor. Then I passed out again, for how long, I've no idea.

My next visitor was the head of security for the hospital. I asked him if I was in trouble. "No," he said, but he wanted to talk to me about a few things.

"So why does the head of security take it upon himself to visit insignificant little me?" I inquired.

Mr. Security Chief informed me, "You scared a lot of people when you were first brought into the hospital," but he would not go into details when I pressed him, telling me, "You really don't want to know."

Dammit. I had visions of what happened when my demons came out while I was being restrained at Brookside Hospital six years earlier. I could only imagine what my Defense System might have done while they were taking my clothes off or trying to intubate me.

I felt so ashamed. And I apologized, stating, "I didn't mean to scare anyone, and shouldn't have, had I died as I'd intended."

Then we talked for a bit about that. How had I survived, and how close to death had I come? He informed me that not long after I arrived, I had become nonresponsive, and was in mild, but brief coma. It had been touch and go for awhile. It'd been far too late to pump my stomach or to administer activated charcoal. All that remained was to see if I had ingested enough poisons to cause systemic failure.

"You came quite close to permanently damaging your internal organs," Mr. Security told me. "It's harder to kill yourself by those means than you might think." He advised me that over-the-counter sleeping pills had been made almost overdose-proof, deliberately so, to avoid a situation where people could discreetly, cheaply, purchase a painless and easy death.

Which seemed unnecessarily cruel to me. An unfortunate byproduct of our overly litigious society, where someone or something else always has to take the blame for influencing or enabling another person's willful actions. Why couldn't there be a suicide pill for the terminally depressed? The manufacturer wasn't forcing me to put the pill in my mouth, they would just be compassionate enough to provide one. I'd have paid $50, $100, even a whole week's paycheck, for a painless one that worked inside an hour.

Taking the three hundred pills had been quite an ordeal in itself. But as I was far too robust from the combination of my youth, manual labor jobs and martial arts, I probably would have needed about five to six hundred to do it. Assuming I managed to ingest all six hundred, I would have had an agonizing, protracted death, as my internal organs became necrotic and died systematically. Far from the graceful, painless sleep I had envisioned.

When I asked about the supposed lethality of drinking antifreeze, he shared with me a professional anecdote. During his time here at the hospital he had known a guy that would overdose on antifreeze every other week.

He would drink a liter of the stuff, and when that didn't kill him, he was back in the emergency room after a liter and a half. He had also been an alcoholic and developed quite a body tolerance. He came close to death after two liters. After four failed attempts to kill himself with vehicle antifreeze, he had finally shot himself in the head.

"What is the point of having warnings about overdosing on OTC meds and drinking antifreeze? Why do the pill bottles always say, 'If accidental ingestion or overdose, call poison control etc.' if you can't actually die from these things easily?" I mused aloud.

"Because some people have died on smaller doses in the past. We all have different tolerances for what is lethal." Mr. Security answered.

I tried to reconstruct my last moments. Something was missing, some other element that was supposed to be part of the plan. Hypothermia. I had been out in the cold for hours, languishing on the frozen ground. I brought up exposure to the elements.

"If you really wanted to catch hypothermia, why didn't you take off your shoes and socks?" He inquired. "You could have poured water on yourself too. You didn't think of that either."

Perhaps, I thought wryly, even the antifreeze in my blood had helped me. Like some sort of arctic deep-sea creature which makes its own version internally to stay alive. Alas, I never got the plastic bag over my head. Asphyxiation was supposed to seal my fate.

I was just inept, and not as prepared as I thought I was. I didn't have access to the internet back then, so I did not have the ability to quickly locate and compare information regarding methods used in failed and successful suicides. Had I discovered something like the suicide discussions on bulletin boards that exist on the internet these days, almost certainly, I would not be alive right now.

"What happens next?" I asked.

"When you have recovered enough, it is policy to have you brought upstairs for assessment in the psychiatric unit," Mr. Security replied.

I nodded with acceptance. I had expected this. *Why is it, that the psych ward in these places is always upstairs?* I pondered. Never ground level or in the basement. It's almost always the top floor. Probably to reduce the speed an escapee can exit the building, or to segregate "mental" patients from chance encounters with the "normal" patients.

I was moved into a different hospital room and slept for another day. Then brought upstairs to the psych unit in a wheelchair. I slept heavily for most of that day as well.

My second day on the psych ward I had to participate in the structure and go to group meetings. I could barely make out other people's faces from a few feet away because my eyeglasses were still in my car where I left them.

When I got to speak with the unit social worker, I was told I had to stay here for a minimum of a week instead of the usual seventy-two hour hold. This was because of the seriousness of my suicide attempt. The psychiatrist would make the decision as to when I could be released. I would get my first visit with him in a couple of days.

Now I knew the primary gatekeeper I needed to get by. To do that, I would need energy and awareness to back up my guile. In short, I needed my wits about me to pull off "normalcy" convincingly.

My body was damaged. My lower back hurt and my legs felt like rubber and shook whenever I stood up. Walking was still a deliberate exercise. I had injured my kidneys and liver and was still in a little bit of shock. I needed to repair myself. The rooms, and the ward in general, were small and there was not much space for what I intended.

I found a short hall, blocked at the far end by the expected magnetic doors. This hall had the least foot traffic and was partially out of view of the community areas. I did some yoga stretches and karate routines, but ran out of gas real fast.

That's when I remembered a book I had read in my late teens, called *Opening the Energy Gates of Your Body* by Bruce Frantzis. It is an illustrated, instructional guide to beginner chi gung. When I first read the book, I didn't have the patience or the insight needed to pursue the standing meditation exercises, but I did memorize an approximation of the primary set of movements covered in the text.

The author himself, a martial arts master and yoga adept, had used chi gung to recover from a nearly fatal case of hepatitis, picked up during a stay in India. He credited chi gung for regenerating his liver. I began to go through the prescribed movements, one after the other, determined to regain my former level of energy for purposes of my impending performance.

The material worked. I felt better, cleaner and lighter. With a surge of renewed energy, I did a few more sets of yoga, followed by karate forms. I finished my workout with more of the chi gung. In this place, with reasonably healthy food, no drugs or cigarettes, I found myself physically healing somewhat from my ordeal, thanks to the routine of mind-body discipline and a somewhat less polluted environment.

The fourth day on the ward I was feeling strong enough to deal with my impending interview and assessment. That afternoon I finally got a chance to speak to the psychiatrist, Dr. Solano. In order not to arouse too many suspicions, I spun a great lie, coating it with many truths. I was probably a bit too glib with my mental health lingo, because Solano realized that I was quite familiar with the system.

I denied his request to access my juvenile records. I told him I had no family, and there was no one to call. Dr. Solano tried to push Prozac (which was still going strong as the number one antidepressant at that time) on me several times during the course of our conversation, and every time he did, I gave him a variation on my usual condemnation speech about psych meds.

Only on a cold day in hell would I ever be on antidepressants. You see, in my perspective, life was about suffering, sadness and pain. I had absorbed the idea growing up at home.

When I had lost my hearing in my left ear as a teenager from my untreated ear infection, I complained to my mother, "It isn't fair!" And Sarah tried (and failed) to console me by saying something like, "We must all bear our crosses and sufferings. They are tests of faith, given to us by God to humble and teach us."

As opposed to the actual truth, which at the time was more like, "We are too far into the hole from the cost overruns of building the unfinished house in Marlborough to be able to pay the astronomical medical bill that would've been incurred by taking you to the emergency room. So we took a gamble with your health and hearing and you didn't die. Your right ear works fine, so don't be too upset, mmkay?"

Although I was not remotely Christian anymore, deep down I believed that turning off your brain's ability to be depressed with psych meds was cheating. Without depression, how could a person fully appreciate how awful life really was and be motivated to do something permanent about it?

About twenty minutes later, Solano was convinced that I'd simply had a bad lapse of judgment. He told me I had to complete my five day stay, but as long as I had no issues and requested no services, there was nothing stopping me from walking out at the end of the week. That's exactly what happened. I endured another day or so of group therapy meetings and the endless downtime, watching TV (which I couldn't see anyway without my glasses).

I had called my brother Byron from a payphone on the psych unit, and he was coming to pick me up. I just kept my cool and continued my exercises. Not just for the sake of appearance, but because I felt better doing them. I would bide my time and not screw up by being honest about my emotions or intentions. Soon I would be out, and after a day or two I would kill myself.

There was nothing to pack, as I had come with nothing but the clothes I was wearing. I would have to recover my personal effects from the police station and retrieve my car from a tow yard.

In the last few hours of my stay there I met with one of the psych nurses to talk about my discharge. It is fairly standard practice for such places to have a follow up interview to discuss coping strategies, in the event of relapse. It helps cover the hospital's liability.

Nurse Angie was an older woman, possibly in her fifties. Probably in charge of this shift, judging by the nurses who deferred to her. Like many veteran nurses, she was direct and to the point.

"So," she began, "Will we be seeing you again?"

"Ideally, no," I replied. "If I had any plans of trying it again, I'd get it right this time. Like I told Dr. Solano, this was all just a bad time for me and I got overwhelmed. In my vulnerable state, I acted impulsively."

I continued, trying to appear nonchalant. "It's not likely to happen again. If I am feeling morbid, I know to look for support and try to get help."

Which is exactly what you are supposed to say if you really want to be out of those places.

"May I talk with you privately for a moment?" she asked.

I nodded and we walked several feet off to the side, away from the nurses station and anyone else.

"You may have fooled your doctor and perhaps everyone else too, but you do not fool me," she stated.

A knot of anxiety formed in my throat and stomach. I fought to keep my body language and emotions neutral. I said nothing and waited Angie out for the next thing she would say.

"You wrote your own Will," she stated. "That was no impulse suicide attempt. You meant to kill yourself," Angie continued, nodding to herself with conviction. "You truly do not want to be here anymore. Yes, I've seen your kind before."

I fidgeted. How had she seen through me so easily? Her sympathetic understanding was killing me, right where I was standing. I felt exposed. Naked. I dreaded what she might say next, so I went on the offense.

"You can not keep me here," I replied with effort. "There is nothing you can say or do that will keep me here if I were planning on trying again."

"I know," she said. "My guess is, you will probably try again very soon after you walk out those doors, and you probably will succeed."

With that statement, I could no longer hide my private agony, and tears escaped to roll down my cheeks. I dared not nod my head in agreement with her. I could barely speak. I turned my head and gazed at the wall so she could not look me in the eye for the confirmation that was surely there.

"I just ask that before you try again, you think about it for awhile. Things do get better." she stated.

I shook my head in negation. *No. Not for me*, I thought to myself.

"Just think about it, that's all I ask. Wait a bit before trying again." she advised me.

I felt like a kid momentarily, standing there. Her empathy was so genuine. Barely audible, I croaked out my sentiment.

"I wish you had been my mother."

Angie smiled and we embraced. I told her that I'd think about it but would promise nothing more. Satisfied, she returned to her duties.

My brother picked me up, offering me a cigarette, which I took gladly after a week of not smoking. He didn't pester me about my experience. He drove me here and there to pick up my belongings and to finally retrieve my car. I was glad to be out again, away from the florescent lights and dismal aura of depression in the acute psychiatric ward.

Finally, I was alone. I drove around some country back roads for awhile, ruminating on my next course of action. I motored over to Tyler's home and he greeted me enthusiastically. He talked me into what is known in mental health circles as a "safety contract."

"Promise me," Tyler begged, "That you'll never try to kill yourself again."

"Dude," I said, shaking my head from side to side. Then I spoke softly, slowly and seriously for emphasis,

"I c a n n o t d o t h a t ."

So we came to a different agreement. After listening to him talk for awhile, I finally reassured him, "I'll attempt to stick around for one more year." I agreed dishonestly, just to make him feel better in the present moment. His personal pain at what I had done to myself was affecting me in my current state. But I doubted I would stick around for more than one, maybe two weeks.

Tyler asked me if there was anything I wanted. I told him I wanted cigarettes, coffee, some pot and to be left alone. He agreed readily, stating, "I will buy you as many cigarettes as you want, if it will help you stay among the living for awhile longer."

I took my coffee and smokes out to a wooden bench swing on the front lawn which overlooked a withered field of broken cornstalks. The last of the snow seemed to have melted away for good this year, while I had been indisposed. The air was warmer, as spring advanced. The property was bound on three sides by lines of trees, fields and behind it, the Merrimack River flowed, swift and deep.

The dirt and gravel driveway was easily a couple hundred feet long. I could barely see rural traffic through the trees in the distance. I would spot anyone coming down this driveway a long way in advance. With the house at my back, I felt safe and secure. Only two people in the world knew exactly where I was, and I doubted they would be forthcoming with that information.

I needed uninterrupted, undisturbed privacy and solitude so I could think and recover. It felt good to sit and do nothing. In truth there was nothing to do. I had closed down my life and all of its limbs. I had said my goodbyes to every friend and family member during my suicide attempt.

I was not expected anywhere, nor particularly wanted either. No one was dependent on me for anything. I had no responsibilities or deadlines, no pressures or stresses. The only thing I wanted to do was withdraw and sit quietly and be undisturbed. I was truly at loose ends for the first time I could remember.

Tyler and my brother took it upon themselves to protect me from the world. They would bring me coffee and cigarettes, or a pipe packed with weed. They'd smoke with me in silence for a few minutes and then wander off to leave me be, without my asking. I was deeply grateful to both of them.

On the evening of my suicide attempt, when I had embraced my death, I had been truly at peace with myself. I'd really relaxed. As though I had achieved the eye of the storm, existentially. I wanted to feel that inner stillness and peace again. It was still there, but much diminished, like coming down from an acid trip. A fast-fading echo of what I had felt that night in my car.

I liked how I felt when I was passionately aware of my spirituality. I liked how I felt now. Reborn into a life with no immediate obligation and with all the time in the world.

My initial goals were quite humble. I tried to figure out how not give in to suicidality, when I had no compelling reason to live another day or another minute, whatsoever. If I could sit still and keep my thoughts quiet (with the aid of marijuana and meditation breathing exercises) I did not feel imminently suicidal. Hour by hour, I continued to make a conscious decision to stay alive by simply not acting at all. I sat very still, with my hands in my lap and my feet up on the other side of the swing.

I stared into the distance and did not comb my memories or dawdle in my imagination. I just allowed myself to be. To absorb and be absorbed by the natural environment around me. It became a ritual and was critical to my short term survival.

One day at a time was how I decided to live. I would not worry about tomorrow, next month or next year. Only get through this day, today, without hurting myself or others. Go to bed at night. Repeat again the next day.

I would get up in the morning and head to the swing with my coffee, to smoke and sit quietly. I would drink my cup and smoke two cigarettes before doing anything. Modeling and imitating the ritual of my foster father, Roland, from years earlier.

After awhile, I would get up and walk around the gravel driveway, compulsively performing various martial arts and fitness routines to speed my healing along. I was still easily exhausted by laborious activity. My legs remained unsteady if I stood up for long. It took awhile before I was as physically capable as I had been, prior to my overdose.

Then I would return to the swing to sit and rest and contemplate. All day long and into the evening I did this. After several days, I came to a number of conclusions.

My first was that I had succeeded in not harming myself or anyone else. The second was that I had no real desire to do so either. The third realization was born from those observations and because of my current lifestyle. Life was not so bad if I could live it like this.

There was no reason for me to be hospitalized or in jail, if I did not bring attention to myself by my actions. No need to be confined or treated, if I was not a threat to myself or the general public. I could exist with a small measure of happiness and sanity for as long as I could avoid other people and their behavior. Their illnesses and convictions. The ofttimes disastrous ramifications of the best and worst intentions of those that take it upon themselves to intervene.

The solution to the bulk of my existential problems seemed obvious to me then. I would avoid everyone on this planet as much as possible, indefinitely. Not just for my safety, but for theirs as well. I would exile myself from society and continue to try to live a studious life of peace and contemplation. To live only one day at a time, and see what the Universe had in store for me in the wake of my survival.

I felt strongly that I had no right to partake of society until I was mentally healthy and could contribute meaningfully to the lives of people around me. Until I could master living with myself, it was best that I not live with or be around others for long. How long that might take, or if it was even possible, was beyond my reckoning.

For the longest time, years really, I did not want to be "helped." I didn't mind counseling per se, but I was not in a place, during my teens especially, where I could be honest with myself about how I really felt. Previous attempts at therapy had little value to me because I didn't know how to articulate what was really bothering me deep down.

I didn't view my symptoms, from the so-called "mania" to my post traumatic stress paranoia, to my intense rages as being "mental illness" in the sense of something that needs "treatment." The very idea of losing those symptoms to the blunting effects of psychiatric drugs caused me intense panic. As a consequence, very little other than idle small talk ever got accomplished during the years that I did have access to regular counseling.

I'd always felt that if I could somehow psychically project the events of my life into someone else's mind, they too would get depressed or go crazy, and then they would finally understand my perspective. Existential depression is not "just" a chemical imbalance. I evolved into this state of mind, it took years for it to get so profound.

I felt that I was fully entitled to my depression, and no, I don't want anybody to take it away from me, it's all I've ever known. I was incapable of imagining myself as a person without depression. I could grudgingly allow myself occasional happy moments, but I felt that this darkness would always be a part of my life, an undercurrent, just waiting for stress to drag me back down into it.

When you've been depressed for so many years, you come to see real happiness as something that can only happen to other people. It leads to a sense that you've been chosen by the gods or were born under a bad star and that having a rough childhood, struggling as an adult, not being able to trust or open up to people, not being able to live a "normal life" and being depressed, is what your destiny is all about.

If I was ever going to recover, or find a reason to live and become whole and well, it would be up to me to do it. To find a way. There was no one else who could do that for me, but me. I could not expect help from any quarter. This problem was mine and mine alone.

At this point in my life, I was in a position to follow the calling of my heart and do what I really wanted to do. And what I wanted most was: To be left alone.

In order to pursue my own life, I would need to change things. I couldn't sit here on this swing forever, nor could I expect to perpetually mooch off of friends and relatives just because I couldn't handle life. I needed to be able to support myself so I could put myself in a position to pursue my solitude.

To do that, I would need to leave the safety of my current situation, re-enter society and get a job again to have a source of money. Which meant dealing with people. For that I braced myself and procrastinated a few days longer, reluctant to break my tranquil routine.

As luck would have it, my brother called and told me about a job possibility that he thought might interest me. So I headed back north to where our apartment was and spent the night in my own room again. The next day we went to a site where an outdoor carnival was setting up for the season.

The chief engineer for Bourget Amusements, a guy named Mack, showed us around. I applied as a contractor to operate the merry-go-round while my brother got the giant plastic Fun Slide. Pay was in cash, weekly, and not much, as we were first-season greenhorns.

For the remainder of spring and throughout the summer we toured various towns, large and small, all over greater New England. Invariably we set up at a sports field or in a Walmart parking lot. We'd run for four days, break everything down and move to the next site.

We got Tyler a job there too, operating the inflatable structure called The Bounce. Every other day or so we exchanged our pooled funds for an enormous amount of marijuana. We ate fast food three times a day. When we set up the rides far away from our residences, we slept in our cars alongside the camper trailers and RVs of the seasoned carnies.

It was not unusual for plain clothes police officers to come out of nowhere and escort one of the carnies away from their rides. Certainly not all, but most everyone that was seasonally employed by this carnival was a social misfit, outcast, mental health case or felon. People who had trouble finding or keeping any other kind of work. My brother and I fit right in.

We were more or less professional during the day while we operated, but at night drug and alcohol abuse was rampant. Assault and battery between carnies was often a near-daily occurrence. In fact, never before or since have I been in so many fist fights with complete strangers in so short a period of time. Aside from that, it was mostly fun. It was such a vital and hands-on job with so many hazards that one had to pay attention to what was going on. It helped get me back into shape.

As the summer wore down, I revealed the plan that had been slowly developing in my mind to Tyler and my brother. I had decided that the best thing I could do to stack the odds in favor for my immediate and long term future was to get out of Dodge. Within one hundred miles of my hometown lived everyone that I had ever harmed or who had harmed me.

There was my mother's family, however disorganized and dysfunctional. There was nothing I could do to save my younger siblings from becoming more damaged by living with my mother, year after year. I was helpless to effect them in any way until they were adults, by which time they would have at least as many problems as I did. Everyone on that side of my family was sick in some way. They would be of no help to me.

Unlike all the blue-collar relatives and welfare cases on my mother's side of the family, everyone on my father's side had college degrees. They are quite well-educated. Most of my aunts and uncles had moved far away from each other as adults. Getting them all into one house together for anything other than Thanksgiving or Christmas Day was like herding stray cats.

Relatives from that group that I interacted with the most were: My aunt Myra, my grandparents and my father. My illness had been a burden to all of them, especially financially. It didn't help matters that I deeply resented all four of them on many levels. Years might go by, but these persons would always suspect my mental health status and be afraid of me. The best thing I could do for them would be to leave them all alone, permanently. They had suffered enough because of me.

Then there were the kids that had picked on me from my grade school and junior high years. Now adults, I was increasingly encountering them anywhere from the workplace to the shopping mall. There was my ex, Gene, whom I had almost killed along with myself because of my misery during our suicide pact. What if I ran into my old social worker or my stepfather? I wanted revenge too much, and the temptation and possibility of coincidental encounters was too great a chance to take. There were too many people in so short a radius whom had hurt me and upon whom I craved vengeance, unrelentingly.

The only way to escape all that and get a genuine fresh start would be to move far away. I knew a place existed where I would not be persecuted and jailed for using the only drug that had acceptable benefits to my mental health. A place where possession of marijuana had been decriminalized by the will of the voting public.

In California I wouldn't have to suffer recurring and predictable bouts of seasonal affective disorder. It was a place that did not die each year and become so cold that you would perish without adequate heat and clothing. California required, quite literally, less energy to simply stay alive. I wouldn't need to winterize my car, shovel snow or purchase winter clothes.

Out West I could gain all those stress reducing benefits. There, I could stack the odds of survival and increase my general comfort level without hurting or impacting anyone else. The possibility of being confronted by, or confronting, those whom I had issues with was highly unlikely. Best of all, everything would be new to my eyes. No going through neighborhoods that held haunting memories. No driving by institutions that I'd once lived in. No more sadness attached to all the places that were special to me when I was last in a relationship.

I sold off most of my possessions, and my T-Bird as scrap metal. That car was meant to be driven only by me. It held within its metal chassis a psychic imprint of my suicide attempt. I didn't want anyone else driving it ever again. My expensive car stereo I traded to Tyler for a supply of weed.

Before the month of October ended, I made my idea become reality. The cold was beginning to creep back, and colorful fall foliage was dropping to the ground with greater haste. Alone, on a Greyhound bus bound for a place I'd never been to before, I was carried away from my home state and from all places familiar into an uncertain future. Suffused with the conviction that self-imposed exile was not only the best thing for everyone, but the only way I could guarantee I'd be left alone. It felt like an escape.

CHAPTER 14

THROUGH A GLASS, DARKLY

I arrived in California without issue. My friend Julian, who had migrated to the Sacramento area two years earlier, picked me up from the bus station. It turned out that other friends and their relatives had also moved here and everyone was cohabiting in one large household.

The house was tense, with so many people living together. I had arrived just as everyone was about to split up and move into different housing arrangements. They'd each been saving up for their new residences during the time they had already spent out here together. They could not offer me much more than a spot on the carpet floor to sleep on. I was grateful. I didn't have any latitude to play tourist or be a guest of the house. I needed to get to work right away.

My first temp job in California was working for the Adopt-a-Highway program. I was dropped off at the side of an unfamiliar expressway, in an orange safety vest and with several giant, black plastic bags. My assignment was to pick up the trash that had collected amidst the dry brown grass, which lay alongside an almost perfectly level highway that ran in both directions for as far as the eye could see. For the better part of the day I fumed while I collected Californian's garbage as traffic streamed by, gusting me with their passage.

Once I had enough money for a month's rent and deposit, I struck out on my own. Using the classified section of the *Sacramento Bee* (a local newspaper), I found a cheap apartment in the inner city. My friends dropped me off downtown and wished me luck.

Rent was due in less than a month and I had no time to waste. Public transit brought me to the edge of the industrial zone and I began walking from building to building, looking for "help wanted" signs.

Out of sheer desperation I took a job that I would never in a million years have picked if I had had a choice. The only job I could find was in a telemarketing company. They were hiring inexperienced people quickly and without the obligatory three week wait.

Let me just say this, there is a specific place in hell where career telemarketers go when they die. My job was trying to con senior citizens on fixed incomes into agreeing to regularly donate money to a dubious charity.

When I wasn't scamming them, I had to cold-call hard working folks in the deep South, to tell them they had won free financing on a brand new Ford (which was a lie). My job was to obtain an appointment from the people on the other end of the phone, that they would go to their nearest Ford dealership on a specific day. There were bonus cash incentives for the operators who got the most confirmed appointments for that project.

These telemarketing scams benefited none of the people I solicited. It was disheartening work and my performance was lackluster. I didn't have the motivation or the ability to hustle people into doing things I didn't believe in or agree with.

I was torn between my better judgment and the need to survive. It was only a matter of time before I was let go as an underperformer. I decided to beat them to it and I quit out of disgust, two months into the job. I just wanted an honest pay for an honest day of hard work that harmed no one. There had to be something better than telemarketing out there that I could find.

During this time period I had another psychotic episode. What I did not know when I moved into the cheapest apartment I could find was that it was located in a dangerous part of Sacramento. Oak Park was a low-income neighborhood, inhabited primarily by African Americans and Latinos.

The space I lived in was just a single large room with no furnishings, except a rickety bed with a stained mattress. Ants streamed through the cracks in the floor. When you switched on the lone over-head light bulb, cockroaches scurried back into the cracks in the ceiling from where they had come. Wasn't there a law against infestations in public housing?

The musty, mildewed building with its various insects was intolerable to be in for long. Naturally, I went outside to explore my surroundings, just to get out. Here was the leading edge of a small ghetto.

I made one major mistake when I moved into Oak Park which put me in real danger. I had purchased some weed locally, and it was far more potent than anything I had ever smoked back in New England. I was high, feeling good and flirtatious.

Since no one here knew me, I did not feel confined to wearing my military-style clothing. I put on some makeup, did my hair and put on a skirt and heels and took a walk in my outfit. I still didn't appreciate where I was. Not until cars started pulling over to my side of the road and complete strangers were hailing me. No, I don't want a ride!

Then there were the glares from the women standing idly at the street intersections. My fun walk was quickly becoming a nightmare of harassment, cold stares and unasked-for attention. What the hell was wrong with these people?

A particular set of headlights got my attention as they came towards me. This was the third time that this particular sport utility vehicle had passed me. Did these people think I was a hooker or something?

When the same car was coming towards me for the fourth time, my danger sense flared. As it passed by me, I slipped up an alleyway, and started walking on a parallel street. I was no longer having fun and I was far too stoned to feel confident in a chance physical confrontation. This had become a bad trip and I wanted to get home, now.

The SUV appeared again, and was coming straight towards me. This time there was no other traffic and no bystanders or street walkers. It's tires screeched on the pavement as it braked hard to stop next to me. Now I could see its occupants clearly. Two Latino males sat in the front.

Before the vehicle had come to a complete stop, the door was opened and a short, stocky, swarthy man in a grey t-shirt and blue jeans exited the vehicle. Without a word, he advanced on me, while his buddy kept the engine running.

Not one person in the world knew where I was just then. Thoughts about women in Latin American countries, who had no rights and were dominated by a cult of masculinity and male chauvinism, flashed through my mind. How many women have died over the years because of male sexual violence. I was determined that I was not going to be one of them. My instincts, training and PTSD reflexes served me then.

I stayed moving and constantly tried to keep parked cars interposed between me and the man coming for me purposefully, who still had not said anything. These guys would probably dump my body into a ditch when they were done with me. No way was that going to be my fate.

In an instant I torqued my heel to the side, pushed down and snapped the straps holding the shoe to my foot. I repeated the action with my other foot. That delay allowed the stranger to come even closer and he finally spoke,

"Where are you going, baby?"

His voice, trying to sound so casual, made all the hairs on my neck stand up. My skin crawled with equal parts disgust and outrage. With one smooth motion I stooped to grab both heels by their broken straps and ran barefoot at full speed down the road.

I ran down one street and up another. I took random lefts and rights until I was sure that I had gotten rid of my pursuers. I was now lost, and had no idea where I was, relative to my apartment. I made one more impulsive street change, and immediately regretted it. Every other street light had been broken or was out. It would have been pitch-black in places, but for the light of the moon.

Unseen African American women, smoking weed in the shadows, discussed me as I walked by.

"Damn, that's a lot of white to be showing off around here, girlfriend," said one.

"They be thin-skinned bitches," indicted another when I didn't reply.

"She be lucky if she ain't raped by the time she gets to the end of this street, dressed like that," quipped the first woman.

What in the world is wrong with everyone in this neighborhood? I thought to myself as I walked on, my pulse still pounding heavily and my legs shaking. This was just a normal day in the life of low-income, inner city dwellers. I was a country bumpkin at heart. I was not prepared for this, and my normal judgment had been skewed massively by the extreme potency of the cannabis that I had smoked.

Somehow I found my apartment again. I rushed upstairs and into my room. Cockroaches ran across the ceiling and hid as I flicked on the light. I sat down on my bed and almost cried, I was so mad at myself and this neighborhood.

Furious, I cleaned off the stupid makeup and nail polish. I put up my hair and donned my armor. I put on every shred of concealing black clothing, including gloves, until I looked like a Russian agent from an intrigue and espionage movie.

I put on my ass-kicking boots. I slipped knives up each sleeve, another one down the small of my back, and strapped one to my calf. I fastened a short length of severed electrical cord around my wrist. A garrote, for really close encounters.

Let's try this again, I thought. Let's see one of these people try to rape or hustle me now. I walked out of the apartment, ready and willing to kill someone, I was that angry.

In this place, who would notice or care? Nearly every day that I had lived here I had heard gunshots, even in broad daylight! I had seen people beat each other up at the bus stop for no obvious reason. I once witnessed a man take apart and reassemble his semi-automatic pistol in the back seat of the bus. It was like being in a third world country.

Everyone you meet on the street suddenly wants something from you, just because you are there. I got used to hearing "Got a smoke?" "Got any change?" as I walked down Broadway, day or night, rain or shine. Then there were the hustlers that idle outside of convenience store entrances, who ask you first, "You looking for something?" and after you shake your head, "No!" and continue walking inside, they follow that with, "You got something?"

One night, I looked out my bedroom window and saw a police helicopter searchlight panning over a group of young black males, all running in one direction together. The authoritative voice from the megaphone demanded futilely that they surrender and be arrested.

Locals would beat their dogs out in the open. The homeless and their little shopping-cart camps invaded the overgrown and littered parking lots of long gone businesses. People were openly dealing drugs on the street while prostitutes advertised their wares with revealing clothing and exaggerated hip and shoulder movements. The deep, throbbing bass of gangster rap pulsed out of beat-up and run-down cars driving on shiny new chrome-plated rims.

The smell of urine and cheap beer assailed your nostrils as you passed by bums, sitting on the sidewalk and trying to sell you broken electronics and worthless knickknacks scrounged from dumpster diving. You'd glance about and catch people standing around, muttering constantly to themselves, totally unselfconscious about it. Screams of unseen domestic disturbances could be heard when you walked past apartment buildings.

It was a carnival of madness. As though homeless shelters, mental hospitals and jails had been emptied and their occupants all lived right here, in Oak Park, Sacramento. An outdoor prison without walls, where the patients and prisoners intermingled. This place was enough to drive a sane person crazy. And I was not the most stable of people at the time.

This whole neighborhood triggered me and kept me in combat mode constantly. I could not relax for an instant. I dared not allow myself to get too high and become oblivious to my surroundings again. I never knew, from one day to the next, if I would be an unwilling witness to brazen criminal activity, or if the cops were going to raid someone's building nearby.

On one of those nights, when I could not sleep because of the noise of the cities' inhabitants, I finally snapped. I opened my window wide and from the second floor screamed into the night until I was hoarse, *"Shut up! Shut up! All of you just stop fighting and shut the fuck up!"*

I put on my black clothing and my array of knives again and took a walk around the neighborhood but came back without killing someone. My hands were shaking with unbridled anger as I went upstairs, my need still unfulfilled.

I laid on my bed while lurid and homicidal thoughts raced through my mind. The wailing, hissing, and crying of the feral cats foraging in the dumpster below my window at ground level penetrated my thoughts. Sleep was impossible. The noise within my mind and outside, was too much. I sprang out of bed and wanted to find out if I had the resolve to be a cold-blooded killer, right now. I put on my heavy leather gloves and went downstairs.

Baited by the smell of the piece of tuna I had brought with me, one of the starving feral cats came over to me. Instantly, I snatched it up by the neck. I stood upright and held it at arm's length and paused, savoring its struggle as it tried to free itself in vain. This thing was just another abandoned and unwanted life form. Just like me. Most likely, this creature once lived in someone's home, or with a family, and got fed regularly. Maybe it even had a favorite spot on the window sill, to look outdoors.

Like mine, this creature's current state of existence was completely pointless. I doubted anyone knew where it was or how low it had fallen. I doubted anyone would care if it disappeared forever. Animal shelters put down unwanted or nuisance animals by the thousands, every year. There was nothing to feel guilty about. I rationalized it as I stood there: I am doing it a favor.

I strangled that animal with one hand. It's claws could not penetrate my leather gloves and jacket. As it struggled mightily to escape, I felt that ancient force of demonic rage come alive inside me once again. And this dark power flowed all throughout my body, providing all the strength I needed to finish it off. Once it was dead, I hurled it callously over my shoulder into the trash, where we both belonged.

There is a heady, seductive sense of power that comes over you when you snatch the life out of something with your own hands. When you kill an animal out of repressed anger and frustration, some part of you knows deep down how good it would feel to stop a human being like that. The emotional payoff from the release of internal pressure would be that much bigger and more satisfying.

It was like flirting with a heroin addiction. I knew that if I ever did one person like this, I wouldn't be able to stop myself from indulging again and again. Before I moved here, this level of rage would've only been triggered by encountering people from my past. This neighborhood was teeming with a disposable assortment of surrogate targets.

Back in my apartment, the noise from the feral cats had ceased and I let out a deep breath. No one had seen me or investigated. I felt not the slightest twinge of remorse for what I had just done. *It's a savage world out there.* I thought to myself. *Damn thing pissed me off.*

Hour after hour passed and still I could not sleep. I became convinced that my mind was uncontrollably projecting my thoughts into other people's minds, and that sooner or later someone would call the police. I battled a powerful, paranoid compulsion to prepare myself for their arrival. My anxiety and dread of what seemed at the time to be inevitable, overwhelmed and froze me into indecision.

They are coming for you. They are going to find you.

I tried desperately to quiet my brain down so that no one could telepathically home in on me. But trying to shut out the voices and turn off my telepathic broadcasts only seemed to make them louder.

They know what you are thinking. They are going to lock you away.

It seemed my future could now take one of two paths. I would either end up in a small grey cinder block room with one tiny, barred window near the ceiling. Strapped to a gurney in four point restraints, with a permanent Trilafon drip inserted intravenously, for the rest of my life. Or I'd be hunted down by law enforcement and shot like a dangerous animal. It was only a matter of time before one or the other happened.

You are not even human anymore. You're a beast. You should run. Now.

I thought about killing myself, right then and there, in order to save myself that fate. I took one of my knives, palpated my neck for major arteries or veins and, upon finding one, began pressing the tip of the knife into the pulse. I thought about my promise to my friend Tyler, not to kill myself for a year, and about the nurse in the hospital psych ward who had told me confidently that "Things do get better." I laughed out loud maniacally and screamed, "You should see me now, lady!"

I sat there on my small lumpy mattress in my dilapidated one room apartment, dwelling on my most recent overdose. I remembered how calm and collected I was before and after the ordeal, how peaceful and fulfilled I had been when I was sitting in the swing, staring out across the corn fields, undisturbed, day after day.

Why couldn't I have that again? Why couldn't I stay on some rustic farm in a remote place, be fed two meals a day, and be left alone for however many months or years it might take before I could deal with life? Instead I was once again broke, jobless, suicidal and within an inch of seriously harming the next human being to cross my path.

Who was I to think that I, of all people, deserved better than this? What had I ever done to earn anything better than what these people had going on here? Answer: Nothing. I had rarely, if ever, done anything for anyone other than myself. I was just as criminal, just as dangerous, just as psychologically damaged as everyone else that lived in this shit hole. I belonged here with the rest of them.

I couldn't keep a job. I had dropped out of high school and had no college degree. Employers didn't care about how many books I had read as a kid. I hated working in fast food and retail or anyplace where I was forced to be social and cheerful in order to create a desirable and satisfactory "customer experience."

Fitful sleep caught up with me at last and I had several nightmares of being hunted and hounded by faceless people who wanted to take me and have me locked down in a psychiatric prison for life. I survived that night by willing myself not to move. I awoke to find myself still free. No one had tracked me to this apartment by hearing my thoughts. No one knew what I had done or what I was thinking. I knew it had been a delusion, but I couldn't shake the feeling that I had simply been lucky.

The next day I took the bus downtown to where my friend Julian's aunt Lacey was employed. I apologized profusely in advance for the burden I was about to dump on her as I walked into her office. My pride stung as I realized one of my biggest fears. I was about to ask someone for mercy, for help, because I couldn't handle it on my own anymore.

I told her that I was terribly stressed out from living in the hood, barely able to keep myself from having a complete nervous breakdown and that I wanted to kill myself, badly. I was almost out of money. I didn't know what to do. I hadn't been stoned in days and the pressure and noise in my mind was driving me crazy. I felt so ashamed for failing to be able to survive without help. But I wanted to tell someone before I hurt myself and I had no one else to turn to.

After discussing my situation with her husband over the phone for a few minutes, Lacey told me that they would help me. She left work early that day for me. I retrieved my personal belongings from my apartment and left the key behind.

- PART THREE -

CHAPTER 15

THE TAO OF HEALING

It was a great relief to leave Oak Park. Lacey drove us into the suburbs of Citrus Heights, to their beautiful apartment, which sported a spacious, ivy-covered balcony. I got to use a modern, functioning shower again and did my laundry. Eddie gave me some money to buy cigarettes with.

I enjoyed a healthy, home-cooked meal for the first time in months. They got me stoned and we watched television for awhile. This day had indeed been better than the previous one. I slept well that night, despite how on-edge and wary I'd become.

The next day, Julian picked me up in his truck, an hour before he normally went in to work. He worked in a warehouse, that was situated at the edge of an enormous industrial park. He dropped me off at the far side of the lot, telling me he would meet me for lunch and wished me good hunting.

Building after building I walked into, inquiring if there was any help wanted. I had no plan or method and was canvassing the entire lot. Assuming there was work to be found, I would simply take the first job I was offered, and make the best of it.

After two hours of filling out job applications and getting the usual, "We don't have anything for you now, but we will call you if we need you." I got lucky.

It was an aluminum and steel pipe factory. They primarily manufactured fire extinguisher pipe, cut to length, and fitted with threads and ends. At full production there was one person doing the cutting, one person doing the threading, and one person fitting the ends.

At the time when I started, the pipe cutter was doing the threading as well. The boss, a heavy-set, white-haired older man named Simon told me, "I was considering putting up a 'help wanted' sign within a week or two."

With the beginning of spring, the construction season got going and business went up. The job paid nine dollars an hour, for forty hours a week. That was like a fortune to me at the time and a huge relief. With a regular paycheck, I could begin to resurrect my life and get back to work, rebuilding the first two tiers of my own Maslow's Hierarchy of Needs.

After six weeks of saving, I had enough money to strike out on my own once again. My new neighborhood was not great, but it was an improvement over the last one I had lived in. The apartment complex was situated right next to several major bus and rail routes. I was able to catch a ride with the foreman of the pipe shop, who passed that way to get to work.

The apartment itself was clean and decently modern. No bugs or leaks. I furnished it with items left behind in a vacant room across the hallway. I felt reasonably safe again.

My new job was the most punishing physical labor I've ever done. All day long I stood on my feet at a machine. With it, I briskly threaded hundreds of lengths of heavy steel pipe, daily. For weeks, I came home from work dead-tired, with arms like lead that would barely move. My hands and wrists thickened from the stress and strain of handling long steel all day. Grease, oil and flecks of metal stained my palms, fingers and cuticles. No amount of scrubbing could get it all out for as long as I worked there.

As business picked up, overtime became mandatory and I now worked six days a week. On Sundays I studiously relaxed. I was now making more money than I could spend, but I didn't have much free time to shop. All my bills were paid promptly. I could afford to smoke as much weed as I wanted. I got up before dawn to drink coffee and smoke pot. I sat in my easy chair, in the waning darkness, and relaxed an hour before work.

I worked so hard that I didn't have much energy to think. I came home fatigued and mildly euphoric from a job where I lifted weights all day. After work, I went home and I got stoned and sat relaxing. I ate simple food, alone. I smoked some more pot before bed. Then I did it all over again the next day.

I had made a good choice moving to Sacramento. The weather was perfect. Every day was sun and blue skies. Once the rainy season had passed, it was over one hundred and eighty days before I would see a single, large, moisture-bearing cloud.

Sunday was the only day I ventured out into the public for long. I would take the light-rail down to the mall complexes. I'd take myself to a movie and lunch. Sometimes, I went clothes or book shopping. Then I would go back home.

As I was walking home from the rail terminal one Sunday afternoon, I was overtaken by three plain clothes cops in an unmarked car. As I had no reason to feel guilty, I was congenial when they pulled up to me. They asked me for my ID (I had a California one by then) and I told them that I lived right up the road. I was employed locally. This was my one day off, and I had gone to the movies. I had no outstanding warrants nor was I on parole.

They searched me and found my small pipe and a gram of marijuana concealed in my pack of cigarettes. They didn't even confiscate it.

"Is this little bud all you have on you?" one cop asked as he handed the pack of smokes back to me.

"Yes sir." I replied honestly. "May I ask what this is all about?"

"We got a call about someone brandishing a butcher knife and threatening people at the rail station a few minutes ago." he told me. "The suspect matched your description. You can go, thank you for cooperating."

"You're welcome," I replied. "Good luck."

That was it. I smiled triumphantly as I walked the rest of the way home. At the time, had I been in Nevada or New England or some place where conservative provincials had enacted a "zero tolerance policy" I could very well have been further detained, jailed, even had my home searched. All for an insignificant amount of a naturally occurring plant whose chemical properties helped me stay sane and keep the voices quiet.

It seemed like the cops of California were enlightened. That, and obviously they had real crime to spend their resources on. I loved this state. This was my new home.

A lot of people are misled about the life of someone who is a cannabis user. They imagine it's like hard drugs. They've heard that marijuana ruins lives and destroys those that use it. Some have been misled into thinking that it causes dementia, psychosis or schizophrenia. That misinformation is mostly the result of disingenuous government propaganda.

The reality is, that there are thousands upon thousands of functional marijuana users just in California alone. Every single one of my west coast friends smoked pot. They all had jobs. They didn't draw much attention to themselves. They paid their rent and taxes on time.

There's definitely a learning curve to living your life under the influence of mind-altering medication. I had made plenty of mistakes when I first started. Now I strived at least to insure that there would be a minimum of collateral damage from my drug use.

Thousands of miles away from my family, even if I got in trouble, it would not spill over onto them. I had no dependents. I was not in a relationship. I lived alone. I did my job well. The only person who would be effected by my drug use was me.

I could've begun saving up for a car, but I did not. I didn't need a car to survive. No more dealing with parking and towing fees. No more insurance payments, inspection fees, repair bills or oil changes. It was an avoidable mental and financial stress. One less thing to worry about.

It was much easier to survive like this, implementing my minimal-social-contact strategy. There was not much to get agitated about. As long as I stayed away from people, they couldn't hurt me and I would not want to hurt them.

When I first moved into this apartment, the other renters were more or less okay. After a few weeks, a family of loud and obnoxious tenants moved in. With them came a huge increase of unsavory traffic in the building. At that particular time in the '90s, Sacramento was considered the methamphetamine capital of

America. There was a good bet that my new neighbors were dealing crystal meth, also known as "crank."

Now crank is a hard drug that can and does destroy people's bodies and brains, not to mention their lives. The new neighbor's undisciplined children urinated outdoors on the side of the apartment, in plain view of other units. Later on, the cops began to show up regularly, beating on doors.

The gun shots in the parking lot one night were the last straw. Coming home from work that day, I looked up to the ceiling and spoke aloud to the Universe. "I can't live here anymore, my nerves are triggered constantly. I am going to go crazy again. I feel in danger and I need a safer place. Please find me something."

It turned out that the landlord owned another apartment building in a different neighborhood. At the time the dot-com bubble was still expanding and the Sacramento area was losing residents. As people streamed to the Bay Area and Silicon Valley, quality apartments were freed up, cheaper now than they had been in ages. I ended up with a two bedroom apartment, all to myself, for the price of a single. It was clean and modern. Plumbing, heating and air conditioning, all worked. The bathroom came with a huge tub and a strong, hot shower. A porch with a sliding glass door opened onto a tiny, fenced in back yard.

I had tons of space and so few possessions that only the living room looked lived in. My bedroom and the spare room were completely unfurnished. Empty book cases, a lamp stand and small end tables materialized across the street later that week, along with a sign that said "Free." I liberated these furnishings before public works crews removed them.

Life just kept improving. I couldn't believe my good fortune. When I explored my new neighborhood, I found a nearby road that let to a park which, it turned out, was the American River Parkway and wildlife conservancy.

It extended along the American River in both directions. There were signs which warned visitors that coyotes, mountain lions and rattlesnakes were indigenous to the area and could occasionally be seen. It was raw nature, ripe for the exploring.

When I got back to my apartment, I rolled and smoked a joint, celebrating. I sat there basking in my gratitude towards the Universe. I gazed at my book collection that occupied my new shelves. There was my science fiction collection. Then there was my martial arts books and occult manuals. I walked over and selected a book on yoga and opened it randomly letting the Universe guide my eyes. My eyes caught the definition of living a yoga lifestyle.

A true yoga lifestyle is not merely going through the movements involved in the physical training. To be a true yogi, one most live a life of health and simplicity. A yogi is not concerned solely with proper exercise. An aspiring yogi must strive to continuously engage in proper breathing, relaxation, diet, exercise, personal activity and meditation. By following this lifestyle, the yogi will eventually gain mental and physical health. With purification, meditation and practice, the yogi can overcome her personal demons to attain spiritual freedom through enlightenment.

Tears of spiritual recognition of universal truth came to my eyes. Some part of me, wanted this. Needed it. Knew what I had to do. I felt closer to having real purpose than I had in a long time. My life suddenly had a meaning again. This was the calling of my heart and I listened to it.

For the last year I had lived entirely one day at a time, concerned only with surviving the waking hours without hurting myself or others. My last suicide attempt had completely dislodged any remaining social compulsion to get a "real life." Going to college, working on a career, getting married or having a family, these were all things other people did. People who had lives and plans for the future. That kind of life was not for the likes of me. I had enough on my plate with simply trying to survive myself and my existence.

As for emulating the path of the yogi, I knew not where it would lead. I was not thinking in terms of enlightenment or understanding the meaning of life per se. I just wanted to know if it was possible to be a little more happy, and more content with the life that I had. I wished to continue to have peace in my life and I wanted to be left alone in my deliberate solitude, so I could continue Becoming. For as long as it would take. Bearing only as much stress as I felt capable of, moment after moment.

A few months after my twenty-first birthday, with only the Universe as my witness, I made this commitment to pursue a more spiritual life. From now on I would live a life devoted to mind-body discipline. Every day would be spent gradually aligning myself with my simple goals. And from now on, every day would be training day. This was the beginning of my recovery.

The next weekend I spent hundreds of dollars on self-help books. Within a month, my bookcase had an occult, wellness, psychology and spiritual development section to rival a small book store. Books covering everything from nutrition and diet, internal martial arts, crystal healing and homeopathic remedies, to Traditional Chinese Medicine filled my shelves.

I poured over manuals on acupuncture and flower essences. I studied vibrational healing, the Rolfing Handbook and taught myself chi gung from books. I deliberately arranged my home to accommodate my lifestyle and preserve my sanity. I kept my home neat and clean at all times. This was relatively easy to accomplish, without children, pets or roommates.

One half of my living room was converted into a small dojo/yoga studio, complete with an altar and shrine dedicated to my personal cosmos. With the Shoji panel lamps, Buddha statuettes, decorative fans and bamboo scrolls on the wall, my space had a definite East Asian feel to it, which satisfied my inner Sinophile that had sprouted ever since my teenage trip to Hong Kong.

The other half of the room was devoted to studious relaxation, reading and contemplation. The smells of aromatherapy and incense mingled with the pot smoke. The sounds of Tibetan bowls, dijeridoos and humpbacked whales, coming from my stereo speakers, provided a positive ambiance, conducive to quietude and healing.

I hung wind chimes out on my patio. I brought home bright green plants and flowers. Altogether, I built a private sanctuary customized to my tastes. It was not as radical of a lifestyle change as living the monastic life in the middle of nowhere. The life of an urban recluse was as close as I could get, and still be able to live independently.

For the next two and a half years, I would live, change and grow in this place. I would learn how to take care of myself and preserve my physical, emotional and mental health. I chose to begin an open-ended experiment in self-healing, using myself as the test subject. I became my own experiment, and utilizing trial and error and changing variables I would observe the results as honestly and objectively as I could.

* * *

I didn't know how to eat healthy. No one ever taught me how to cook or what kinds of food were good for you. I bought several books on nutrition and diet and began to experiment. I started studying food-labels with a discriminating eye and became appalled at how pervasive certain elements like sodium, trans-fats and high-fructose corn syrup were in the general food supply.

At that time, I drank about two liters of Pepsi-cola and ten cups of coffee (with sugar) daily. I quit my addictions to sugar and caffeine over the course of a weekend. That was a painful two days, as I endured incredible wrap-around headaches, my skin itched unceasingly and I felt like I couldn't sit still for a minute. When that weekend was over I really felt better and I had a clear sense, internally, that the huge amount of unnecessary chemicals that I put through my body had negatively impacted my physical and mental health; in nutritional health lingo, I'd been toxic.

The first time I tried to swallow a handful of broad spectrum vitamins, I thought I was going to die. My throat spasmed shut. My body involuntarily broke into a sweat and started to tremor. My breath was becoming shorter and my pulse raced. I was having an extreme anxiety attack. Then, I suddenly understood intuitively, my body thought I was trying to kill it again.

I wrapped my arms around myself and crooned to my body as though it were a scared animal. I talked myself down until I was relaxed enough to try again. Methodically, one capsule at a time, I got over my primal fear and swallowed them all.

I took up fasting once a week. I started eating organic foods. I became a vegetarian for awhile and later tried the raw food vegan diet as well.

It occurred to me after reading those nutrition books, that I'd been partially dehydrating myself for some years now. It seemed a simple enough thing to remedy; after all, water was healthy and drinking it seemed like common sense. Why didn't I think of it before?

My body-consciousness gave me the answer: Increased water consumption leads to more visits to the bathroom to urinate. My body remembered how much pain that the increased need to urinate caused because of the continuously losing battle against dry mouth when I was forced to take lithium to treat manic depressive symptoms. I had gained a ridiculous amount of water fat, had suffered agonizing pain from what seemed at that time like a perpetual urinary tract infection. Thus, I avoided water unconsciously.

I had to sit down and gently coax myself to drink volumes of clear water. A little more each day, until I was pushing upwards of a gallon of water through my system a day. The effects of hydrating myself like this would be different now, since the toxic effects of that artificially induced lithium imbalance had long ago ceased manipulating my body chemistry. My energy level continued to surge and headaches became more infrequent. As a consequence of quitting all that sugar and salt as well as increasing my water intake, my skin looked much better, even younger.

Although detox and nutritional awareness made me much healthier, those things did not fundamentally change my deeper psychological issues. The healthy living choices merely optimized my physical wellness, allowing me to inhabit a better functioning organism with greater clarity of thought.

My diet was one of the factors of my life I had control over. I could deliberately stack similar factors in my favor. I trained myself to listen acutely to my body and pay attention to the short and long term effects of how ingesting various substances – or abstaining from them – made me feel.

I was heavily influenced by traditional yoga and Ayurveda, but my real interest lay in understanding Chinese medical theory and healing practices. The Chinese manuals, covering subjects like herbalism, energy healing (chi gung) and acupuncture theory, were, generally speaking, deeper and more complete than their Japanese counterparts, like Reiki and Shiatsu. I studied both, the Chinese and Japanese methods, to increase my understanding and perspective.

Some parts of Chinese medical theory bear a superficial resemblance to Western understanding of physics. The big word you hear among Western people discussing the subject is chi. Chi is considered to mean energy.

In a nutshell, some Chinese believe, that everything in the universe is comprised of different vibrations of energy, including solid matter. Thus, the sun, moon, water, trees and the earth itself can be said to be different kinds of chi. All natural effects, including biological processes and things like the weather and the changing seasons are considered to be chi, manifesting and fluctuating in natural ways.

The base premise of Chinese medical theory is, that if all your chi is free to flow and change naturally, you would be physically and mentally healthy. Keeping oneself in balance, internally as well as externally, is therefore the key to long term wellness and illness prevention.

These ideas, Taoist thought and Chinese medical theory, had considerable influence on me. With this framework I began to see my existence in terms of body-mind balancing. I could make a practice of going inside myself to find and correct all toxic manifestations of energy. I had all the rest of my life to pursue this.

CHAPTER 16

As Above, So Below

It was only a matter of time before I ran into my first real internal obstacle. I was not just physically hooked on smoking cigarettes, but psychologically and emotionally as well. It was part of my self-image. Every single one of my friends and most everyone in my family smoked. Smoking was an ingrained social ritual as well as a coping mechanism.

I found it hard to imagine myself as a nonsmoker. What would I do with my hands? What would I do on my fifteen minute work breaks, or while I was waiting for a bus? How would my friends react?

I looked for ways in which to motivate myself into quitting and found that my ego and vanity provided the shortest route to the solution. Quitting smoking was good for my health and bank account and even helped the environment. It would make me stronger and more physically "pure" than my smoking peers.

At that time, I fell short of total smoking cessation and instead tried to make it more of a ritual. I would smoke only one Camel Light in the morning before work. I had one after dinner and one before bed. I made my smoking a private act, designed to enjoy the experience. No more impulsively lighting up anymore.

After two months of controlled smoking, I got fed up with my lack of conviction. At exactly that time I was reading in the newspaper of the legal actions against Big Tobacco. Scientific evidence revealed that cigarettes had been engineered to be highly addictive. I never even had a chance. As a fetus I had been bathed in nicotine regularly when my mother carried me. I had probably been withdrawing from it when I was born.

Given the permanent exposure to it, my teen addiction was a foregone conclusion. As I thought about it, I became momentarily enraged at the idea. I felt exploited, manipulated by people I had never seen. In a burst of anger, I hurled my pack of cigarettes across the room and quit for good, then and there.

Going through all those different withdrawals and deprivations, like fasting, changing my diet and quitting smoking, strengthened my will immensely. My success at it only made me more confident of my inner resources. Gradually I became hale and radiated energy from a cleaner and more health-conscious lifestyle.

Slowly, I began to come out of my privacy shell to test my behavior on others. I tried, in my own way, to be around people with similar lifestyle goals and attitudes about wellness. As close to a "support group" as I was ever going to get.

I became a New Age hippie. There was a pocket of spiritual seeker-type people to be found in the small town of Fair Oaks, California. I exposed myself to an ever-increasing number of decent and intelligent folk that had similar interests. Many of them were trying to reconnect with their inner child, find spiritual peace or otherwise resolve their mid-life crises.

I subjected myself willingly to a variety of self-described spiritual healers and facilitators. I briefly reacquired my interest in pagan spirituality and ritual magic. I allowed myself to lie down inside crystal circles and let people lay hands on me, in an attempt to raise my energy vibrations or otherwise heal my spirit. As I became more robust physically, I easily did my full-time manual labor job and still had plenty of energy to spare for my other activities.

In personal development, your resistance to change or lack of vision of what is possible ultimately governs how fast and how deeply you can progress. I was open to the kind of change that would transform me fundamentally. I was ready to give up who I was and become something better and more capable. No one was twisting my arm to undertake this evolution. After my last suicide attempt and resulting near-death experience, I was motivated entirely from within.

I changed the priorities in my various training methods. I shelved my practice of karate indefinitely. Hatha yoga also got the back burner treatment. I gave myself entirely to the Chinese methods of self-repair and resurrected the mind-body discipline that remains to this day the nearest and dearest to me. I began regular sitting meditation practice, once again.

As my textbook knowledge of chi gung theory grew and my self-taught practice continued, I began to notice different effects on my psyche and physicality as a result of it. Chi gung is powerful stuff and it effects your nervous system and subsequently your entire being.

Without guidance, I could spin my wheels aimlessly, or worse, screw up my nervous system. I now had a basic enough grasp of some of the internal aspects of the training to actually hurt myself with it unintentionally. I realized that the time to find proper instruction was at hand.

I contacted the students of, and spoke on the phone with, a couple of the authors of some well known chi gung books. I talked about my training goals and about what some of my problems were, and why I was desperate to find the best instruction available.

As I made phone calls all over the country that day, again and again one name kept coming up. If I wanted to learn the real deal chi gung for martial arts, meditation and self-healing, there was one man, a Taoist master, located not far from me, that was known to be classically trained in all those aspects. His name was Bruce Frantzis.

That was the guy whose book on beginning chi gung *Opening the Energy Gates of Your Body* I had purchased as a teenager, on impulse, because the title had spoken to me from the shelf. Years later, practicing the basic material and movements taught in that book had helped me get back on my feet quickly after my last overdose. I joined Mr. Frantzis' mailing list and anticipated the arrival of the pamphlet that would outline his seminars, workshops and retreats that year. I couldn't wait to begin.

A few months into my job I almost lost the first two fingers on my left hand. One split second gap in attention and my hand got crushed by a machine. I was completely amazed to find my fingers still attached when my hand was freed. The damage was surprisingly non-horrific. The interior of one finger had blown out in a neat line, like an over-boiled hot dog. The finger that did not rupture was ridiculously swollen. I couldn't feel either one at all.

The company paid for me to get stitched up, and my boss gave me a few days off. Nevertheless, there was unsubtle pressure to get back to work as soon as possible. I was needed after all.

I could have used some of my vacation time to take more days off. As a result of wanting to please my boss, live up to expectations, and show everyone how tough I was, I almost certainly delayed the healing of my fingers for quite some time. By never giving them a chance to take a break from the stress and strain of my job, I ended up with nerve damage that lasted for years.

What finally restored full feeling and functioning in my two damaged fingers were specific chi gung techniques that I learned from Master Frantzis later on. With diligent practice I was able to gradually regrow my nerves and awareness. Today my fingers work fine and there is almost no sign that they were ever injured.

As time went on, my new mindful approach to life had other, at times alarming, side-effects. For one, I began to become aware of all this "stuff" inside me, for lack of a more precise word. Flashes of different kinds of physical and emotional pain intruded. Sporadic and inappropriate impulses to harm myself came and went in the blink of an eye. These sensations and increasing awareness of what was flowing around inside me really took off when I got back into a regular practice of meditation, and became progressively more destabilizing as time went on.

When I first tried to get back into stillness meditation, I was appalled at how difficult it was for me to even sit still and keep my mind quiet for five minutes. Meditation had been easier during my early teens, before more life had happened to me. Since then I had acquired all this agitated "stuff" inside me that was making meditation vastly more difficult. One of the things which helped me deal with all this was that I knew from reading books about meditation that it could happen, and so I was slightly prepared for it.

Dark emotions came and went and the pressure in my head intensified. After about ten minutes, at best, I just wanted to scream as loud and as long as I could. Despite this, I stuck with it and persevered daily. The longer I kept at it, the longer my buffer of internal peace would hold up. Eventually, I was sitting quite easily for thirty minutes to an hour. When I sensed I was coming too close to the maelstrom, I backed off, and took a break. In that way, I was able to make considerable progress with meditation on my own.

For awhile it seemed like meditation was really working. I was feeling more at peace with myself and my surroundings for longer periods of time. I became easier to get along with and to be around. I decreased my own stress levels, day to day, and became noticeably calmer as a person.

Listening acutely and paying attention to my insides was becoming more of an ingrained habit. Even when I wasn't trying, I was starting to get continual feedback about my internal states. A kind of low grade version of the agitation storm I had encountered while meditating.

This was hardest to bear at work, where it began to happen all day long. Once my internal juices were flowing from the pace of the work, my inner voice would light up with a litany of complaints about my body.

I would arrive at work in a peaceful state of mind from my morning meditation and workouts. Once I was straining and sweating from handling the cold metal in the concrete walled workshop, the peaceful state vaporized. That's when I began to really understand that the state of your body fundamentally effects your state of mind.

Pain from old injuries, never fully healed, flared up. First in my legs, then in my back and eventually my neck. Then my damaged fingers would start to throb.

As hours ticked by and I was assaulted by so much internal discomfort, my mind became equally agitated. I found myself raving out loud, under my breath, about my lot in life and what a waste of my gifts it was to work here. I found myself angry from the pains, angry at metal pipes, angry at my threading machine. The slightest thing became an instant irritation. The only way to escape it was to work fast enough to stay in the "zone." The runner's high of elevated neurotransmitters. A state where your mind becomes quiet and you are one with the machine.

Where did all this trouble come from? My practices had increased my conscious awareness of and connection to the rest of my body. This "stuff" had been here all along, accumulating over the years. I was now beginning to sense the real me inside.

That issue was one of the many reasons I was so interested in training with Mr. Frantzis. He specialized in methods and techniques to resolve such blockages on the physical, mental and emotional level. It was perfectly timed, it seemed, that I should learn those techniques precisely when I was finally at a place in my life where I was deeply motivated and needed to learn how to deal with all that stuff.

As part of my ongoing quest to understand how I reacted to the world, I did a lot of experiments with sound and light. What I mean by "experiment" is that I would expose myself to different stimulation and then perform an honest self-assessment of how those stimuli made me feel. Subsequently I would sit vigil and observe what kinds of thoughts those emotions were causing.

During one such experiment I tried to live without electric lights for weeks, using only candlelight at night. My night vision improved dramatically after awhile, and overall it was a very peaceful and soft experience to have only sunlight or candlelight illuminating my lair. That kind of environment, relying on natural point sources instead of large over-head artificial lighting, especially at night, seemed to reduce the noise in my head.

In the course of those lighting experiments I discovered that I was quite sensitive to fluorescent lighting. A tiny piece of the agitation/depression puzzle locked into place when I apprehended that. One of my worst years, behavior-wise, had been my time spent in fourth grade at a Catholic school. During that year I got into a lot of trouble. My teachers had complained that I talked back to them, my grades had been plummeting and I didn't have an explanation for my behavior when the faculty or my parents asked me.

The first two periods of class had been spent in a classroom with almost no natural lighting. Sadistic fluorescent strips fluctuated right over our heads. They buzzed inside my brain and I couldn't think. When I told my mother, "I can see the light is moving." (its moving caused me to have painful headaches), Sarah had dismissed me in that tone of voice that meant I was stupid for even bringing it up. "You are so full of it," she had replied smirking, "No one can see light move."

Back then, nobody had made the connection between artificial lighting, oppositional behavior and learning impairment. Since that time, scientific studies were conducted in some schools and it became clear that a certain segment of the student population performed worse under fluorescent lights and better without them.

I had lived a significant portion of my life under their emissions. They were in all the schools and institutional buildings I had been in, as well as in every single retail, manufacturing and industrial workplace I knew. I noticed, that when I was away from them, a small piece of the overall noise in my head was gone.

I also conducted numerous experiments involving sound. I paid attention to how I felt when I was waiting for a bus on busy street versus how I felt when I was walking down the wooded trails in the park. When I was in the woods, my head was quieter. When I was surrounded by vehicles and street noise, the din in my head was louder.

A lot of people are unaware of how sensory stimulus can agitate the mind and body. There are numerous techniques for dealing with it, including meditating in quiet places without distractions. Very useful in this respect is a practice called "withdrawing and cleansing the senses" or some variation of it, which involves deliberately tuning out sight and sound in order to listen internally more carefully.

It became clear to me, that when I was mad or frustrated, I listened to angry, raging music. When I was feeling down, I listened to sad and depressing music. When I got really honest with myself, I realized that the music enhanced the intensity of dark thoughts and feelings. Music to kill yourself by. Listening to it while depressed was a kind of unconscious form of self-abuse.

By absorbing the sounds and lyrics I was picking at the emotional wounds. I kept myself worked up by dwelling over my various trials and misfortunes. Misery I had on tap and I poured myself a draught every time I gave in to the urge to go on those extended self-pity sessions. Along with the chain smoking and sitting in the dark, dressed for a funeral, it had made me feel worse, not better. On some level, I had always known that I did it deliberately, to keep the pain of the memory from becoming stagnant. It was hard to let go of this particular compulsion, even after I identified my behavior and the reasons for it.

There came a day when I found all my favorite music to be totally unappealing. I turned on some kind of angst-ridden heavy metal when I came home from work, and it was repulsive. I acutely felt the negative impact of the wailing guitars on my emotional states.

I couldn't turn it off fast enough. When I did, my insides quickly settled down in relief. It felt good to simply exist in total quiet. I took notes of that too. Just to confirm the experience, I switched it on again, and instantly the music caused spikes of disruption on my nerves. I didn't want to feel disrupted anymore and so I turned it off again.

It seemed I needed to replace my music now and I experimented with different kinds. I played mating songs of humpbacked whales and the tones of Tibetan bells. I once played nothing but Gregorian chants for weeks. All day long and all night the whole apartment resonated with the voices of the monks. It was very peaceful.

Through these experiments, involving exposure to different light and sound, I became sensitive to how varying environmental stimulation can change your conscious and subconscious thoughts and feelings. It helped me appreciate how and why a quiet retreat like my apartment was so much more spiritually healing than my living situation at the Hell House or in Oak Park or in any of the group homes and psych facilities that I had once lived in.

I also conducted these stimulation and reaction experiments on the unwitting general public. I would spend a few hours sitting quietly in the park by the river and then go to a busy mall. While I was there I would listen intently to the thoughts and feelings that being around other people created. Invariably, I always preferred to be at home in my sanctuary, or down by the river, as opposed to being around crowded and bustling places. I grew to become very fond of spending long periods of time alone by myself. In an apartment devoid of noisy pets, roommates and relatives. I controlled how much and what kind of noise was going on at all times.

Contrary to my own experience, I've known a number of people who cannot simply sit in silence for long before they crave stimulation and turn on the TV or call up someone on the phone. Others claim that they have to be in the company of someone else. That they suffer anxiety attacks if they are alone. I can imagine it, but find it hard to empathize with. Over-stimulation and my unceasing awareness of the possibility of violent behavior from people in my company were clearly two of my biggest sources of anxiety.

It seems that a great many people lack the ability to honestly self-analyze, self-diagnose and self-therapy. Failing that, a lot of folks with significant mental health problems only end up making life worse for themselves.

Some would argue that it is difficult to take responsibility for that which you have no insight into. But how common is it for people with mental illness to bring their life to a screeching halt and then proceed to spend months and years cultivating self-analysis and practicing introspective meditation in search of a greater understanding into their own behavior and the underlying motivators for it?

If you are serious about mental health recovery then I think you should distance yourself from anyone who is modeling mental illness and who is herself poorly functioning. Otherwise you end up partaking of their false dilemmas, projections and their reoccurring, emotion-laden and energy-draining dramas. Recovery while in a prison or mental institution seems as unlikely to me as it would be if one lived in the midst of domestic violence. They are all places where you are in perpetual danger and so are not safe and sane environments.

Ideally, you want to surround yourself with mentally stable, highly functioning people. But if you are suffering, how will you attract stable people to help you? If you are a self-destructive loser, a liar, intemperate and volatile, why should anyone have anything to do with you? For a healthy person, there is nothing to gain from contact with someone who is mentally ill, except huge amounts of stress, frustration and confusion.

Misery loves company and attention. I didn't want to hang out with people at my own "level." I did not want to burden sane people with my madness. That was one of the primary motivators for me to live in solitude. The best solution seemed to be to stay away from everybody, until I had my head on reasonably straight.

* * *

Despite my progress in mind-body disciplines, the noise in my body and mind was becoming progressively louder as of late. As I pondered possible causes, it dawned on me that I was smoking a lot less pot. When I had first settled down with my new job and could afford to have a drug habit again, I had been easily smoking upwards of two ounces of marijuana a week. Roughly speaking, it took about three to four finger-sized joints daily to keep the voices away and not brood endlessly about my past. Now I was smoking only one joint per day. Since I didn't drink and no longer smoked cigarettes, smoking pot after a hard day's work took the place of a couple of beers that many blue-collar workers traditionally consume instead.

Coming home from the factory, I had only so much time before my aikido and tai chi classes started. Thereafter, I would typically wander down to the river to keep practicing what I had learned, sitting and meditating until nightfall. I was just too busy now to get high all the time. The pains in my body and the voices in my head, previously muffled by the drug, began to come back.

This was an expected side effect of coming off my "meds." I could've wimped out and hid from my problems by smoking more again. Upping my dose, as it were, to deal with a trouble spot. After having personally experienced using both psych meds and recreational drugs, my discovery in both cases was that my problems were still lurking underneath those chemical effects, completely unchanged.

Covering up symptoms is not to be confused with healing. Using substances in that manner has another unfortunate side effect which is to retard your ability to perceive and gain access to the deepest layers of your consciousness. It is unfortunate but, real lasting mental healing just can't be attained while a person is on the kinds of drugs that are available in this day and age.

As an alternative to masking or blunting my symptoms chemically, I could instead allow them to manifest and use their appearance and my subsequent suffering as a realistic guidepost and indicator of my progress at stabilizing my inner world. Meditation practice is partly about peeling through all those layers of consciousness in order to apprehend the more subtle qualities and essence of your innermost Being. Even the Buddha himself would have trouble meditating under three, four or five psychotropic drugs.

Certainly, my upbringing and subsequent institutionalization were disadvantageous in the extreme, but I took responsibility for my mental and emotional problems. By "taking responsibility" I mean that I did not foist off the causes of my issues to genetics, astrology charts, chemical imbalances or the will of the gods. Nor did I see my problems as being something that was up to someone else to fix or out of my control. I had the unmitigated gall and ego to believe that I could eventually understand and heal myself of my mental illness.

As my cannabis consumption declined, I found that my psycho-emotional issues were still there, inside of me. My problems were like an unfinished phone conversation with someone who was still waiting on the other line. Getting stoned regularly had not diminished them in the slightest. Now that I was slowing down my life and paying careful attention, all those unfinished phone calls were vying for my immediate attention.

Soon after I became exposed to Bruce Frantzis' meditation teachings, I had a serious sit-down with myself to honestly analyze my previous meditation training and assess my current goals. I had been first taught meditation at the age of thirteen by a crowd of intelligent and eclectic older kids. By the time I turned eighteen, I had absorbed at least a dozen distinct meditation techniques from different sources.

If you are in my age group and had met me back then, you could have easily been misled into thinking I was a young meditation master. I had learned a few nifty parlor tricks that could dazzle the uninitiated as to my bona fide ability. Yet here I was, in my early twenties, with at least seven years of on-off meditation, and I was still trying to kill myself. Where were all the beneficial and stabilizing long-term effects of meditation? What was I doing wrong?

As I learned to discriminate between one meditation training and another, I came to a judgment. From Master Frantzis I had learned that meditation was the complete cessation of conscious projective thought. It is internal stillness. Genuine meditation practice inevitably leads to that state. In terms of self-healing and self-mastery, I could parse the different teachings I knew at that time into true meditation paths and false ones.

That led me to pull out every single book on my shelves that contained the word "meditation." What I was looking for was patterns. I isolated similarities and differences. Some techniques were designed to create bliss states or to manifest various forms of spiritual energy while others facilitated out-of-body experiences. I had, at various times, experimented with all of them.

Affirmations, guided visualizations and aura meditations are not real meditation. Nor is contemplating a picture of a beautiful lotus or a gazing at a trippy fractal pattern real meditation. You are probably not going to progress in meditation by staring at a lava lamp and smoking a joint while listening to Enya. That's relaxation and zoning out on a wave of euphoria while getting lost in free associations.

Meditation is zoning in, with a mindset and intention of vigilance. I think you should be highly suspect of anyone who tells you they can cause you to enter a "real" meditative state with a pattern of colors or tones or by vibrating crystals. Meditation is hard work. It's not something anyone can do for you. You have to train your brain yourself.

You are not doing real meditation if you are under the influence of acid, mushrooms or other entheogens. If you practice those sorts of things for years, like I did, and you find yourself wondering why you are still suffering, like I did, perhaps you should come to the same conclusion as I did.

Even the Buddha himself, at one point, had to learn proper practice from someone. It is known that he sought out instruction from mystics and hermits. Although no one knows for sure exactly what the Buddha learned before he went out into the wilderness, we can reasonably assume he learned some kind of yoga involving concentrating the mind and internal awareness, because that was what was floating around in that area at the time.

But what is the best way to learn this stuff? Wasn't I supposed to have a guru? Should I move to Tibet or India in search of a teacher? Should I go to Japan and join a Zen sect? Would I be better off making a pilgrimage to China to live the monastic life?

I didn't want to have no choice but to remain a vegetarian or be celibate. I did practice those things, but only when it suited my immediate goals. Taking orders or strict vows was not going to work for me. Same with nonviolence. I refused to turn the other cheek, and I was certainly not above the concept of preemptive attack if I was genuinely threatened.

Another problem to be considered was my mental health issues. I had visions of being woken up at an ashram by a fellow acolyte to attend morning meditation. I might unintentionally punch someone who touched me in my sleep because of the PTSD.

My psychological problems, combined with my current economic situation, meant that moving to Asia and living in a communal setting was probably a very bad idea. Without a grant or other financial support I would run out of money real fast. I was not prepared for life abroad for any duration. Also, I didn't really want to move. I liked the set up I had now. If I could keep my life situation the same as it was and continue to practice meditation at my own pace, according to my own need, then that was what I would do.

Bruce Frantzis' extensive background ultimately sealed the deal for me. He had already done his spiritual quest and had made the pilgrimage to the Far East. He had trained under gurus. Bruce had studied and practiced different meditation and martial arts traditions in their native settings over the course of twenty years. In short, he had exactly the education that I had always wanted. He knew about all those things I had been busy trying to learn on my own during these past years.

He is a repository of information about traditional Chinese medicine as well as Taoist, Buddhist and yoga meditation practices. And his incredible story does not end there. He had suffered a terrible car accident that basically destroyed him physically. His back had been broken in several places and his skull and pelvis were severely injured. Against medical advice, he had refused a spinal fusion and instead went on to regenerate his spine, using the chi gung healing techniques he had learned in China, until he was effective in martial arts once again.

The strength of his mind and his determination to remedy his circumstances made me feel a spiritual kinship with him. Bruce's credentials and experience were beyond any doubt. He had exactly what I was looking for in terms of martial arts, self-healing, and meditation. He would be the ideal teacher for me. With these considerations in mind, I decided to give up on ideas about a pilgrimage to India or China and instead give myself to his teachings.

When I first met Master Frantzis, he was not taking on personal students. My only access route to his teachings was to take his seminars and retreats alongside everyone else, when and where they were available. His instruction did not come cheap either.

I barely made enough money to make all my ends meet and attend his programs too. As it was, I had to make hard decisions in order to do it all. With the money I was saving, I certainly could have eventually bought a used car or more shoes or better quality food. Instead, I saved up every penny for months, just to attend a single retreat. Only by diverting almost all my financial resources could I hope to train with him. So that is what I did.

It was January 1998 when Bruce's martial arts teachings first became available to me. This was an opportunity I had fantasized about since I had read his mini-biography, included in his *Opening the Energy Gates of Your Body* book, seven years ago. He was then in his early fifties and presented an energetic and portly figure of average height. His head, from the base of his skull to his close-cropped beard, bears an uncanny resemblance to marble busts of the Greek historian Thucydides. He walks with a slow, measured gait that belies his ability to move in an instant with phenomenal grace and explosive power.

Instruction took place in a community church located in a small town north of the Bay, started in the evening and ended late. I had to take a half day off from work and a Greyhound bus from Sacramento to San Francisco where I changed to local transit that would take me to the rural location. Altogether, that was about a three hour affair, just to get there, one way.

Naturally, I had to punch into work at the factory at seven a.m. the next day. After class, I sat in the rain at night, waiting for the bus to take me back into the city. Once there, I could either take the last bus and be stranded in Sacramento around one o'clock in the morning. Or wait the whole night in SF and get on the earliest line back north, where I'd arrive at six, then take local rail to my home by six-thirty. Jump on my bike and, without any sleep, off to work. Maybe, if I was lucky, I had time for a shower.

Usually I carried a change of socks and underwear, toothbrush, gloves, warm beret and heavy sweater in a backpack. Every book Mr. Frantzis had ever written by then was tucked in too. I passed the time until dawn practicing the stuff I had just learned, in a parking garage, city park or some other unobtrusive place.

I had come to the decision to empty my cup and abandon the plethora of meditation techniques and occult methods that I knew, as they now represented conflicts of interest. I put aside all that which I had learned from books, videos and other teachers. I devoted myself to Mr. Frantzis' material, as I became more involved in his Taoist Water Method approach.

From Bruce, I learned what to train, how to train and why one should train in the order that he presented. I learned a specific technique from him and his students that would end up being the single most important tool in my eventual mental health recovery.

I also learned a systematic method that would enable me to process the content of my inner world with that technique most effectively.

My self-directed meditation and chi gung practice had finally begun to heal me in small ways. At the beginning I had made great strides, experienced increased energy, growing awareness and quietude. But over time my steps seemed to cover less ground. During my healing process I came face to face with the immediate limits of my knowledge. When I tried to meditate deeper, I was ejected out of the mind state of calm and assaulted with a rush of internal noise, emotions, images and personal demons.

When I practiced chi gung for prolonged periods, terrible emotions of self-destruction, anger and sadness came over me completely unbidden. What I needed was another vehicle to deliver me to a state of meditation so I could continue the work of self-healing. At that point, I had practiced meditation while sitting, kneeling, standing and lying down and had reached my limits with how long I could do any of them. Right at this time, as I was running out of ideas how to deal with all this, I started learning Bruce's dissolving practice and how to perform proper meditation.

It is also possible to perform meditation and achieve quality stillness through moving practices. I learned how to dissolve myself, using my awareness during the tai chi form. I gradually incorporated the techniques of sitting meditation into the form as well. It was through the form practice that I was slowly able to find a path that led to deeper meditation. Stillness through motion.

In my private, self-directed healing sessions, I listened carefully to my feelings and intuitions. One of the first clear communications I received from my body was tension. Somehow, over the course of my life, the energy of my body had become tightly coiled up like a spring and had simply stayed that way. I found myself constantly straining at all times to do something. I held myself in an eternal readiness, braced for impact. But why?

Even after I left my home and had become strong enough not to be a target at school anymore, the danger to myself never let up. I was locked into a state of perpetual fight or flight. I perceived ongoing threats to my person from living in psychiatric hospitals, group homes and later at various jobs and scary low income neighborhoods I had lived in.

Meditation and marijuana had only superficially calmed me down. I could not truly relax, because deep inside, I was at combat readiness at all times. Like Lt. Onada Hiroo guarding his post, who couldn't believe that the war was really over. For me, the war was not over either. Even when I was in the solitude and sanctuary of my home I was still stuck in combat-mode. Restless. Wary. Suspicious.

I'd get into fights with ten different people before I'd been awake for an hour, and they were all in my mind. I imagined a home invasion robbery on me, and so I kept weapons of every conceivable shape and size concealed everywhere in my apartment within easy reach. That's what it's like to have post traumatic stress. You are stuck with a paranoid survival reflex and you are always thinking about your security and you tend to obsess about life and death.

Over time, this all pervading tension throughout my body made me rigid. My muscles were tense. I had hard knots of tissue and bands of adhesions through my arms, legs and back. The more I paid attention, the more it felt like I was wearing an invisible corset, or straitjacket. My own body functioned like a torture device.

The practice of tai chi gradually began to soften my body. From my wrists and forearms to my back and legs, my entire body began to thaw. As I practiced meditation breathing and taught myself to move slowly, carefully, and deliberately, the muscles of my entire body began to relax and let go.

Initially I moved like a rusty machine. My movements jerky. My arms and legs trembled with ingrained tension when I slowed my movements down. The pervasive rigidity of my tissues and muscles acted like a brake. I was uncoordinated, and felt acutely disconnected inside myself, all over.

In the initial stages, my whole body was actively fighting against this new way of moving. Why? Because relaxing translated into giving up my defense. Even though I knew it intellectually, it took a bit of internal adjustment before my body realized that this was a superior way of moving through space.

After awhile, my body figured out by itself, that by being re-laxed I could actually be more prepared. Without internal resistance holding me back, I could move my entire body much faster. By relaxing, I was always recharging, whereas by being tense all the time, I was constantly burning my internal reserves while keeping my stress levels high.

At first I despaired when I realized how much work it would take to transform my body with this method. The more I listened to myself, the more problems I found. There seemed to be no end of them. I felt like I had running all my life in the opposite direc-tion of where I wanted to be. It was daunting.

Despite the setbacks, I was determined to stick with it. It did not take long before my body craved for more of what tai chi was doing to it. I had absolutely no idea who I would be further down the line if I kept at it, but I was curious and wanted to find out. Already I was changing.

Tai chi made me feel amazing. After a series of short forms I felt calm, centered, and relaxed. My mind was quiet. I stood straighter and more confidently. I felt content. The longer I did it, the better it became. I wanted those feelings to continue, so after a short rest I did another few sets.

During break time at work, instead of hanging out with the other employees who were eating or smoking, I went outside and did tai chi in the steel yard. It helped mitigate the muscle tension from manual labor and revitalized me for the next few hours. I'm sure I must have looked eccentric or even pretentious, but alas, I couldn't bring myself to care what others thought about me. It was their loss that they could not tell at a glance how awesome tai chi was, and how much happier it might make them if they practiced it too.

Gradually, practicing tai chi became my primary coping mechanism for everything.

If I was tired, tai chi picked me up.

If I felt tense, tai chi relaxed me.

If I was angry, tai chi calmed me back down.

If my body hurt, I did tai chi and it felt better.

If anything destabilized me in the slightest, the solution was to immediately do tai chi and it brought me back to balance.

It occupied as much of my time as I could reasonably set aside for it. I did tai chi when I got up in the morning, and before I punched into work. I did tai chi after work, and before going to bed. The changes to every facet of my being as a result of this tai chi lifestyle were phenomenal.

One of the first things that began to vacate my inner world was my anger. Experiencing myself as a centered person resulted in long, anger-free periods during my day. I was more relaxed and calm. Consequently, I put people around me more at ease, because they no longer had to deal with the usual wariness and nervousness that I inspired. Before that, I had made them feel uneasy and wary, because that was how I felt inside.

Without constant tension, anxiety, fear, anger or sadness my body became healthier. Previously, when I had been angry and depressed all the time I also used to get sick easily. Ever since I took up tai chi, I rarely catch colds or the flu, and if I do I tend to get over it quickly.

I found myself smiling much more often and I laughed out loud when I caught my reflection in a building window. For the longest time I had had nothing to smile about. Now, I felt great!

Tai chi was making me softer, not just physically, but emotionally and mentally as well. As my body changed, my mind changed. Correspondingly, as my mind changed, so to did the way I carried my body. There was de facto evidence that this was happening. Had anyone else been paying attention, they would not have failed to recognize major changes.

On the emotional level, I felt more relaxed and not constantly on edge anymore. When I laughed, it was not forced, or strained, but genuine. What might have made me furious before was now a mild irritation that could be dealt with without going off. My hair trigger temper was being defused. I had not hit or yelled at anything or anyone in quite awhile.

On the mental level, I found myself considering other options and points of view more often. No longer was everything cut and dry, black and white, one extreme or another. My very thoughts themselves were becoming less rigid and more flexible.

This method of self-repair has a synergistic effect on your whole life. When your mind, body and feelings are calm, stable and very alive, you radiate positive energy around you. As that happens, instead of repelling people away from you with negative vibes, you start to attract them. One experience I had, about a year and half into this, I'll never forget, because it really cemented my faith in my purpose.

On one particular weekend I had been fasting the whole day and had practiced meditation and tai chi all morning. I had aikido class that afternoon and there was a hour-long meditation sit afterwards for those that wanted to stay. By the end of the meditation sit I had basically been doing this stuff for six to eight hours over the course of the day. I was the last one to get off the mat, after everyone else went home. Finally I got up, stretched, and went to change into my street clothes.

When I came out of the changing room, I met one of the aikido instructors as he was closing up the office. He was a spry, easygoing man in his mid forties, and he was just standing there, staring at me. I smiled at him and met his gaze levelly with my own.

As he stood there, both his eyes became moist. I asked him, "What's wrong?"

He said to me then, "You have a glow about you I can see from over here. There is light coming out of your eyes. You look so completely at peace with yourself."

Then he said wistfully, "Ah God, I wish I had gotten into this when I was your age. Maybe you are picking up where you left off from another life. I can't say for sure about that," he mused, "but this is clearly what you were meant to do."

Certainly, not every day was like that, not by far. Nor should I have expected it to be. That had been a particularly good day. Mostly because I had spent the entire time free of all stress and obligation, willing and able to work on myself continuously.

* * *

When I was doing tai chi or sitting meditation, I was always working on dissolving myself. Dissolving gave me a means to work directly with whatever problem was at hand. Be it tension, frustration, anxiety, flashbacks, old injuries, aches and pains. Every out of place or destabilizing sensation that was filtering into my consciousness became subject to this dissolving practice.

Dissolving is a process whereby you gradually turn your awareness inward and begin to systematically patrol your body, looking for signs of internal discomfort. When you locate some kind of tension, pain or something that feels out of place, you deliberately coalesce your attention into that place of discomfort. As your awareness of that area increases, you focus on relaxing and letting go of whatever that "stuff" may be.

This is not merely targeted relaxation, which at first was all that I was capable of. As I stuck with it and paid close attention, I found that different degrees of relaxation are possible. I allowed myself to surrender into relaxation instead of trying hard to relax. Over time, the process became more effortless. I achieved a state where focusing my awareness yielded a greater degree of emotional, psychological and physical release, with a minimal amount of applied intent. I had finally made the transition from relaxing into dissolving.

One of my earliest mistakes with this technique was over-dissolving. I would dissolve-bomb myself. My concentration would surge into blocks and tension. I would focus much like a laser cutting through steel. I did make progress, yet often that kind of focusing just increased my agitation. It stirred up my stuff and did not fully release it. I poured huge amounts of concentration into a tense or painful place inside myself, getting only a little bit of dissolving in return.

Nevertheless, the effort was not a complete waste. One day, I was sitting and dissolving, my concentration batteries were almost drained. But I wanted to keep dissolving this one particular place in my back that was really bugging me.

When I had only a thread of awareness to work with, that was when I noticed a subtle change. I kept this tiny bit of relaxed attention going, and then after awhile, the pain dissolved very gently, with little fanfare, seemingly all by itself. Instead of trying to blast my energy blocks into tiny particles, I was now gently melting them, like the spring sun thawing winter ice.

Previously, I had always been in a hurry to dissolve, and so when I burned all this concentration up in a short amount of time, I moved on to another tension without fully ridding myself of the previous one. In my haste to get all this physical pain and emotional baggage out of me, I worked a lot harder than I actually needed to.

Once I independently discovered this minimalistic approach to dissolving and cultivated the patience for the block to fully dissolve when it was good and ready to go, my practice took off. I was doing without doing, which is a Taoist ideal.

What changed my overall rate of progress, and for that matter my entire approach to life, was trying to embody the Taoist 70 percent rule of moderation that I learned from Bruce Frantzis. The idea of this principle is that you only apply 70 percent of your available resources to a given problem or situation. If you keep your energy expenditures or your stress tolerance at that level, you will always have that 30 percent or so in reserve.

The rule also applies to practicing tai chi, chi gung and meditation. As a beginner, I did not know exactly where my limits were and it was easy for me to cross the line past 70 percent to 90 percent without noticing it. Before I experientially understood the wisdom of that approach, I was burning myself out unknowingly.

Even beyond that, it is very useful for dealing with life in general. You can apply it to nearly everything you do, for example, in dealing with other people. With this new awareness I could gauge accurately when I had had enough of being social. When the moment came, I would take my leave before I became irritated or anxious by being around folks for too long. It's a formula for reducing your overall stress levels, no matter what you are doing.

Within your body, where exactly do you do all this dissolving? If you just want to rid yourself of assorted physical pains and tensions in your body, you can dissolve anywhere you feel the need. Your arms, legs, fingers and toes can all be dissolved and you may feel better as a result.

If your intention is to dissolve emotional, mental and spiritual blocks, then you need to work primarily with your entire spinal column and your internal organs. You are going to want to dissolve your head, your neck, upper body, intestines, your pelvis and genitals. From skull to sacrum and all along your central core, that is where you are going to target your dissolving practices because this is where the bulk of your problems are most likely going to be.

Your fixations and triggers may seem to be connected to other places in your body, by association with past events, but the real residence is going to be somewhere between your head, heart and bowels, with your central nervous system being the primary connecting element and access pathway.

How is it possible that you can do this at all? The answer lies in what is called the *Eight Bodies of Being*. I learned the concept of these eight levels of existence from Mr. Frantzis' writings and seminars.

The Eight Bodies of Being comprise the totality of our experience of being alive. These eight different levels include our physicality and our "chi." Chi includes the actual biochemical electricity that flows throughout our bodies and our conscious awareness. The next two levels are the emotional and the mental.

Those are the first four Bodies. The next four include our psychic perceptions, the body of causality (our karma) followed by the body of individuality or our "spirit." The final level is Universal Consciousness.

I realize that not everyone believes in karma, psychic abilities or souls. Those are interesting subjects, open to interpretation or debate. The four Bodies of Being that comprise the second tier of our existence can be considered our "higher" functions. In terms of spiritual development, they are considered advanced levels and are not immediately germane to what we are working on.

The first four levels, comprising our physical body, awareness, emotions and thoughts are more "mundane." For purposes of mental illness recovery we need concern ourselves only with the first four, because they are the easiest to work with and the most readily sensed.

So far, I covered the essential basics for what followed.

First was the understanding that liberating myself of internal blocks would lead to becoming healthier physically, mentally and emotionally.

Second was using the dissolving practice to resolve those blocks.

Third, governing my approach to resolving my issues, was following the 70 percent rule of moderation.

Fourth and final was actually dissolving the first four Bodies of Being with my intent.

These different "Bodies" all occupy the same space like a multi-dimensional hologram. A possible analogy is white light passing through a prism. As the light passes through the prism, the entire spectrum of color is found to be within it.

Meditation allowed me to experientially sense these different colors contained within the whole of my being. Dissolving gave me a means to resolve the issues bound up within the different colors. Freeing myself of the problems within those first four levels of Being became my singular, overriding passion for a long time.

Gaining access to those levels may seem abstract, but it's easier to do than one might think. Since all these Bodies of Being occupy the same space, it's only a matter of time before working on one of them gives you access to another.

At one point, during one of my dissolving sessions, I was working on gently dissolving the region of my left eye, temple and cheek. After awhile, a powerful flashback of my mother's hand slamming into my face came over me, completely unbidden. I felt the shock of the blow to my face, as though it had just happened. I could feel the heat from the reddening imprint of her fingers on my cheek.

While reliving this past trauma, I became spontaneously angry, sad and vengeful. My thoughts became diverted momentarily, as I felt the urge to strike my mother in return. I saw in my mind's eye a vengeance scenario in which my mother slapped me and I slapped her back (which I strongly felt the urge to do when it had first happened). In that moment I was no longer meditating but reacting to an ancient and still unresolved trigger.

My point is this: The episode was not triggered by psychoanalyzing my past, but by working with my body. In this case, concentrating attentively on the flesh and bones of my face had resulted in contacting a very real blockage of sorts. A part of my body where my emotions and certain attending memories could be consciously triggered and refreshed. When that happened, I was witnessing the real-time interplay of the first four Bodies of Being (physicality, energy, emotion and thought).

As I continued to dissolve my face and the felt sensation of my mother's hand on my cheek, the energy block gradually resolved and gently released. As it did, the muscles of my face on that side rippled and spasmed momentarily. As the trembling passed, I felt my pain go away. With the physical memory of the event released, my sadness and the indignant rage evaporated. When I replayed the scene (my mother slapping me) in my head again, I no longer felt as though I had just been struck a second ago. There was no attending impulse or thought for revenge. That event no longer had any power over me.

In a way, my experience was comparable to the fable of Androcles and the Lion, an analogy Mr. Frantzis himself often uses to describe the process. When Androcles removed the thorn in the lion's paw, the lion calmed down and stopped eating people. Dissolving gave me a workable means of removing all my "thorns," no matter where they were located, how deeply they had pierced me, or for how long they had been there.

My success at removing one of these mental and emotional thorns increased my resolve to continue. Those distressing events and the triggers that were still embedded in me served to continuously exacerbate my PTSD. Their existence was the reason why I was perpetually ready to fight anything and anyone at all times. Subconsciously, I was always expecting something bad to happen. That created an ongoing state of anxiety, so subtle that I never became aware of it unless I paid attention.

Besides emotional wounds and scars were those from various car accidents, industrial work injuries, martial arts and sports. Dissolving just my hands was very revealing, because I had all manner of micro flashbacks manifest from the time when I had punched walls out of anger up to the moment when my fingers were crushed in a machine. Fear of loss arose, as I dissolved my still damaged fingers.

Much of the current disconnection and damage that I suffered now I had done to myself, when I didn't care if I lived or died. In my extreme mental and emotional states I had run roughshod over my body and I was now starting to comprehend the effects of that lifestyle.

By doing tai chi and meditation according to Taoist tenets, I viscerally learned how changing the mind would change the body and vice versa. I gradually became an ongoing example of "as above, so below" within the microcosm of my subjective world.

CHAPTER 17

DEPROGRAMMING

Over the years, my body had suffered some substantial abuse from which it never fully recovered. One particularly severe accident had been a gymnastic stunt gone wrong. My forward flip ended abruptly when my head smashed into the ground, resulting in a seriously damaged cervical spine.

At the time, I tested my fingers and toes and there was no tingling, so I carried on as though nothing had happened. In the frantic inner pace of my teens I never made the connection between the neck accident and the chronic pain and dysfunction that soon followed.

The short term consequences were a stiff neck and excruciating headaches. Years later, the damaged tissues in my neck interfered with the natural pulsing in the Eustachian canals, which pressurizes your ears. As a consequence, the ability of my ears to rid themselves of wax build up was impaired, which resulted in temporarily losing my hearing in both ears about once a year.

In the same year, I threw out my right shoulder during a softball game and tore the muscles underneath both of my shoulder blades while trying to help push a truck out of a ditch. I didn't want to appear hurt or vulnerable to adults or group home residents and so I just toughed it out. But the pain never really went away and I got used to suppressing it and not paying attention to the discomfort.

Flash forward to when I was twenty-two and I worked at the pipe factory in Sacramento. I was rotating a twenty-foot long steel pipe over my head when my arm locked up and became paralyzed. I felt an electrical shock flash through my arm from shoulder to wrist, and my hand began to get cold. I had to dodge out of the way as the pipe came crashing down.

I relied on my arms to make a living. No arm, no work, no money. I did a few chi gung sets in the privacy of the restroom, which seemed to restore functioning to my arm somewhat. The accident and the resulting paralysis was extremely unsettling and so I sought out help.

The weekend after it happened I visited an outdoor alternative healing fair. There were massage therapists and yoga demonstrations. I talked with a local Rolfing facilitator and received some sample processing. As I made my rounds, I found a chiropractor who was offering free spinal health exams, so I stepped up to get one.

Dennis wasn't "merely" a chiropractor. He radiated compassion, and you got a sense that he was always listening and paying attention to you. He was very experienced in deep tissue work (like myofascia release) and was a certified Reiki healing practitioner. When I told him about my interests in chi gung and tai chi, we hit it off immediately.

Dennis set about various measurements of my whole body and posture as I stood on scales, one for each foot. We discovered that I was putting ten more pounds of force through my right leg than my left. He explained how the unequal force distribution would wear down my joints asymmetrically.

Furthermore, we found that my left shoulder rode higher than the right one. Bands of adhesions (from unhealed injuries) in my middle back created a tension in my upper body. My right shoulder, neck, and back muscles were larger than the corresponding muscles on my left side. And there were distortions in the tissues themselves, around those muscles, owing to my body's attempt to compensate for these various tensions.

Dennis was having a sale of sorts. I would have to pay for the X-rays, but get two free visits worth of adjustments or something like that. With anticipation and some trepidation, I awaited my visits and the results of my upper body X-rays.

When he finally showed me the pictures of my skeleton and the condition of my neck, I despaired. There was scarring along my neck vertebrae and bony growths. The vertebrae above and below the damaged ones were bigger from calcification and the muscles around them more developed as they had taken over the load. I had cervical vertebrae degeneration going on. I could see the scars in those close ups.

The reason for my transitory arm paralysis became clear in those images. The first two ribs underneath my clavicle had migrated upwards over time. The right side rib was almost touching my clavicle and the left and opposite side rib was getting close. The proximity of my ribs to my clavicle put pressure on the nerves in my arms and the right side had basically short circuited when I lifted the steel pipe over my head.

In my lower back, my floating ribs were fusing to the ribs above them because of the rigid bands of fascia that my body had grown to compensate for upper back strain. The way I wore my body, constantly straining and tensing, combined with my ignoring of all my accumulating injuries over the years, had resulted in neurological damage.

No wonder I was getting grey hair in my twenties. Although I had become a lot healthier recently, those X-rays were evidence that all was not as well as I'd thought. When I got home I allowed myself to feel sorry for what had happened to me. No one had abused my body more than I did. For the majority of my injuries I had no one to blame but myself.

I started seeing Dennis for adjustments. Since I had no health insurance, I paid for it out of pocket. Initially we had great results. One of his first adjustments was to my skull. When he pulled my skull and stretched my neck vertebrae, I saw stars and my ears popped. Immediately after that, some of the noise in my head was gone, I sat straighter and felt better all the way down to my toes. It even altered my gait, as I walked about with a new spring in my step.

One result of that specific adjustment effected my lymph nodes. Ever since I fell sick as a child and lost most of my hearing in my left ear, there was one swollen, rock hard lymph node behind my ear that never drained or softened over the years. Within a week of treatment, the swelling was gone as though it had never been there.

Unfortunately, my ribs were a more difficult problem. He cracked my back this way and that. He put physical pressure on my ribs to bring them down. He applied heat, magnets, electro-stimulation and transmitted Reiki healing into my upper body. It had very little effect.

There was only so much money I could throw at ineffective treatment. He didn't want to give up trying and I knew he was good. His knowledge and techniques just could not counter the forces that caused my ribs to migrate like they had. Eventually, I stopped seeing him regularly. I certainly couldn't afford osteopathy or surgery to my ribs. So what was I to do?

At about that time the possibility of self-healing opened up soon after the need arose. Master Bruce Frantzis was holding a retreat on spinal chi gung that summer. He'd teach the material he had used to regenerate his broken back.

According to the pamphlet I received, I would learn how to pulse my entire body to improve circulation. My glands, organs, blood pressure and even the cerebrospinal flow could all be effected with certain breathing techniques. I would learn to control every vertebrae in my spine and move them in any direction at will. There were other levels to that training, including how to use the spinal chi gung within the tai chi form or during meditation. The idea of learning how to control the vertebrae in my spine was what sealed the deal. I needed to learn this more than his other offerings that summer.

My work at the pipe factory would only continue to exacerbate the condition of my arm and ribs. With great reluctance I left the company and found employment elsewhere. I congratulated myself for having actually kept a job for a whole year, which was a new record.

Fortunately, I got a new and much more interesting job working in the assembly department of a custom metal fabrication shop. It was good money, and after several months I had saved enough for the up and coming chi gung retreat.

The end of the summer was fast approaching and my friend Julian drove me to Mr. Frantzis' scheduled retreat deep in the heart of Sonoma County. While there, I ran into some emotional problems.

It was day two or three of the retreat, and we were all busy learning how to breathe in such a way that the movement of the breath would cause the entire body, not just the chest and back, to expand and contract. In the process, we were pumping our spines and pulsing our internal organs. Master Frantzis had warned us that one possible result of this kind of breathing could be spontaneous emotional release.

I had been largely stable the last six months. Yet now, out of nowhere, I felt an overwhelming urge to kill myself right there on the spot. While meditation had already helped me quite a bit to get this far, it only took a few hours of proper breathing to come into contact with the mass of emotional pain that I still carried around inside me. With tears in my eyes, I walked over to where Bruce was sitting, overseeing everyone's practice.

I told him about the sudden surge of powerful depressing emotions and he replied that it was not unusual for young people to feel self-destructive when they have no purpose in life. He observed how intense and agitated I had become, and told me that I was constantly straining too hard internally. Bruce said that he could feel my chi-energy emanating from me and stated, "Your nervous system is stuck on maximum output." Like running your car at full throttle all the time. "Sooner or later," he informed me, "you exhaust yourself, and that recurring cycle of central nervous system fatigue is part of the reason behind your depression."

He added, "This is what you need to do: You need to stop hurting yourself. You need to learn to dissolve properly and do it. And you need to get over yourself."

Get over myself? I thought silently. Who did he think he was? How dare he? He had no idea what I had been through and survived. I thought I understood the whole self-harm thing. After all, I'd quit smoking, taken up tai chi and was learning how to relax. I was trying to practice the 70 percent rule of moderation. What did he mean, stop hurting myself?

I said to him, "Ah, you are right. I've been so blind. I am so stupid!"

He replied, "Stop. You're hurting yourself right now."
I froze.

"You're not stupid," Master Frantzis stated. "You made it here, didn't you?" he asked. "You came to learn how to heal yourself. That's not stupid. Who told you that you were stupid?"

I thanked him for his advice, and, not wanting to monopolize his attention, I walked off to sit for a moment and collect myself before engaging in the lesson plan again. Where had I learned I was stupid? My stepfather used to brow beat me again and again, repeatedly telling me I was stupid during my childhood. My mother had done the same.

"For the love of St. Mike, how can you be so stupid? God, you are so stupid sometimes. You are stupid for even asking!" my parents had drilled into me.

Over the years, part of me had internalized the name "stupid." It was a label I owned. I had effectively taken over for my parents and abused myself with it ever since I left the Hell House. In that instant I realized that my strings were still being pulled by this form of self-injury. I had done some stupid things over the years. But I had also done a lot of intelligent things over the years.

I was not fundamentally a stupid person. The label did not apply to me. As that realization sunk in, a great weight was lifted from me. In the moment of apprehension I understood what Bruce meant about hurting myself. Henceforth I would be on the lookout for other ways that I might be doing it.

Self-injury is not limited to substance abuse, cutting, or other physical forms of self-harm. It is possible to injure yourself psychologically and emotionally too. I might as well have been mentally flogging myself with a cat-o-nine-tails, like a religious ascetic, for my mistakes and shortcomings.

Some readers will recognize, that my interaction with Mr. Frantzis amounted to a cognitive behavioral therapy lesson. Once I was sensitized to the idea, I was able to effectively perform this kind of therapy on myself over the years. I became my own therapist, as I examined all my thoughts and tried to find out where I had first obtained certain ideas about myself.

The key to success with this method, whether you do it to yourself or have a facilitator, is self-honesty. You must agree not to bullshit yourself. You have to become an objective coach to your inner psyche and give yourself a brutally honest summation of the reality of your situation. Ever since my last suicide attempt I found myself possessing this brutally (desperately) honest self-critique, and I improved as I kept on using it.

I was not the only person whose emotional stuff had been churned up by this powerful form of chi gung. Towards the end of the retreat Mr. Frantzis gave a lecture on how to use spinal chi gung during meditation and how to use the dissolving technique to get over the stuff that was coming up in practice.

Bruce went on to talk about the injuries people can experience, physically, emotionally, or mentally, over the course of their lives. He discussed the notion that there is a certain terminal level of insult or abuse a person can take and beyond which, there is no hope for recovery. That person will never "get over it."

He talked for a bit about his broken back, and that people had told him he would never recover. Using these Chinese energy healing and physical therapy techniques, he had recovered psychologically as well as physically. He then related two other stories of recovery.

The first was about a man who had survived the Holocaust during World War II. He had been spared because his services were needed, pulling the dead bodies out of the gas showers and carting them off to the ovens to be incinerated.

The things he did and witnessed were traumatic in the extreme. That is something you might think no one could ever get over. Many years later he recovered from it enough to be able to share his story with others.

The second story was just as poignant.

One day, many years earlier, Bruce had been discussing his various problems with one of his primary teachers in China, and he made the mistake of saying something along of the lines of, "It isn't fair." His master responded with something like, "Oh really? You think that your life isn't fair, or that you've had it rough? Come with me."

Mr. Frantzis was introduced to a woman who had survived the social upheaval of the Cultural Revolution. At one point, the Red Army had been garrisoned near her village and she had drawn the attention of one of the officers. He had selected her to sexually entertain his son, and when she refused he turned her over to his troops. She spent the next week being gang raped and tortured.

Bruce explained that in a Confucian society what happened to her was a shame on her and her immediate family and also her ancestors. There was no possible social recovery from that. She must've been overwhelmed with the urge to kill herself, yet she didn't.

Although she still bore the physical scars and could never have children, she had come to grips with it and learned to live with herself. She was quite capable of calmly relating this horrendous event to a perfect stranger. She considered herself lucky, because she had witnessed even more awful things happen to other people during those revolutionary times.

When I considered my own past and compared it to those two stories, I realized that I had had it comparatively easy. For one, we lucked out that our parents were too religious and self-righteous to ever become substance abusers or alcoholics. We were spared sexual abuse too.

Even so, I had often beat my breast, looked up at the sky and asked, "Why God, why? Why did this happen to me? It's so unfair!" I was angry at the world, bemoaning my fate, and demanding that the Universe reveal to me the meaning of it all. I felt ashamed that I had fallen so completely apart as a consequence of my life's events.

Bruce's teacher was right. Life was not fair. There were never any guarantees that it was supposed to be. There is no inherent "meaning" when people are made to suffer. Shit happens, in a less than perfect world.

Those two stories of recovery became a benchmark for me. Now I knew that my own recovery was possible. With the dissolving technique I possessed the skills needed to overcome my past. That was how I was supposed to "get over myself." But sometimes it takes more than one kind of feedback for the totality of an idea to sink in.

Not long after the chi gung retreat I was hanging out with another of Mr. Frantzis' students. Noah was a handsome, intelligent, and also peremptory young man, a year older than I. Despite his personality shortcomings, he was quite adept at some of Mr. Frantzis' material. I recognized he had developed real skill and I was willing to put up with his rough edges in order to learn.

We sat in his apartment, talking about dissolving and meditation. At one point, I began to bring up my past. I started talking about the child abuse and life in institutions and I became intense. My voice became tinged with bitterness and anger. I leaned forward in my seat and was talking rapidly while my hands were shaking.

He interrupted me and said, "Look at yourself. You were calm and collected before talking about your past. Do you realize how worked up you are? You are still a slave to your inner world and you have to dissolve that stuff, so that it no longer has any power over you."

This shocked me into silence as I scanned my insides and found it was true. It had taken less than a minute for me to go from calm to boiling, simply by thinking about my past. My energy was so agitated that I was like radioactive material, spewing toxic emotions into his apartment. I had become downright manic for a few moments. Noah gave me a lot of other good pointers and revealed some advanced technical material to me. But nothing he taught me was as useful, or as profound, as that one observation about my reactions.

When I got back to my home, I immediately went meditating in pursuit of emotional triggers, with the intent on getting rid of them, once and for all. I knew exactly how to find them. All I had to do was rake over my memories, one event at a time, and deal with whatever came up. A thought or a memory trigger would cause a change in my emotional state, which would lead to a shift in my physical and mental states as well.

At first, there seemed to be no end of them, and for a time I even despaired. As I inventoried the morass of chaotic emotions, I would encounter dark signs and onerous voices that warned me off of the feelings I was scanning.

"Abandon all hope, ye who enter here," lamented one.

"Turn back while you still can," cried another bleakly.

"Here, there be dragons," whispered a third.

My heart was blocked up all over, and every memory seemed tinged with some kind of charge that I could do without. Dissolving those things brought me great relief, as my emotions smoothed out and the overall noise in my head quieted down as a result. At other times I did not pursue specific memories and instead patrolled my body core, from head to waist, dredging for possible triggers I was not consciously aware of. Not all the stuff inside me was as easily defined as blockages resulting from a specific physical or emotional event.

Often I did not know what I was working on. One pain seemed connected to an issue completely unrelated to what I was feeling at the time. Instead of clear flashbacks of a previous life event, I felt disconnection and blackness inside me. Sourceless seeming rage, anxiety and dread, commingled with various aches and pains visited me as vague memories churned at the edge of my awareness.

Sometimes, dissolving a block was fairly straight forward. I dissolved a pain in my shoulder and I felt immediate relief and more calm. Other times, it was not so simple. I might be dissolving one issue and in the process I detected another issue underneath it which covered a third one, and so on.

During those sessions, I followed the 70 percent rule of moderation and withdrew from my meditation to settle down before I became too unhinged. I would reflect upon and replay the struggle. I analyzed my mistakes and made changes to my strategy. Then I would step up, go back inside and face the whirlwind again.

As time went on, my ability to persist and stay focused in that chaos increased. Eventually I found that I had cleared a portion of my inner sky. Intrusive thoughts and turbulent feelings spontaneously abated when I reached the eye of my inner storm. When that happened, I felt profoundly still inside and at peace with myself. There was no emotional pain or suffering for awhile.

Effective dissolving removes your psycho-emotional triggers in both the conscious and subconscious mind and there is no more coping with them. They are just gone, like they never existed. Over time I dissolved dozens of these kinds of issues, irrespective of their order of primacy. Each success strengthened my will to continue and increased the effectiveness of my dissolving ability.

As I located and dissolved the many wounds in my heart, my inner sensitivity and concentration ability continued to grow. Eventually, I perceived this increase in capability. I decided the time had come to get rid of one of the deepest, most powerful psycho-emotional triggers inside me, one way or another.

It was an old trigger and my parents were directly responsible for its existence. When I was a kid, they never respected me, my privacy, or even my sleep. Tim and Sarah were both rageaholics, and when they worked up a good angry, it was not unusual for one or the other of them to come bursting into my room at night, grab me by my hair or feet and drag me out of a sound sleep, out of bed, for a screaming, shouting and slapping session.

As a consequence, I developed a subconscious hypervigilance that had played havoc with my stress levels and my immune system. It was one of the reasons I used to get sick so easily. It interfered with my concentration at school the morning after one of those episodes and was partly why I was so obsessed with the martial arts.

After leaving home, I had to endure "room checks" at various institutions in the middle of the night. My door would crack open, and I would be instantly woken from sleep to a bolt upright sitting position, my heart pounding, my breast heaving, sleep dazed, shaking and completely ready to fight anything. That had happened several times a night, for years.

Year after year, the events in my life never allowed me to stand down and begin to heal. I had become so used to insecurity in my life, that I never relaxed, not even in sleep. The slightest thing could trigger my fight or flight reflexes and I would wake up in my apartment, reaching for the nearest weapon, while listening acutely to my surroundings.

This continued to happen even after I had my apartment sanctuary located in a decent neighborhood. Every so often a late shift worker would come home and shut their car door; hearing the clunk, I would snap awake, thinking my stepfather had come home from work and the punishments were about to begin. Alternately, someone in the upstairs apartment might slam a door or occasionally stomp heavily across the floor and I would have flashbacks of the fights in our home. My pulse would pound in my ears and sweat might break out, even when I was sitting still, reading a book.

When I realized I could search for triggers and disarm them, and that, that particular string was still being pulled by abuse that was long past, I decided I had had enough. Those random outdoor and domestic sounds could be used to access the internal blocks and release them. With that in mind, I began another experiment.

I stayed awake one weekend in search of this trigger. I sat in an easy chair in complete darkness and practiced meditation throughout the night. I waited and sat vigil on my internal world.

Sure enough, eventually someone slammed their car door in the parking lot. It seemed ridiculously loud on account that I was listening for it so carefully. In an instant I acutely felt the biological processes involved.

The sound triggered an impulse that went down my spine and punched me in the lower back. My adrenal glands released, energy shot back up my spine. External sounds became muffled while my awareness increased sharply. My legs shook and I needed to urinate. Intense anxiety, a sense of danger, and a desperate need to run for my life overwhelmed me.

In that moment, I moved to counter the spell that was coming over me. My awareness coalesced around the sense of anxiety, and time slowed down. I could feel where the action-impulse began and ended. I talked myself down and told myself, that everything was okay and that I was safe. There was no one trying to hurt me, and if there were, I was here to protect me. I whispered calming thoughts down my nerves.

As this occurred, I simultaneously reversed the series of events that were triggered in me. I dissolved all sense of fear that seemed to pulse outward from the vicinity of my kidneys. I eased my foot off the gas and took deep calming breaths. I was safe. My parents were eight years and three thousand miles away and could not touch me. I was not in a group home or on a psych ward. There was nothing to be afraid of. Remain calm.

All of this happened in the space of seconds. Time resumed its normal pace again. I had faced my reactions and my fear. I had lain in wait for it, like a spider in a web, and intercepted it as it happened. I allowed the impulses and feelings to wash over me and then reversed their course. Tiny jitters passed as my adrenaline level normalized.

That trigger was gone. I had liberated myself of another of the strings that I had danced to for so long. The ever-predictable car-being-parked and resulting door closing woke me up once again later that week and I lay there, with my eyes open, listening. That was it. No adrenaline dump. No fight or flight response. Just that sense of listening to be sure I was safe, before falling back into restful sleep. That post-traumatic stress reflex never visited me again.

When I would go on internal missions to find my issues, I would conjure an event that I knew bothered me and allow myself to fully relive the experience. Generally speaking, sooner or later the trigger would present itself, and I would dissolve it at a physical, emotional, and mental level until it was gone. But other times it was not that easy.

As the months wore on I went over the faces of my family and recalled incidents of various kinds of abuse. I recalled memories from the institutions and I dissolved them too. I dissolved all the loss, the indignant rage, the anxiety and fear, anything that disturbed my inner world. It was during this process, in my early twenties, when I finally understood the manic component of manic depression.

At some point I discovered a simple truth. As long as my mind was quiet, it would never be manic. Mania and stillness are mutually exclusive. Your mind can not accelerate itself and work your energy up to the level of exalted euphoria when you consciously abort or let go of mental or emotional reactions to stimuli on a moment-by-moment basis.

Initially I had achieved this by holding my mind still. That had worked for me in Tobey School, when I was under intense pressure to conceal any manic symptoms from observing staff and counselors. In that case, I had to perform for about four weeks in order to prove I wasn't experiencing a manic phase. But I knew that I couldn't control my thoughts forever through sheer force of will. I had to train my mind to arrive at stillness naturally. The potential for mania would always be there, unless I fundamentally changed the way my mind worked and reacted to things.

I always did this work in complete solitude, with hours of free time at my disposal. I started from a baseline of calm, when I was at the emotional "equator," so-to-speak. As a result of my success at it, I had longer and longer periods when my mind sat quietly, with no obsessive ruminations, no churning thoughts, or flight of ideas.

There were also periods when my inner world was deceptively calm, like the stillness before the storm. My approach then was to listen carefully and attentively, as though I were trying to detect an intruder in my home.

Eventually I discovered a very specific process which could be observed internally, that led to mania. It could happen quite quickly. But when I was internally slowed down by meditation, this process became very apparent. I would think a thought or feel a feeling and it would cause me to speed up inside. On a scale of zero to one hundred (with zero indicating relative calm, and one hundred being flown blown mania), I was able to observe how I stepped on the gas and sped myself up.

All it would take was one thought which led to another and another, like chain lightning. As each thought branched, it picked up a greater charge and intensity, triggering various emotions as well. As the psychic and emotional intensity of my inner world increased, it resulted in a flight of ideas, a fascination for trivia and momentous-seeming grandiose inspiration. As that progressed, I wanted to run around and do a thousand different things.

As I continued to listen and experiment, I found that I could begin to sense, very acutely, what caused mania and exactly when the onset occurred. At first, the transition between zero and one hundred was quite fast. Mania seemed to literally come out of nowhere. Eventually, I was able to perceive exactly when I was pressing on the gas and giving energy to my thoughts.

In time, I began to sense by degrees precisely when I went from zero to forty, then sixty, then eighty. Later still, I was able to accurately detect when I went from zero to one. When I dissolved the thoughts and feelings that were accelerating me internally, I gained the ability to reverse the process of a manic episode.

That is how I was able to observe that mania does not just magically materialize "out of nowhere." In the process, I discovered that I myself produced the elation and racing thoughts. Mania occurs because of the things we think and feel, and the things we do as a result of the things we think and feel. We get so caught up in sensory distractions and keeping busy in our own minds that for many of us with the bipolar diagnosis, mania does seem to come "out of nowhere."

I am convinced that we allow mania to possess us, by not paying attention to the balance of our inner world. With training, you can catch yourself shifting out of calm and arrest the movement of your mind before you are destabilized. My psychiatrist was wrong. Mania was most definitely not out of my conscious control.

* * *

During the rainy season, the Sacramento area is stricken with so-called Tule fog. This is no mere fog, but a dense cloud which descends to ground level. It can cover the entire Central Valley up to the Sierras. Visibility in this fog can be as far as eighty feet or none at all.

In the month of my twenty-third birthday, the fog was particularly persistent. Usually gone by mid-afternoon, it often did not dissipate until night time. The all-pervasive grayness absorbed a lot of light and you couldn't see the sun for days, even weeks.

One day I came home from work and I just felt tired for no good reason. I really didn't have the motivation to go down to the park and work out. I had no motivation for anything at all. I felt gloomy. Then a quiet voice in my head whispered, "There is just no point in doing anything, anymore."

I recognized it instantly as a depression thought. It was so out of synch with how my inner world, emotions and thoughts had been lately, that it alarmed me. This wasn't right. There didn't seem to be an immediate reason to be depressed. Which part of the depression equation had changed – and why now?

As I considered that, I wondered too, when exactly had I been depressed last? It took awhile before I calculated that I hadn't been depressed in two years. I smiled as I realized that it was true. I had not been counting, just living in the moment, one day at a time.

Immediately I dropped whatever was in my hand. I closed my eyes and listened very carefully to my inner world.

Tell me what is wrong.

After a moments pause, without conscious thought, I turned on my heel, walked outside and gazed up at the sky. The sun was a dim, circular patch of white, blanketed by grey mist. It's weakened rays couldn't penetrate the Tule cloud that sat on the ground. It had now been four weeks since I'd seen or felt the warm and yellow rays. More than anything right then, I felt that I wanted, no, needed to see the sun again.

I called Julian and asked him if we could go on a drive out of this fog for a few hours. He picked me up in his truck and we set off down the highway. Miles of gloom passed until we were starting to go up in elevation. We reached Auburn, a thousand feet above sea level, and I asked Julian to pull over.

As I got out of the truck, I gazed down upon the valley. The whole Sacramento area was gone, hidden by the fantastic cloud that hovered over everything. I took off my jacket and allowed my bare arms and face to absorb the warm rays and the perfect blue sky. Energy, purpose and motivation surged through my limbs and my brief depressed state was utterly gone, evaporated.

We headed further north, up to about six thousand feet, and stopped again. For an hour, I did my tai chi, basking in the warm friendly glow of the sun. The heat sunk into my flesh and bones and I was totally revitalized. The fog persisted another couple weeks, but my fleeting depressive feelings did not return.

Another piece of the depression puzzle box snicked into place. I now understood viscerally what I had known intellectually. Namely, that I was affected by the weather. That malaise had been the onset of seasonal affective disorder, brought about by a prolonged lack of sunlight. Because I was paying attention to my inner world, I was able to accurately perceive the problem at an intuitive level and could reverse it before it got worse.

I remember how we had grown up as kids. My mother and I had always become depressed during the onset of winter. Short and cold days, a house surround by hills, and staying inside all the time, forced by my stepfather's oppressive mandate to turn off almost every light in the house when not in use. All these factors minimized our exposure to a healthy amount of illumination. We always seemed to bounce back during spring, when the days grew longer and we could go outside more often.

I had done the right thing by fleeing the mercurial, bipolar-like climate of New England to stabilize my emotions. The weather itself had been a recurring issue in my overall personal depression puzzle. The Tule fog never again was as severe for the rest of the years that I lived in the Sacramento area.

* * *

One afternoon, as I was waiting for the bus, several other would-be riders strolled up and joined me. I observed an elderly man who constantly kept rubbernecking in the direction the bus would eventually come. He paced and grimaced and muttered to himself. Others joined the grey haired man in rubbernecking, checking their watches, fidgeting and pacing. I was perfectly content to stand there, breathing, being fully present in the here and now. The bus would come, sooner or later. Wonder and worry would not hasten its arrival.

Throughout my childhood, my parents would cajole me to physically slow down. In my mid-teens my other relatives implored me to slow down my talking speed. I was always moving or speaking too fast whenever I was in proximity to adults, it seemed.

"Wendiddalaswoncomby?" one of them asked me.

"I beg pardon?" I replied.

"Can you tell me when the last bus came by?"

"Sorry, but I just missed it myself before you got here."

Roles had changed in only a few short years. Now it was other people who talked or moved too fast and I was the one asking them to slow down and repeat. While I was calm, they were the ones racing along inside, impelled by their habits, schedules and troubles.

Practicing tai chi and meditation gradually slowed down the rushing pace of my thoughts and feelings that had so often been a source for "typical" manic symptoms like power-eating, power-walking, and power-talking. Clearly, this lifestyle was making major changes to my inner landscape, and hence, to my entire character, the longer I kept at it.

Every morning I got up while it was still dark outside. I biked down into the park and rode to the edge of the American River. In the pre-dawn light I practiced tai chi along its hard clay banks. Then I would sit in meditation and watch the sun rise. Afterward, I cycled out of the park to get to work.

In the evenings I reversed the process. I went back down to the river after eating dinner. I did my chi gung exercises and meditated as the sun set and practiced tai chi long after darkness had fallen. Then I biked home and went to bed. Other than my job, I had not a care in the world. This routine and my devotion to the Chinese methods of self-repair was my life.

Gradually, I became one with nature and the elements. I spent so much time outside that my body acclimated to all forms of weather. I practiced even when it was raining out, or cold. I could tell the approximate time of day (plus or minus an hour) just by sensing the position of the sun; I didn't need to look directly at it to tell where it was.

On weekends I spent the entire day, from dawn till dusk, training like this. My backpack contained bottles of water and tea, bags of trail mix, and all of Mr. Frantzis' books. I practiced in two to four hour shifts, with breaks in between to eat lunch or to explore the quiet, riparian areas of the park via the bike path.

This path, also known as the Jedediah Smith Memorial Trail, is a winding route which shadows the American River for miles. It is one of the largest purpose-built bike paths in the nation. The trail, along with the river and the extensive acreage of American River Parkway offer a broad range of recreational activities, from camping, cycling and fishing to white water rafting and gold panning.

The Parkway is home to a phenomenal range of plants and wildlife. On an average summer day one might see hawks predating on voles. Long legged herons step delicately in the shallows while turkeys roam the underbrush. Voracious jade dragonflies with bodies as thick as a pencil flit about, feeding on insects of opportunity.

A number of short paved roads and dirt paths grant access to vast fields overrun with yellow starthistle, whose long, pointed spines perpetually endanger every rubber tire that trespasses. Stands of grey pine and blue oak as well as groves of manzanita offer shaded places to practice during the heat of day.

On moonlit nights, the lunar glow revealed the nocturnal activities of the local fauna. A pair of enormous white owls hunted the sky overhead. Deer walked right by, singly and in groups. A juvenile rattlesnake passed once within inches of where I sat, hissing and rattling as it slithered on its way. The sounds of coyotes, calling out mournfully to each other, permeated the night air long after most visitors had left the park.

In the mornings, a tenuous mist covered the river and spilled over its banks. Salmon breached the surface in search of food. Sometimes I found my clothes damp from having unintentionally spent the entire night meditating outdoors.

The longer I kept that routine, the stronger my mind became and the more comfortable I was with being me. I realized one day, as I watched the sun come up over the horizon, that I loved my life. This moment had been waiting for me since my last suicide attempt.

Some of my older friends now had higher paying jobs or new titles. Others were getting married, having children. They were buying condos and home entertainment systems. They had credit cards and new cars. It was easy to see that all my friends were passing me by in terms of social climbing, status and financial security. They were involved in all these heavy adult concerns, and quite frankly, it was easy for me to stay unattached. I didn't want to alter my lifestyle to catch up with them. I didn't need the stress of having more things to worry about.

Mostly, I went over to where all my friends were hanging out on a Friday or Saturday evening, to smoke a joint, have a beer and watch *Babylon 5* and *The Simpsons* with them. Then we would all go back to our own worlds. Mine was down by the river at the edge of the woods.

CHAPTER 18

RECONSTRUCTION

A few months earlier I had learned some martial arts techniques that used strong movements involving the elbows. Very specific postures called for dropping your elbow down your center line resulting in an internal downward pressure that went through the arm and shoulder, into the shoulder blades and created a force vector along my ribs.

These elbow sinking techniques, when combined with the breathing and pulsing movements I had learned at the spinal chi gung retreat eight months earlier, served to create a continual wave of inner-directed downward pressure on my upper body when I practiced. As a result, something horrible and wonderful was about to happen.

Where my chiropractor's abilities had ended, the chi gung had taken over. The first ribs on both sides of my chest that had been slowly migrating upwards from years of bracing tension, began to migrate back down to their natural position, considerably faster than they had gone up. There was little warning that this was about to happen, apart from my body's attempt to communicate this to me via sensations of impending doom a few days in advance.

Dreadful anxiety began to come over me in periodic waves throughout the day. I would be doing my tasks at work when suddenly a strange feeling would wash over me, tinged with a knowing that something awful was going to happen soon. Generally speaking, I was mostly calm at that point in my life, so the anxiety attacks were definitely out of place. But recently a critical amount of connective tissue had finally softened to the point of being unable to unnaturally support my first ribs anymore. When that happened, my upward-migrating ribs began to come back down. First the left one, then, about a week later, the right.

The process was unbelievably destabilizing. When it began, I could not exert any force into my left arm without feeling excruciating, mind-blanking bursts of pain. There was a grating, grinding sound issuing from my ribs with an accompanying sense of ripping on the inside as I articulated my arm.

No way could I perform my job functions in this condition. I couldn't even ride my bike home from work. A coworker drove me home on lunch break, with my bike in the back of his truck.

When he dropped me off, I went into my sanctum to meditate. As I deep-scanned my body and performed internal systems checks, I figured out what was going on. I gained a sense of my inner events as a kind of plate tectonics.

The next day, I couldn't even hold a cup of coffee in my left hand. The weight of the cup put sheer forces through all the muscles of my arm and shoulder, directly onto my rib, and the dragging-down effect caused a tearing sensation that made me scream out loud. I would be calling in sick to work today.

This was not good. As long as I didn't move, everything seemed okay. The minute I tried to do anything involving my left arm, all hell broke loose.

In my practice I had been doing the opposite of what my chiropractor had tried with no effect. For sustained periods of time, I held these various postures and used the spinal chi gung to put tiny force vectors on my ribs from the inside. As I did this, I tried to listen acutely to what they were doing to my insides, second by second. I was trying to cause my ribs come down. I had no idea that it would happen like this.

There was one posture that I was doing quite a bit of. It involved holding one arm out with fingers stretched and the elbow sinking and it had put considerable downward pressure on my ribs. Now, as I tried to hold that posture as gently as I could, electrical spasms rippled across my pectoral muscles, neck and face. That whole area was heavily inflamed and sweat poured off of me. On impulse, I went over to my mirrored closet door.

Amazed, I saw that my left shoulder was substantially lower than it had been before. The internal changes were now visibly obvious on the outside. My whole upper body was starting to sink down. How long would it take before it stopped? I had no way of knowing. You can't force the body to heal or change much faster than it's capable of.

After a week away from work, it was apparent that I could not guarantee any functional stability on a day-to-day basis. I lived paycheck-to-paycheck at the current job I had. Saving up for various teachings and the occasional chiropractor visit stretched my finances to the max, and I had little in the way of savings. I went to my boss to get my last paycheck. She couldn't keep my position open. I needed to be replaced if I could not show up and punch in on time.

Sometimes, folks can be daft and blissfully simple, even with the best of intentions. When my boss, a petite older woman named Virginia, asked me, "Why don't you just get surgery on your ribs?" my jaw almost dropped to the floor. I was flabbergasted with sheer incredulity.

Who did she think I was? She paid me $300 a week to push boxes around in a warehouse. She knew I was unmarried and had no health insurance. Where was the money for the consultations with specialists, for assessments, and the surgery going to come from? Who was going to pay my cost of living during this down-time?

Those were my immediate concerns. Keeping a roof over my head when I didn't have the means to do so anymore. I couldn't go on workers compensation because it was not work that caused me to be disabled.

My chiropractor put me on limited disability, which took a couple weeks before it was all sorted out. When I got my first check, it was about $100 and I was appalled. This would feed me for a month. No more organic foods, herbal teas, and quality vitamins until further notice.

My money supply was drying up. My rent was paid, up to a point. My deposit could cover another month and that was it. I would be evicted if I couldn't pay. I had about ten weeks before I would lose my beloved apartment sanctuary that had allowed me to create a safe and sane space to heal for the last two and a half years.

I felt pangs of regret at the situation I was in. My isolationist and anti-social attitude that I felt I needed to maintain, in order to foster a healing environment of personal growth, was working against me. I had no family support to speak of. My few friends couldn't help me much and my lack of social networks meant also no support from others.

Without a job for the next ten weeks, I worked on myself all day long or as much as I could endure. If I was going to be healed, it was up to me to continue the process. I certainly did not want to go back to where I was with my lung expansion volume being slowly reduced over time as my ribs fused together.

The longer it went on, the more I did endure. I could perform a certain amount of the most gentle tai chi and chi gung before my ribs became inflamed and the electrical shocks resumed. At those times I could do nothing but sit absolutely still and endure it. With the inflammation and shocks I also experienced palsy. My left shoulder would jerk up and my head would twitch to the left to meet it. That was part of the actual tissue change.

The muscles in my neck, shoulders and upper back had two conflicting nervous system impulses. The first impulse was the old ingrained pattern. That impulse caused my shoulders to tense and rise and my neck to contract and stiffen as I braced for the impact of life. The second and new impulse that I was deliberately patterning into myself was to relax, and let go, and to release.

Sometimes my shoulder would float back up to its old elevation for a bit. At others, it settled down until the tip of my shoulder was lower than my clavicle. Occasionally the impulses clashed in an electrical storm which rippled visibly in micro-twitches across the skin of my face, neck and chest. Then I would just sit there and twitch, and twitch, and twitch some more.

With those two ribs seemingly floating around, combined with the pain and weakness and the muscle seizures, I felt always on the verge of completely coming apart at the seams. Not just physically but emotionally and mentally also, because it's all connected, and what happens on one level invariably causes an effect at another. While I was being mindful of and fully present in the midst of that maelstrom, I was working directly with the first four Bodies of Being according to Taoist theory.

It was a great blow to my ego to find myself disabled in my early twenties. Unless you had a trained eye or witnessed one of my electrical storms firsthand, it didn't look like there was anything obviously wrong with me. Actually just the opposite. When my shoulder was settled down, I had better all-over body alignments and moved more gracefully.

On good days I could carry a bag or two of groceries in my left hand just fine. On bad days I couldn't even move my arm at all without shrieking in agony.

That made me feel really insecure. To know that I could not even handle light loads was one thing. But what would happen if I got assaulted? I couldn't wrestle, block, or hit back with that arm. For the first time in years I couldn't expect to be able to defend myself effectively. The awareness of my current physical vulnerability, combined with the pressure of the clock ticking down on how long I could live here without income, caused me the first real stress in years.

I did my best to handle it by continuing to dissolve. I lived one day at a time, even one hour at a time, trying to maintain balance and peace in my inner world.

When you are stuck indoors and there is nothing you can do except sit still hour after hour, there is no escape from your inner world. Tai chi was of limited value as a distraction. There was only so much of it I could do before the external movements caused internal movements that were too much for me to take.

When I sat back down from one of these short, cautious, exploratory tai chi routines, repressed grief, rage, and anxiety I had no idea still existed, tore out from my insides and overwhelmed me in huge waves. I would just start weeping. It was like someone was randomly hitting my emotional switches or whimsically changing my hormone balance.

One moment I would be carefully wrapping my awareness around my ribs and using deep breathing to pressurize them, and the next second I wanted to kill myself. I wanted to give up. It felt like I had been fighting and holding on forever.

I couldn't always be sure whether I was actually healing or hurting myself. I wanted to smash my head into a wall in frustration. Feeling that particular impulse, made me realize that my rationality was beginning to slip and slide as well.

This injury proved to have one advantage. It created a fissure of vulnerability that went straight to my core where I held my deepest feelings about myself. That rift in my psyche served as an access point to get inside and accurately sense what was going on at a deeper level.

It might have taken years for some of these emotional memories to percolate up on their own as time allowed them to heal at their own pace. This was a perfect opportunity to go inside myself and do some major psychological and emotional house cleaning while these issues were right at hand, begging for resolution.

For the better part of a year I had been working on gaining precision control of my various vertebrae. When I showed these techniques to my chiropractor, he told me respectfully, "You might know more about spinal repair than I do." He asked me to come in and demonstrate that material to several of his colleagues. When I did so the next day, they were duly impressed. I told them not to worry about me setting up shop and taking their business. "Controlling your body like this is not easy to learn, or easy to do and in this day and age, most people are going to opt for a quick adjustment rather than take the time to learn spinal chi gung." I explained.

In the process of dealing with my ribs I had to delve deeper into the material itself in ways that seemed a natural extension of what I learned already. After awhile, I was able to move one individual rib at a time. Because of this, I could directly effect the speed at which they came down. It was apparent that with some control over my spine and ribs I was directly affecting my nervous system, and there was a real risk that I could screw myself up good with these techniques if I overdid it. I had to be very aware and pay close attention to my internal feedback, for when something felt right or wrong.

If I messed up my neurological functioning, there was no one I could turn to for help. I was on my own and it remained to be seen whether I was too far in over my head. Mr. Frantzis had used this chi gung to fix his broken back. I had developed a belief in myself and my abilities in recent years and I sensed I could do this if I stuck with it. I didn't have any other choice.

I passed the ten weeks that followed after losing my job either in my apartment or at the American River, trying desperately to heal myself. I was able to dissolve and resolve all manner of attachments, aversions, fixations, feelings and all this dark matter inside me that had no name or function but obscured my consciousness and imposed gaps in my awareness wherever I found it.

As I dissolved this stuff, my sanity and stability came back more solid and certain than before. Every couple of days I was a new person, freed from the bondage of some of my emotional and psychological pain. It distinctly felt like growing up. I was finally getting over myself. By practicing gentleness, I had cultivated a certain amount of affection towards the organism that carried my consciousness. It had been through a lot. I didn't want to hurt it anymore, unnecessarily.

At the zero hour, I called the only person that might possibly be able to help me. Back East in my hometown, my brother shared a house with another guy I knew from junior high, and there was some room where I could chill out for awhile. After almost exactly three years to the month, I returned to New Hampshire to recuperate from my disability.

* * *

Things did not bode well from the moment my brother picked me up. He didn't have any kind of room in his car for my things. As soon as my stuff was somehow squashed in, most of the visibility in the windows was gone.

Then, as if driving down the highway without obstruction free windows didn't call out for notice, his car seemed deliberately decorated inside and out to attract attention from highway patrol. And he drove in the left lane. Very fast.

I had survived the last three years by maintaining a studiously low profile and now Byron was drawing attention to us both. I had arrived in New England calm and relaxed, and within thirty minutes of driving to his place I was struggling to keep my cool and not to succumb to anxiety for my safety and anger at him for subjecting me to this.

The situation quickly got worse upon arriving at his apartment, for it was a complete disaster. It was absolutely disgusting, with bottles, trash and junk piled everywhere. The kitchen, the bathroom, his other rooms were all unclean and chaotic. After years of living in my spare and organized environment, his slovenliness was a constant assault on my stress levels.

He had cleared a patch on the floor where I might put my bedroll. When I woke up the next day, it was to the sound of something skittering across the hardwood floor. I opened one eye in time to see a piece of cat feces, lying mere inches from my face. It was not there long, as an enormous and overfed cat streaked by, attacking it's own refuse and batting it across the floor in another direction like a hockey puck.

As I looked around further, I saw my brother at his desk, smoking a cigarette. A grey haze hovered about his head while he studied something on his computer monitor. To come awake into such a grungy and unpleasant space, with cat poop skating by my head, in a enclosed room filling up with fresh cigarette smoke, made me instantly regret coming here.

This arrangement could not and did not last long.

Some of my old friends from junior high lived together in a huge house nearby. As luck would have it, they had an untenanted bedroom I could use for the time being.

I was not entirely freeloading. I had enough money to buy my own food for awhile. I had brought gifts of potent botanicals from the west coast that stupefied them to their delight while I regaled them with stories of life on the other side of the country, living near big city culture.

The best part of this arrangement was the park across the street. It was not the American River Conservancy, but it was reasonably spacious for a small town park. It provided a wide open area where I could practice internal martial arts outdoors.

I noticed an interesting thing as I spent several hours a day outdoors, acclimating myself to the increasingly cold temperatures. Falling leaves and some partly cloudy skies didn't seem to dent my emotional stability at all. The consistent practice of meditation and tai chi had slowly grown in me a core of emotional and cognitive stability that I could rely on. I now enjoyed the changing seasons.

My old friends and classmates partied hard, several times a week. I found the house filled with strangers on weekends. The alcohol flowed and the rooms filled up with loud music, smoke and conversation. Going to a party and having a few beers in that communal fog and noise did not pop any of my screws loose. It didn't make me manic. I always knew when I was approaching my safety tolerance. When I reached it, I went back to my room or to the park to meditate and decompress. I had tons of time to myself to work on healing. I did party a little and had to deal with a house full of people when I had lived only with myself for so long.

This situation however, was not ideal. I still had no job and my money was almost spent. With my sanctuary apartment gone, I would've been homeless without the generosity of my old school friends. On top of that, I had this lingering internal healing process going on, with no indication as to when it would end. My future was completely up in the air.

Under these circumstances, and adding the increasingly dreary weather and all the stress I was under, it would be reasonable to expect that I might be a little depressed. But I wasn't. My self-esteem and inner purpose never wavered. I took it one day at a time and paid attention to my inner states while striving to remain calm and centered, no matter what I was facing.

For the next three months I lived there, working on physical therapy. I integrated myself better than I had ever been before. I seemed to have brought some of California's warm weather with me, because the snow was late this year and it was not until mid-December, when it finally came down hard and covered the ground for the rest of winter.

After New Year the rent was going up. My housemates needed to rent my room to a paying tenant. I got a fresh infusion of a couple hundred dollars cash. A last minute gift from my father, who was back in the area for the holidays. With less than two months to go before my twenty-fourth birthday, I headed back to California. In the event that I had to live on the street again, my chances of survival were higher if I lived in a place without snow and freezing temperatures.

When I arrived in Sacramento, Glenda, an older woman whom I had met at an aikido and yoga studio, picked me up. She let me stay with her for a couple days, to clean up and get some real sleep. Then she drove me down to a homeless shelter and wished me good luck.

It took me two or three days to figure out that the homeless outreach programs were a bad joke, created only to make Sacramento city officials feel better about themselves. In practice, it's not that dissimilar from other institutional programs. You spend ages standing around, waiting in the food line. Waiting for the buses to take you to the emergency overflow shelters. Waiting to be told to get off the bus, and take a bed and a sleeping bag.

To actually get a room in the program, you had to spend hours in lines to be present at specific times of the day when the available rooms were announced. If you weren't in the line at the right time, you lost the room or your place on the list. There was no time, between morning buses, breakfast and dinner lines and staying available to keep your spot on the waiting list for a room, to actually take the time to range as far as job hunting requires.

You were stuck by an umbilicus of policy and structure to get any of these benefits. If you came back too late, you missed dinner, a bed in the emergency overflow shelter and a chance at a long term indoor bed. It seemed inherently designed to keep needy people bound to those services. It certainly gave the outreach program employees a paycheck.

This was just not going to do and that's when I become a transitory homeless person. I had to be careful while lugging around my things (my books and such were all in storage at my friend Julian's place), so as not to overdo it so soon on my ribs, just in case. I spent several nights sleeping in the park, under the bridge that carries Sunrise Boulevard over the American River.

It was the rainy season, which meant job hunting in torrential, wind-driven diagonal downpours. My dietary staple consisted of sandwiches I made from canned tuna and whole grain bread. When you are outdoors, at the fringes of an urban area, and you are aware of other homeless camps nearby, you don't really sleep, but doze intermittently. It was like an indefinite camping trip that you are ill prepared for.

After awhile it gets harder and harder to keep decent looking, enough at least to score a job interview. You haven't showered in days and your clothes stink. You are carrying all your stuff around like a hermit crab. That was quite stressful and it was a struggle to stay optimistic for awhile.

A lot of people equate homelessness with mental health issues. People don't look you in the eye anymore if they think you're homeless. It's hard for a potential employer to take the risk to go out on a limb and give that smelly and unkempt person a job. The circumstances are self-perpetuating and there are too many pressures holding you down when you don't have a physical address, a phone number or a place to clean yourself up. Once you drop off the edge of civilized society like that, it's hard to climb back up.

Even with my tai chi to keep me in shape, I was losing weight and couldn't sleep well. I was always hungry and I was starting to look a bit haggard. I did get gloomy and bummed out. I never actually got mortally depressed or felt like hurting myself and ending it all. Somewhere out there someone was suffering worse than I was. I told myself that, again and again, until I accepted it and made the best of it, while it lasted.

One day I stopped by my old employer's factory on impulse, to see if they were hiring again. While I was waiting for the boss to come off the factory floor, I made quick use of the restroom, to arrange my hair, brush my teeth and wash my face before seeing him.

We sat down in Paul's office and I begged him for one day's work, paid in cash, so I could continue my job hunt. He agreed. Then he asked me what happened after they laid me off some eight months ago. I gave him the whole story, as candidly as I could.

I told him about the structural problems, and being unable to work the warehouse job that had followed this one. I told Paul about the disability and how I spent the last five months rebuilding my body so I could work again. I felt strong enough to do manual labor again and I needed a job desperately, so I could get some kind of normalcy and safety back in my life.

"Well, don't worry," Paul said, "you are not spending another night outside." I would be coming home with him and his wife after work that day. He gave me a job, even though there wasn't much for me to do besides sweep the floors and count inventory until the rainy season was really over. He loaned me a thousand dollars to get a room share tenancy, buy new clothes, and a new mountain bike to get me to work.

I spent a couple of days at their luxury home in El Dorado Hills, eating sumptuous meals with my employers. My boss's wife, Jody, had washed all my clothes while I was taking a long bath in their giant tub. When I was finally alone, I cried. I was so grateful. I just wanted my simple and uncomplicated life back, and with a job and fresh capital I could do that.

They understood, that from time to time I might need a break to avoid stressing my ribs. I had invested a lot of effort to restoring stable function in my arms. As long as I didn't fall back in production, I could take time out and keep my own schedule, work half days, or go home early. It was a one-of-a-kind deal that allowed me to work on my body and not push my limits while still being able to pay the bills.

Occasionally, when they flew back to the east coast to take week long vacations in Martha's Vineyard, they paid me to watch their huge, expensive house and to feed their geriatric pets. They told me to help myself to anything I wanted. It was a chance to do better for them than I had done with my grandparents, the last time someone had taken me in.

I kept my full-time job with them for the next three and a half years, before the economic fallout from September 11, 2001, began closing down small business in the industrial sector. Theirs was one of the ones that fell, eventually. Before it did, I earned several raises and ran my own department in the shop, taking care of the custom electrical wiring for the computer server racks and workstations that we fabricated there.

Paul, my boss, and his wife Jody really took me in. Perhaps they felt I deserved a little better than I'd had. Thanks to their generosity, I climbed back out of the hole and got my life back the way I wanted it.

A few weeks later I moved into a modern home in a good neighborhood. Although officially I had to share the house with its owner, a yuppie businessman-type guy, I practically had the house and entire backyard all to myself because he was hardly ever at home.

I got back to practicing in the park again, next to the American River. On the weekends I gradually created a stone platform in the middle of the river and a stepping stone path that allowed me to walk out to it without getting my feet wet. It was big and stable enough to practice standing trainings or have a long sit. I spent hundreds of hours practicing mind-body disciplines on my stone platform.

Eventually, meditating for ten, twelve hours at a time became no big deal. My experience repairing my ribs and getting tons of emotional and psychological pain out of me, allowed me to keep my mind centered easily. It took me ten minutes or less to get into it. I had no desire to move from where I felt so completely at peace with myself and at one with the purest forms of nature.

I didn't really have to move if I didn't want to, aside from biological needs. I stayed there, hour after hour, utterly content to simply be. I was fully present and in the moment, with absolutely nothing on my mind, and nothing that needed to be done.

That may seem anachronistic in our culture, something most people never imagine themselves doing. Our hectic pace of life and over-reliance on caffeinated beverages with extra-extra sugar to keep us going really makes what I was doing impossible for most folks.

But it's not impossible if you really go out of your way to do it. It does take time and training. I didn't get to meditating through an entire day and night the first year. There were levels of concentration that needed to be cultivated. There was a lot of internal disharmony that needed to be overcome before this was even remotely possible for me. I'd always imagined, ever since I was very young, that I was one of those who could do it. Too much influence from fantasy books and sci-fi movies back then, I suppose.

It's also easy, once you have achieved a certain amount of quality inner peace and respite from your issues, to think you're done. Mission complete. That is when you should be on an even greater lookout for inner disturbances. If you're feeling good all the time, then why keep going? I had been depression free for almost four years at this point. Even the introduction of severe stress into my life, including a two-week stint being homeless, had not destabilized me much or for long.

It's easier to be motivated to meditate when you are actually feeling physical or emotional pain. It gives you impetus to relieve it. When you are not overwrought, melancholic or apoplectic, and you're calm all the time, it can seem like there is nothing to work on.

I became skeptical that I had really figured out and fixed everything that needed to be fixed. I didn't think the Universe would let me off that easy. I knew I had a lot of issues, and at this point I had resolved a large portion of the small and medium sized ones. Enough to improve the quality of my life and my psychological stability significantly.

CHAPTER 19

REVELATIONS

As 1999 closed out and year 2000 approached, my brother Byron came out to be in my vicinity in case something happened. When I say "in case something happened," what I really mean is that we were waiting for the end of the world as we knew it. You can go ahead and laugh. I laugh too when I think about it now. But one of the biggest, longest running sources of my depression was constantly being scared of and ready for the end of the world.

Ever since we were kids we were bombarded with messages that the world was in imminent danger of ending. On television we saw documentaries about the power of the atomic bomb. As a kid I had nightmares about it. I saw the nuclear blast wave ripping through our neighborhood in my dreams. I owned several apocalyptic and post nuclear fallout science fiction books. We had movies titled *Mad Max*, *Wargames*, *Terminator* and *Red Dawn* back then which provided Doomsday scenarios for my fertile imagination.

I could even trace my personal seed of fear and preparedness to a movie I saw as a kid, called *The Day After*, a post-nuclear holocaust film that aired on public television in the early 1980s. That movie subtly traumatized me. I would fantasize about bomb shelters and nuclear winter and doodle detailed mushroom clouds rising over shattered urban landscapes in my notebooks.

Growing up, I realized one day that good grades were not going to open too many doors on the day that civilization reverted to the Stone Age. My parents I'd thought fools for getting mad at us children over poor grades, as the collective quality of our schoolwork gradually declined owing to the accumulating years of stress at home. None of that mattered to me back then. I slowly ceased to care about performing up to expectation. I tuned out whatever the teacher was saying while I imagined graduates of business management courses killing each other in their three-piece suits as they scavenged for food in a post-holocaust wasteland.

To this day, I don't know how the other kids paid attention in class during school. How can people choose what they want to be when they grow up, if there is no world to grow up in? Our whole "culture" seemed asinine to me. I had different ideas: My career track was to become a survivor of WWIII.

The Berlin Wall came down and it didn't happen.

The Soviet Union collapsed and it didn't happen.

The Gulf Wars happened and still, no rain of nukes.

Year 2000 seemed like a good chance for anarchy. People everywhere were already freaking out that computer networks worldwide, unable to handle the change of the millennium, would collapse. My brother and I were effected by Y2K fever too.

We were very well prepared. We had all manner of outdoor survival and paramilitary gear, and, of course, weapons. Our stockpiles included everything from tools and bottled water to batteries and a years supply of Raman noodles. With everything organized, we waited together in Byron's armored four-wheel drive in a remote area overlooking a small town, as the minutes counted down to midnight, December 31, 1999.

Zero hour came and went, nothing happened. But we continued to wait. Thirty minutes. An hour. It takes time for ICBMs to travel around the world and for chaos, looting and rioting to get really rolling. We waited for two hours and then another. We monitored radio stations and scanned the emergency bands. No panic and "War of the Worlds" announcements. No screaming reports of risen dead walking the streets. Nothing. Just another ordinary New Year's Day.

I felt let down and very disappointed. As I explored that feeling, I discovered that deep inside, some part of me wanted it all to go down. Even longed for it. As strange as it may sound, my way of coping with the Cold War panic as a child was to hope Armageddon would happen so we could all quit waiting for it. At the very least we'd get out of school.

After a period, I came to accept that the collapse of civilization was probably never going to happen. There would be major disasters here and there, as humanity fumbles and matures as a species. But it was unlikely that there would be a global Apocalypse. I am sure Byron was also a bit let down. He thought the same way I did. We didn't want to be the ones caught with our pants down because of denial or inability to seriously consider that kind of reality. He stuck around for awhile to see some of northern California. Ultimately, he ended up moving back East.

* * *

It was not long after the anticlimactic finale to Y2K, when I went inside my mind to deliberately root out lingering emotional blocks, traumas, and assorted demons. In my current state I would often sit for hours every day, for weeks, without finding anything that needed resolving.

Since I didn't seem to have anything concrete to work with, I focused on the more intangible aspects of my inner world. A lot of people who get really involved in meditation sooner or later encounter various kinds of disconnection and fog inside themselves. Areas that seem to resist opening themselves up to your awareness. These places are gaps in your consciousness.

This gapping can manifest in the form of twenty minutes of spaced out limbo during a two hour meditation session, or it can be several micro-gaps in your conscious awareness that occur in a single second. Trying to penetrate these gaps can be like walking into an unfamiliar and pitch-black room that you are navigating with one arm outstretched.

"Dark matter" is the colloquial term I use to describe obstacles that present themselves to your mind's eye and which can interrupt continual mindfulness. Inside or beyond them you can find all manner of physical or emotional pain and memories that you've tried really hard to forget.

Sometimes these dark areas have nothing at all to do with emotional issues. Mental fog in particular can be the result of physical trauma to the head. All manner of central nervous system depressants can induce this fog. It can be caused by electro-convulsive therapy and chemotherapy as well as by antipsychotics.

Internal fog may not have any apparent source whatsoever. It's just there, clouding your inner landscape. These dark gaps can conceal both good and bad things about ourselves or an assortment of mundane and exotic issues. Regardless of its cause, dark matter distorts our self-image and obfuscates our true nature. Dissolving through it is of supreme importance if you are trying to resolve your spiritual problems and become fully present.

During that time I had an appointment with the Sacramento DMV to renew my I.D. and had to take public transit through a familiar neighborhood, Oak Park, to get there. As a consequence of clearing out the psychological and emotional turbulence inside myself, I became more sensitive to what we might call "static" or "bad vibes" coming from other people.

As the locals boarded the bus, I could acutely feel sadness, anger and other negative static coming from them. Their mental and emotional states polluted the area around them. It was easy to pick up if you were paying attention to how quiet it had been before that person came along.

Later that day, as I was sitting and dissolving any lingering static I might have picked up from my sojourn downtown, I felt smug about my abilities. At least I made sure I was calm and relaxed before I went out into public, and as a result couldn't possibly be adding to the ambient negativity in the world. On the heels of that train of thought, my cold inner rational voice woke up with a start and its tone dripped with undisguised ridicule and sarcasm as it mocked me.

Of course you don't know anything about poisoning your own life and the lives of people around you.

You've never scowled or frowned and given people hard stares. You've never spun lies and deceptions.

You've never stalked or intimidated or assaulted anyone, right? You think you're virtuous now – that's what it is, isn't it?

Do you honestly think a couple years of hiding in the woods, literally sitting on your ass, avoiding the world, somehow offsets all the things you've done to others?

You stand accused of being a gross emotional polluter and are hereby charged with dumping millions of gallons of anger, hate and depression into the world for other people to feel.

How do you plead?

In that moment, images of nearly every single act of violence that I ever committed visited me all once. Vivid, anger-filled flashbacks were set loose to strobe across my inner eye. As I freshly relived those experiences, I became the walls that I had punched and slapped, when my temper was out control. I was just a piece of Sheetrock or wood paneling minding my own business when, out of nowhere, I was attacked and a great discharge of rage was buried into my atoms.

I felt and experienced the effects of every negative emotion that I had unwittingly discharged into the air over the years. A terrible truth became obvious to me: I myself had been one of the biggest emotional polluters that I'd ever met. In a flash of insight, the scales were lifted from my eyes and I understood the terrible crime that I had committed upon my fellow human being because of my vanity, my ego, and my presumption. I had truly believed I was special, and that somehow I had been chosen to suffer. In my anger and my desire to attach special meaning to my experiences, I had assumed I was right and the world was wrong.

I had gone from sitting in a half lotus with my spine erect, to curled up in a fetal ball on the floor, writhing and twisting. The force that pulled me down seemed to increase in magnitude in proportion to my growing awareness of the profundity of this monstrous accusation. Heat began to flash all through me.

A distant sound of wailing, tinged with agonizing grief, was coming from somewhere. Sweat started to pour off me. Any second now, I thought, I was going to smell smoke. I gnashed my teeth, pulled my hair, and clawed my face with my fingernails. Then my entire body seemed to ignite all at once from the intensity of my inner loathing. As I lay there, burning, being consumed by a spiritual conflagration, my thoughts and inner turbulence churned on.

How could I have been such a fool, and not seen what I was doing?

Was I really just a horrible person, pretending to be a good one?

Has all this work been for nothing?

My whole being was wracked with an incredible spiritual pain. A composite agony made of wounded pride, loss and helplessness, as well as an unfinished duty of righteous revenge and a mounting sense of deep remorse. A part of me believed that I needed to be hurt far worse that this to atone. That maybe it might even be best if I just died. Then I would never hurt anyone again. I didn't deserve to be alive.

"Please, kill me," I begged to the Universe aloud through clenched teeth.

But an inner voice spoke to me then and told me that I truly had not known better when I did what I did. It was a new awareness. A new level of responsibility.

Within that knowing was the realization that I didn't need to die or be endlessly chastised for what I'd done. There wasn't any virtue or redemption to be had in more self-punishment or recrimination. So I found it within me to forgive myself for my ignorance, and the soul-fire was extinguished. A tremendous weight was lifted from me.

Once I had forgiven myself, I gained the ability to forgive others. My thoughts went to the black book of names in my mind, to people who had it coming to them. For a long time, I felt the only way to take the pressure out of my mind would be to seriously maim these people someday, sooner or later, so I could look them in the eye and ask, "Has the idea that someone might come back to exact revenge for your crimes ever occurred to you?" Or similarly, "Do you now feel remorse for what you did to me?"

To cope with traumatic events, some people dissociate or develop amnesia. But my mind used to replay traumas and violence over and over again in flashbacks and "intrusive thoughts." Those experiences echoed in my head long after they had actually occurred and were a major source of my revenge obsession. Before I learned proper meditation, smoking marijuana was my primary means of dealing with the intensity of those memories.

I took to summoning the faces of everyone that I had really wanted to kill in my life. People whose deaths I thought would make me feel better and relieve the pressure in my head. The first person I ever imagined killing was my stepfather. When I was about eight or nine years old, I had gone so far as to stalk Tim in the middle of the night, holding a 12-inch carver over his chest as he slept.

After I forgave him, I proceeded with my inept social worker, then certain psychiatric staff and the kids from my junior high who had chased me home after school and thrown rocks at me all those years ago. As I dissolved and let go of my hatred for them, a huge chunk of inner compulsion fell away, like an iceberg calved from a glacier. With it went tension, obsessive thoughts, toxic anger, injured pride and an enormous volume of racing, antagonizing voices in my head. One by one, I erased their names out of my black book and in the process I liberated myself of the need to get back at them to even the score.

Perhaps the hardest person to forgive was my mother. Sarah created the family dynamic that had us all currying to win favor and betraying each other. It was a toxic environment that fostered the spying and mistrust, the whispered conversation and secret plotting we did. Then, when she decided that she had had enough, she took her toys and went home, metaphorically speaking; leaving me to deal with the house, my violent stepfather and my neurotic brother. Later she gave me up to the State.

In the last six months before I had turned eighteen, I sent her an emotional letter, asking if she would take me back, allow me to sleep on the floor, go to a local school and get a job to prepare for being a legal adult. In my desire to finish my teenage years in a normal setting, I agreed we could start over and forget the past. Sarah left me in limbo for weeks before I finally got myself out of Bennington School. She never replied to me, and in so doing abandoned me for a third time.

I finally came to grips with the reality that she didn't want me in her life anymore. I accepted it and moved on. Accepting something like that is one thing, but forgiving it? There was too much emotional blood spilled.

There existed in me a childhood love for her that was not merely unrequited, but punished. You can only break someone's heart so many times, until the place where love exists goes cold and dead inside. The truth was that I hated her, knowing intellectually that my hate was a burden. How could I ever find it in me to forgive her?

I found a path to forgiveness through empathy and compassion. I put myself in her shoes, tried to experience her world and see our family life from her eyes. I retraced events from childhood with adult understanding and tried to imagine what she went through to make those decisions.

When I realized that I might have done the exact same thing, I finally developed a little compassion. I knew I was fundamentally not all that different from her. No better and no worse. I forgave us both simultaneously. Tears of relief of no longer having to carry that burden flowed down my face.

When I forgave her, I stopped hating her. That didn't mean that I started loving her. I didn't forgive her because she deserved it, but because it was impeding my growth and emotional stability by preventing me from moving on.

* * *

Meditation and dissolving helped me get over another issue as well. Physical contact with anyone whom I was not immediately sexually involved with (or sparring with) was repugnant to me for a long time. I couldn't stand to be patted on the shoulder, arm or back. Simply performing the obligatory embrace of my relatives when I came to visit in my teens was awkward and unpleasant to me.

It was very threatening to allow any human being inside the "assault zone," an area extending equally in all directions away from me about half as far as I could extend my fist. Consequently, I needed a lot more space between me and other people to feel at ease. Eventually, I was able to dissolve the memories and triggers associated with my revulsion of physical contact. These days I no longer have a problem receiving affection or being near people.

Between 1998 and 1999 Master Bruce Frantzis released two books, *Relaxing into your Being* and *The Great Stillness* about the Taoist Water Method of meditation. Those two books were my bibles, and they were never far from my hand.

Shortly after the first of these books came out, he offered a three hour sit and lecture at a university in Tempe, Arizona. I took a Greyhound bus from Sacramento all the way to Tempe and back again (a sixteen-hour round trip) just to attend that lecture.

In the summer of 2000 he was holding his first west coast meditation retreat covering the material in those two books. I saved up and trained myself for that event months in advance. During that week in Sonoma County I had a number of break-throughs.

On the third day we were meditating and working on gently dissolving tension in our hearts. While I was dissolving, I found myself spontaneously laughing. First a smile. Then a chuckle. Then real mirth.

All my life I had taken everything seriously. So seriously, that I was never able to see the humor in the ironies in my life. Instead I had become cynical, thinking I'd seen it all. Now I giggled like a fool while I was standing in line for the buffet lunch. Once freed of that block on my heart, I was able to appreciate, in a kind of George Carlin-esque way, how funny life could be. I never took myself or life quite as seriously ever again.

Towards the end of the retreat, before the start of our morning sit, I walked over to Bruce. I thanked him for his knowledge and for sharing the Water Method of Taoist meditation with the world. I told him about some of my successes with it and what I was experiencing now.

He shook my hand, congratulating me. Then he asked me to tell the audience what I had told him. I was taken aback for a moment. I had never addressed a group of people like this before. Everyone present seemed to be my elder and my better. People had flown from other countries to be here. I had never talked about my mental health issues in public before.

I stood straight, addressed the gathering and told them what I had told Bruce. I admitted, "Ever since I began Taoist meditation I have been free of depression. I have not considered killing myself in over four years, which is a new record for me." I glanced over to Bruce for a prompt, and he gestured and told me in a low voice, "Tell them the rest of it."

So I talked about my dissolving practice, that over the years I resolved many things and for some time I achieved a level of stability. "Recently I have been going ever deeper into my Being and the ride is becoming pretty wild the closer I get to the heart of my consciousness." I paused, took a breath and continued, "Dedicated meditation practice has made my existence bearable and continues to motivate me to stick around and see what else life has in store for me."

The other attendees erupted in brief but enthusiastic applause. Some were nodding in affirmation. That evening an elderly couple came over to where I sat and asked to sit down and have dinner with me. I accepted them magnanimously. I couldn't imagine why anyone, especially folks three times my age, would want to share space and words with me.

They had been moved by my little speech. Both of them were in a late-life crisis. They had been alive for over six or seven decades. They both felt a strong need to understand what the meaning of their lives had been. I never imagined that some people contemplate suicide towards the end of their life, but it made sense.

In the months following the retreat I kept on meditating. I did about an hour or so of tai chi daily and spent the rest of my spare time in sitting meditation. I used my flexible work hours to compress my production time and to take Mondays and Fridays off. That way I could spend four days in a row meditating in shifts: morning, noon, and night.

As autumn progressed, I took a break. I had spent most of the last five years living this lifestyle and had won freedom from my PTSD symptoms, my schizoid symptoms and all manifestations of manic depression. I had completely forgotten that I had been diagnosed with incurable genetic diseases just ten years earlier. Mental illness no longer had any power over my day to day life. I gave myself a pat on the back for a job well done.

Now that I wasn't driven by a need to do martial arts all the time and taking a break from meditating, it was time to rediscover my other interests. All my life I've loved sketching panorama and scenic backgrounds. I discovered that modern video games were becoming more life-like and realistic every year. I started exploring the world of video game design and environment building.

Employment in the digital gaming industry is very competitive. In order to even consider putting out a resume that would be taken seriously, I would need to be able to do more than edit video game architecture. A functional knowledge of programming languages like Visual Basic and C++ would be essential as well as an investment in expensive modeling and design programs that are commonly used in the industry.

It basically meant I would need to take a couple of years to study it deeply, to get involved in it seriously. It meant prioritizing my life so that when I was not at work at the factory, I was on my computer at home working on graphics design, modeling, and animation. It meant staying abreast of ever-improving gaming technology and reading design publications. It would take up all my time and I didn't want to do that.

So I got back into my daily routine of training tai chi in the mornings and evenings once again. I had no need to do it, but I was driven internally to keep going. It had become such a natural part of my life that I could not do without those things for long. Soon enough I gave in to the inner compulsion to go back and meditate some more.

I can honestly say that at that point in my life I had dissolved and resolved nearly everything that I felt needed dissolving. I was no longer triggered whatsoever by deliberately recollecting traumatic events in my life. The weight of hate, guilt, and revenge was gone. I had no black book of names anymore. The intrusive voices, along with the violent imagery were all gone like they had never even existed in the first place.

There remained only one or two pressing issues to resolve. The nature of identity and purpose. It boiled down to a series of questions:

Who was I?
What did I want?
Was there anything worth living for, long term?
What exactly is this subjective knower and thinker and feeler?
Where is the location of this thing that asks these questions?

If I knew who I was, I would know what I wanted and what my purpose really was.

Over the years my personality had splintered. The first real break had been the creation of the survivor-protector self as a child. Then there was a manic, "grandiose" dreamer self in tandem with a depressive self. Each had its own set of capabilities and idiosyncrasies.

Everything I did seemed like one kind of behavioral performance or another. I was one kind of person when I was at work and another when I was out in public or socializing. A different personality manifested when I had solitude and privacy. I didn't understand the concept of simply "acting naturally" or "being myself." I didn't know which of these masks constituted the genuine "me."

As I had worked over the last few years on exploring the country of the mind, the number of distinctly different personalities had dwindled. At this point in my life I seemed driven by two separate but not entirely definable identities. Which one was the fabricated one and which the intrinsic one? To frame it another way – which was the false self and which was the real self?

That led me on an investigation of how we acquire personality traits, the old "nature or nurture" question. What was genetically determined and how much of my personality was the result of modeling others? As I started to wrap my mind around this topic, I slowly began to come face to face with a deep fear that had periodically gnawed at the fringes of my psyche over the years. What if there was another dimension at work here?

All my life I had been infatuated with ghost stories. While growing up I had some color illustrated children's books on ghosts and hauntings, and these books contained collected stories of phantom trains and boats, haunted woods and hotels.

As I grew older, I became involved in ritual magic and a variety of other occult practices. Some of which entailed channeling spirits, contacting the spirit world and summoning angels and demons by their secret names. I had spent time visiting supposedly haunted houses and cemeteries and tried to open myself to sensing other spirits.

When I had given up on God and turned to Satan to grant me the occult abilities needed to overthrow my oppressors, I had agreed to let my body share space with demons or entities if doing so would give me their powers. In my desperation to be delivered from the state residential treatment facility, I had once drawn an inverted pentagram on the floor of my room, sat in the center of it and prayed to Satan to possess me.

From age fourteen to age twenty I had tried to commit suicide no less than six times, with three of those attempts leading to prolonged states of unconsciousness or incapacitation. In addition, I had also done my share of tripping on hallucinogens. I wondered if the ounces of psilocybin and the half-sheet of LSD that I consumed during my early twenties might have made me vulnerable to spiritual possession somehow.

The last evening of the Taoist meditation retreat a few months earlier had entailed a final question and answer session, along with a lecture by Mr. Frantzis.

I asked Bruce if he believed in spiritual possession. Or more specifically, "In all your twenty years spent in China, India and Japan, have you ever encountered a case where a person seemed possessed?"

He was a moment in consideration before telling me, "Perhaps. Once. Possibly." But then he added, "I couldn't be certain."

I had asked him pointed questions before. A few years earlier, at a weekend chi gung seminar, I had asked Bruce, "How did the yogis and chi gung masters of antiquity discover things like: kundulini energy, chakras and acupuncture meridians in the first place?"

"They discovered those things inside themselves," Bruce told me. "As a result of going within."

Another time I asked him, while we were on lunch break at a retreat, "When you were discovering these techniques as you studied with master after master, you didn't learn the way you are teaching us here." I indicated the group of attendees around us, and continued, "How did you, personally, learn and actualize this material?"

"You really want to know?" Bruce asked rhetorically. "Generally, I was shown a technique once or twice, or had it unambiguously demonstrated on me. Then I was instructed to 'go away and practice,' until I could reproduce the process on my own."

As I ruminated over those past conversations, it became clear to me that the only way to find out conclusively if I was host to more than one kind of spiritual force or entity would be to go inside and find out for myself. I would need to take on this quest with the sincerity and acuity of the ancients who had discovered the seat of their consciousness on their own.

CHAPTER 20

POSSESSING ME

My first major crisis had been related to my mental illness. During the process of healing I became aware of many physical problems as well, results from badly misusing my body. Now, after restoring equilibrium to both of these areas, I entered yet another crisis, a spiritual one. This particular problem could only be solved by delving even deeper into myself to find the most subtle levels of spirit. The fifth, sixth and seventh Bodies of Being, according to Taoist cosmology.

The longer I thought about it the more I obsessed about it. I lay awake at night, analyzing the content of recent dreams and trying to sense if spirits were communicating with me via dream imagery. I started a specific form of occult training, spending hours of my time meditating in front of a full length mirror. I searched the eyes of my reflection long and hard for any glimmer of an alien presence. Who is it that looks, and sees, and perceives itself?

Assuming I was possessed, was this presence male, female, or an alien from another planet or dimension? Was it the ghost of an adult or a child or something else entirely? Possession could explain so many things, from certain voices in my head to specific dreams I'd had and some of my past feelings and behavior. But only if it were really true that those actions were compulsions from another entity inside me.

As my suspicion that my body-mind might be compromised grew, I began having petite anxiety attacks about it throughout the day. I couldn't concentrate at work. The need for this to have some kind of resolution so I could be at ease again was overwhelming. How could I ever be myself and know my wants and desires if I could never be sure who I was from one day or one hour to the next?

Business was slow during the winter months. I asked my boss for an indefinite leave of absence. The first two weeks were paid vacation, but after that I would be relying on my savings. I had enough to buffer myself and keep my bills paid, so I could probably take a month or two off before I was in financial hazard.

Once freed of the obligation to punch in every day, I turned all my energies into figuring out what I needed to do. The first half of the problem would be identifying the alien spirit. The other half of the problem would be figuring out exactly how to exorcise this being, once and for all.

I figured that the only way I could detect the presence of an alien entity would be to be continuously, experientially aware of where my spirit began and ended. In that way, once I knew which energies were me, could I know which energies belonged to some Other. The question then would be, what to do about it.

I spent hours trying to come up with an overall strategy. From a technical aspect there seemed like a finite number of ways for a spirit to enter and possess a human body. What would I do if I was a lost soul, desperately trying to cling to an organism so I could partake of the host's senses, feelings and thoughts?

Perhaps the easiest way to accomplish this would be to permeate the deepest core of my being in order to abide without detection while partaking of my senses. The most likely candidates would be my spine, my internal organs and heart or, most insidiously, my brain.

In any of those places it would have direct access to my nervous system and it could generate impulses and feelings into my subconscious that seemed to be my own. It's very proximity to my inner core could make it that much harder to detect. Much more so than if it was inhabiting an arm or a leg or a digit.

I had always imagined something like being possessed to be a spectacular contest of will that would cause seizures and voice changes and uncontrolled emotions or incoherent babbling, similar to what you see in movies or documentaries about tribal occult practices that involved channeling or trance states.

I couldn't recall a time when something like that had ever happened to me. Indeed, I began to suspect that the real thing would be much more subtle and seditious. Something more akin to a computer virus. Something that would install itself silently, line by line, until it was thoroughly rooted in the structure of the operating system.

It could have happened while I was sleeping, one night at a time. It could have lain dormant until I was least aware, and then built its own network of control, like a spider builds a web at night, unseen. Possession (hypothetically speaking) probably followed the paths of least resistance and acted in natural ways, instead of provoking one giant conniption of special effects.

This entity may have grown with me over time, manifesting in small ways, speaking to my subconscious and infecting me with thoughts or feelings not my own. Over the years it would've come to know my body fairly thoroughly. I doubted that dislodging something that entrenched would be easy. It would require an exorcism that was even more insidious and more subtle than itself.

As to that matter, there seemed only so many ways one could go about it. If I could contain this Other presence, perhaps I could attempt to send it into the light. I could try to coax it to go willingly, or I could resort to brute force.

This Other, if it was truly another spirit, was actually at a disadvantage. I too am a spirit and I had access to my own powers of concentration and awareness. I had immediate control over my voluntary nervous system and physical body. I had the energies of thought and emotion, and the power of the dissolving method at my disposal.

If gently coaxing and dissolving were not enough to eject this spirit, I could burn it out cell by cell, using the force of my will and intent like a supernova shockwave. It would be its presence versus the combined energy of all my Bodies of Being.

I would make this exorcism a ritual beginning with purification. I would draw upon my knowledge of chi gung theory to engineer custom techniques for this job. Techniques I had never been taught previously. This was no longer simply chi gung (energy work) but shen gung (spiritual work).

This entire experiment and process would require an enormous amount of physical and mental energy. I fasted for a day or so and took long baths. For a few days I didn't work on the exorcism itself but instead focused on the energy development practices of chi gung, tai chi and yoga.

Calm and rested, I continued to build a mass of concentrated awareness inside. I gathered my intent and my awareness into specific areas of my lower, middle and upper torso where, according to Taoist theory, energy centers, called *tantiens*, exist as a kind of internal energy transformer station.

Gradually, my overall intensity began to increase the longer I sustained this circulating ball of my concentration through the entire spectrum of my senses. When I perceived that I had attained the limits of the charge I could hold in my mind without it spilling over and causing racing thoughts or physical agitation, I began the process of turning my entire Being into an energy trap.

At this point and for the next week I would sit, stand or lie flat in my bedroom and listen inside like I had never listened before. The goal was to achieve a state of continual stillness and vigilance so complete that I would know the very microsecond a physical urge, an emotional impulse, or a subtle thought or image manifested, that could not possibly be originating from me.

The way to achieve such knowing would be to permeate every level of my being with my full presence and unlimited patience. I would wait out this Other until it made a move. In the instant of its movement, I would know where it was rooted, and I would bring this ball of awareness to bear on it from all sides, surrounding it and contracting around it, like a macrophage containing a foreign body within a cell.

In the process of simulating the act of possession, I believed the simplest way to invade a body to possess it would be to come from up above the host and moving downward through space. Enter the brain at the crown *chakra* and insinuate myself in the basal brain structures and spinal cord.

I had a considerable amount of practice, feeling the deepest levels of my physical structures. I had used that sensitivity to regrow the nerves in my crushed fingers. It had allowed me to control any of my vertebrate at will and eventually enabled me to move a single rib up, down, back or forward without any externally obvious movements at all.

For those reasons, I ruled out the possibility this entity idled away any of its downtime in any of my limbs, otherwise I would have noticed by now. Nor could fleeing to my limbs be an avenue of escape. It would make it even easier to get rid of it if it made that mistake. Instead, I was sure that the likely place would be in my torso, somewhere between brain and bowel (as was the case with my emotional and psychological issues).

To make sure this entity could not escape into the space around me and abide until I was no longer paying attention, I needed to create an energy trap which began outside my body and gradually contracted, catching everything in its way.

Slowly, like a tiny spider, I began the process of walking my awareness – one micron at a time – through space, until a large web of concentration filled the aura surrounding my physical body. With this series of subspace trip wires in place, no foreign presence could escape without my knowing about its attempt immediately. Spinning this web of awareness took most of one day and one night.

During the next day I gradually shrank the net in a series of spherical shells smaller and smaller, until I began to permeate the skin of my physical body from all sides. From there, I created and connected another series of strands throughout my arms and legs, ensuring that nothing could slide into them without triggering my attention.

At that point I began to make passes through my entire body core. The first such pass began at the top of my skull and I worked my way down millimeter by millimeter, until my attention resided in my perineum. Thus far nothing untoward had made itself felt. Perhaps this entity knew its residence was in jeopardy and sought to remain silent to avoid detection.

Of necessity, this was slow going. This downward pass took the better part of another day and night to achieve. After it, I felt even more still and more at ease with my inner world. It was time for the next pass.

A curious effect happened as a result of this process. I spent every second of every waking moment in complete serenity, with the exception of the focal point of my moving awareness. My breathing and heart rate were slow and steady. As a consequence of not burning up a lot of energy, I didn't need to eat or sleep.

If I could compress myself into tiny spaces, so too could this entity, if it borrowed the trick from my own mind. I could not afford to gap my attention even the slightest, for fear that this entity was waiting me out for just that. Which meant, starting from that moment of realization, I couldn't afford to fall asleep until this was over, or I would have to start all over again.

Some Taoists hold to the idea that the space inside us is as unlimited as the space around us. That means, that as far as we can stretch our consciousness outward, we could also coalesce it inwards. In theory, one could try to project one's awareness from the center of our minds outward into deep space itself.

The best analogy I can come up with to impart a sense of what that is like involves astronomy. In 1995 the Hubble telescope was used to gaze at an insignificant patch of relatively empty sky. What it had seen in the farthest reaches of the nothingness, was no less than thousands of galaxies, with more and more of them clumped together the further away it looked into outer space.

As I proceeded with the second pass through, moving back up from my pelvis to my skull, I gained a deeper view into my inner space than anything I had attained previously. As I penetrated the darkest, smallest, and most innocuous corners of my being, I found them. Entire stars, nebulae and galaxies became apparent in my inner vision. I beheld a light inside me that had been hiding all this time.

After another day had elapsed, I gained a new ability. As I continued to investigate the properties of the phenomenon of my awareness itself, I found the place from which all intent came. Before you actually felt a feeling, or thought a thought, or sent an impulse into a limb, there was something behind it that moved first. It was the power-behind-the-power. It made inner dissolving work.

I sat there for awhile, playing with it. The easiest access route involved surrendering into myself without trying to. I felt my motedom then, and realized I was quintessentially attached to this stream of nothingness. I was like krill drifting through this ocean.

When I moved my mind, it seemed invisible. When I was still, it became as plain as day. It was vast, and only by keeping myself utterly still could I sense its movements within and without. On that day I discovered the mindstream.

Aided by the mindstream, on the following day I made my final pass. This time I broke my ball of concentration in half (imagine cellular mitosis). When each sphere of awareness was complete and stable, I folded inner space and jumped one of those spheres to a space a few inches below my perineum. The other sphere I positioned a few inches above my skull.

This final pass I took slower than all the others. I had to be sure. I could not lapse for even a second, or I might miss this alien's last desperate attempt to escape. Any minute now my awareness might make contact with its presence.

I peered into every distant corner in my body-mind being, using my focused attention like a spotlight. My whole awareness now swept downward and upward like solar wind passing through my inner space. I could feel every heart beat. Each full breath now took a minute to complete. My inhalation was so slow and careful that I could feel air pressure moving in my nostrils and sinuses, like a low-density liquid that my lungs were drinking. I could hear my blood moving around the blood vessels in my neck.

Slowly, the downward scan and the upward scan began to merge in the middle. This process occupied yet another sunrise and sunset. Towards the beginning of the next day the two waves finally met in the middle and mixed. A great pulse then emitted from my heart in a soft, silent, and simultaneous explosion and implosion of consciousness.

As my awareness followed behind the wake of each wave, all there was, everything I could sense inside and out, belonged to me. Every cell emitted a familiar beacon of recognition and everywhere there was only a deep stillness to be found.

I was alone.

Everything inside me was me, belonged to me, and came from me. It was perfectly natural and right that it was so. As though a great machine had finally solved a long processed equation, the answer lay right in front of me.

I had never been possessed.

There was no longer anything to be afraid of. I had no reason to leave. I was absolutely and perfectly happy just being me. All of me was a perfectly natural occurrence, like the sun, the moon, and the tides. The perfection of this knowledge and the understanding that I was just fine created another reaction inside me.

A spontaneous energy moved first up, then down my center being. My whole spine shook with its passage. A sense of purpose, serenity and absolute unconditional self-love sprouted forth from the core of my heart and radiated outwards and inwards in every direction. Everywhere it passed it left only peace and profound inner equilibrium.

I knew in that instant that I would never hurt myself again. I was in love with myself as a complete and spiritual being. There was no more hollowness inside me. In place of that ancient emptiness a powerful radiance and hope now existed. As though a tiny star had been born in the core of my Being.

Tears of joy and profound gratitude came then. A moment later, I began laughing too. I sat there laughing and crying and savoring every breath in my born again Being. Nothing would be the same anymore and yet very little had changed. The world still turned. People did what they did.

Inside my world, a newly unified consciousness stretched forth. I possessed myself, and in so doing realized that I would never be possessed by anything else. I was complete now, and my spiritual integrity was sealed from that kind of possibility.

Without warning, my life flashed once more before my eyes. I could see how even the wrong turns and bad decisions had actually served to put me in this place. The harder I struggled, the more I had wanted freedom from it. The more confused I had been, the deeper I had looked into spiritual truths for answers. All the books I had read, each discipline I had investigated, every spiritual teacher I had had, contributed to this current state of being.

There was no inherent meaning or mystery to life at all. Life was to be experienced as it presented itself, and only through the artificial filters with which we view life do we find mystery or meaning that begs to be understood. We have trouble sometimes, as thinking humans, accepting the simplicity and perfection of "mere" existence, and so we search for complexity and divine revelation where none needed to be had at all.

Once the aftershocks of my awakening had passed and I was no longer crying and laughing simultaneously, I stood up and gazed at my reflection in the mirror. There was something ephemeral and vaguely angelic-like about my countenance. There was a glow around my face and head. My eyes were very bright. The static charge around me had caused my curly hair to rise in a corona with a life of its own. Altogether I gazed into the eyes of a singular being deeply at peace with itself.

I owned my self-actualization and I would never allow someone to invalidate me or try to interpret my spiritual experiences into something else that fit into their particular set of filters and biases. What I had attained that morning no one could ever gainsay or take from me. It no longer mattered what others thought of my spiritual state. My own counsel would be sufficient in that matter, for no one knew me better now than I knew myself.

It took about a week or so before this elevated state of consciousness returned to normal. For the next few days I would be simultaneously taken over by these brief fits of spontaneous laughter and joyous tears, during which I must have looked like a mad person.

I decided to venture forth and see how my fellow inhabitants would react to this change in me. I saw other human beings as constellations of light and dark and I could feel their energy emissions from a distance. I didn't have to try to scan them, but merely listened to and interpreted what I sensed, like a radio telescope and observatory.

Their vibes emanated forth like the energy from other galaxies passing through my own. From the quality of their lightness or darkness I could tell when someone was suffering from the confusion of life or if they were truly at peace with themselves. I wanted to share my own inner light and so I went out of my way to make eye contact with people I passed on the street or in the grocery store and parking lot.

When I looked into the eyes of galaxies that were more or less content with themselves, I was met with smiles and relaxed body language. I knew I had this wholesome smile on my face, charged with a secret excitement as though I just won the lottery or discovered I was pregnant. A positive attraction existed between me and those that smiled back.

But when I looked deeply into the eyes of those that were depressed or possessed of self-loathing, they looked away from my light as though it hurt them to behold. No one who was a slave to their inner darkness could sustain my gaze for long.

Some people imagine that they can hide their deepest fears and inner turmoils from others by keeping a poker face. Many can do exactly that, up to a point. Still, your inner states radiate outwards around you. No one whose inner water is clear and who is intimate with spiritual darkness can be deceived for long. It's not magic or mystical sensing. It's self-honesty and clarity of perception. That insight and perception is alluded to in a certain passage in the Tao Te Ching, verse 54. Invariably translated as something like "How do I know the ways of the world? By what is within me."

All things being equal, we all function alike on the emotional and psychological levels. People sometimes tend to think they are aliens sometimes, but they're not. They are misidentified and alienated from themselves. In that alienation and lack of completeness develops an existential void.

A void, which people are always trying to fill, either through drug experiences (with a little help from my friends), by getting high on their bodies own chemistry, (weight-lifting, fighting, extreme sports), or distraction (socializing, workaholism, entertainment, compulsive shopping and consuming). There is no pill or other quick fix for that disorder.

What happens when people lose access to drugs, or their job, or lose loved ones and personal connections? They are diminished and still seeking. They were never complete in the first place, and once their current distraction is removed, they are left with nothing substantial to fall back on. Is it any wonder then that people sometimes become suicidal after such loss?

I had become happy with nothingness. Nothing needed to be done and everything was achieved as a result.

I then decided to see if my friends various distractions had led them to similar peace and resolution. I dropped by the home of one I knew best, Julian.

He had taken me into a group of eclectic and eccentric people when I was a young teenager and was responsible for first teaching me meditation at the age of thirteen, but had abandoned the practice himself years ago.

While I had been on my spiritual quest, he had developed quite a life for himself. He was married now, with a child imminent. He had a solid career and made plenty of money. All the outward signs of social success and adult responsibility he had attained.

We sat at the edge of a sidewalk in his suburban neighborhood and passed some time catching up on recent events. He had noticed that a marked change had come over me and mentioned it as a by-the-way thing. I studied him with my open heart and took his spiritual pulse in one gestalten flicker.

"We've been friends for awhile. Do you mind if I ask you a deeply personal question?" I inquired.

"Go ahead," he assented.

I laid down the conditions of my request.

"I will ask you a question that requires a simple yes or no answer. Do not think about the answer intellectually. Instead, I want you to speak the word that first comes into your mind as the answer to my question. Do not hesitate, but simply state the answer. The first answer will most likely be the honest one."

He agreed to my condition. He had no idea what was coming.

"Do you love yourself and all that you are in this life unconditionally?" I asked calmly and evenly while looking him straight in the eye.

Immediately he gazed at the ground and I felt a glimmer of remorse. His eyes became moist as he answered me in an equally calm voice, "No."

That was the answer I had known he would give. On the outside, he seemed self-possessed and reasonably happy, but I could just tell that on the inside he wasn't as stable as he appeared. Rarely do I ever conduct that experiment on others. Through observation and testing I have confirmed for myself that I can accurately tell when people don't love themselves. I can feel the void inside them.

I don't know for certain that I achieved *the* Great Stillness but I did achieve *a* great stillness. It was enough to transform me significantly. From now on, I would continue to dissolve my inner world, as the static of life itself built up from having a normal, less studiously isolated existence.

It's easy to stay in total bliss and serenity when you are always safe and stress free. The real challenge for being alive is keeping a measure of that stillness while fully engaging with the reality of a modern life, complete with stress, profanity, distraction and other people's often unpleasant personalities.

That experience did not remove all flaws and render me perfect in all ways. I am not a spiritual healer or some kind of transcendent, holier-than-thou guru. I am just a normal human being. As such, I can still be irritated and annoyed. I still make mistakes. I have good days and bad days, just like everyone else.

When I accepted myself and all that I was, I accepted a gem with little inclusions and discolorations here and there. The quality of the overall gem was sufficient for me not to reject it on the basis of those flaws. I will always be a little eccentric and individualistic.

Some folks have a fantasy that people who do a lot of meditation become permanently detached from their emotions and can't ever get angry or sad about things that they read or witness. If you were doing a weekend meditation sit with me, I suppose it might seem like that. But in my day to day life, nothing could be further from the truth.

I can fall in love with ideas and can be outraged at things that offend my sense of rightness. I don't have sourceless anger or sadness "for no reason," like I used to all the years I was growing up and into my young adulthood. I have a constant, up-to-the-minute status and inventory of my feelings. If I am angry or sad, I know why, and ultimately, I decide how long I want to think the thoughts that made me feel those emotions.

I've always been a passionate person, and the years of meditation and energy work only strengthened my emotions, making them more intense, while the clarity that comes with the practice has made me more decisive when it comes to things that I care about. If I never wanted to experience anger, sadness, or excitement, then I would be in retreat all the time, in solitude.

During the years of training preceding that spiritual experience and all the years since, I have never been suicidally or even mildly depressed.

Shortly before my twenty-sixth birthday I finally found a reason to live, and my own inner purpose. In the process of my spiritual recovery, I discovered who I was, and what I wanted, as well as the healing power of genuine and healthy self-love. What I did to myself can not be easily undone and I've been tested more than once over the last ten years.

EPILOGUE

The Brookside psychiatric facility where I received a diagnosis of manic depressive illness (bipolar disorder I), comorbid with schizophrenic tendencies (schizoaffective disorder), was part of a franchise called Charter Hospital which operated similar facilities all up and down the east coast throughout the '80s and '90s. There was very little psychotherapy administered to any of its patients. Instead, the primary treatment consisted of psychiatric medications.

Their treatment policy for teens and adults involved milking the insurance cow until it was dry. As soon as a patient's insurance coverage ran out, they were summarily discharged, regardless of the actual state of their issues. By the time a patient was released, she was so thoroughly medicated, that her lack of immediate symptoms was considered effective treatment.

Ten years after my stay there, the Charter Brookside Hospital in Nashua, New Hampshire came under federal investigation. The government report stated that there was evidence indicating sexual contact between staff and patients, inappropriate use of restraints, and general negligence on the wards. Although it's name would seem to imply otherwise, there never was a brook, stream or creek at its side or anywhere near the place. The facility later closed and was eventually purchased by the Southern New Hampshire Medical Center.

In November of 2008, the Tobey private school for special needs teens was moved into the Thayer Building a short ways down the road (*The Tobey Building was forced to close because of structural code violations and the rising cost of heating its vast and unused areas.*) The Tobey School continued to provide an Individual Education Plan and a lockdown facility for teens with psychiatric disorders until September 2009, when it closed for good. A move which saved the cash strapped State of N.H. over four million dollars annually.

Lake Shore Hospital Inc. in Manchester, New Hampshire, where I spent my second inpatient hospitalization, is no longer in operation. In 2000 the space that it formally occupied was rented by the Easter Seals Foundation and it became an educational facility. The building the psychiatric hospital once resided in sits, ironically, at the end of an industrial park, miles away from the nearest actual lake shore.

The Bennington School for behaviorally challenged teens remains open. The program is still run out of its continually growing campus located on an expansive green acreage near a historical battle monument, not far from where Robert Frost is buried, in the old town cemetery in Bennington, Vermont.

To this day I encountered only two staff and two patients from those places.

The first was Gordon, a staff counselor who had enjoyed tormenting the residents of the Tobey dorms. That nearly ended catastrophically for both of us. The second was my favorite staff, Drew, who once encouraged me to call him if I ever needed anything. When I did, it was because he was one of the few people I didn't owe money to, and I needed one hundred dollars to tide me over before I got my first paycheck from a new job. He gave the money to me.

The first former Bennington School resident that I saw again was Melissa. We met entirely coincidentally, in the parking lot of a Burger King in New Hampshire, about a year and a half after I had left the placement.

When I first had contact with her she was seventeen and had a lot of problems, including depression and substance abuse. Now she was nineteen and expecting a child from her new boyfriend. She told me that, more than anything else, she wanted to be a mother.

Years later I ran into a guy named Neil again, also from Bennington School. Every group home has one or two funny-man types among the residents, and he was one of those who provided occasional comic relief with his attitude and his humor. I vividly remember what he was like back then and I wondered if that might have been a better time. At least back then he was healthy.

At first I didn't recognize him. This old bum, wearing a hood over his head, came up to me one day while I was basking in the sun in the Golden Gate Park in San Francisco, some nine years after the school. He wasn't old though. He was my age. And standing before me, in his smelly and stained clothes that he wore in layers, with his jacket tied around his waist and his backpack over his shoulders, he looked like a vagabond. He told me there was something familiar about me, and it was his voice that made the "recognition switch" trip for me.

Neil was homeless and lived in a nearby camp, hidden in the bushes, with a few other disposed kids. He had done prison time in different states and was once more on the run from the cops. Neil was a heroin and methamphetamine junkie with the skin sores and abscesses to prove it. He was slinging marijuana buds in the park to pay for his habits. To his credit, he readily acknowledged that he had made a lot of bad choices in his life and claimed that he knew he was "stuck" somehow but didn't know how to change himself.

Oak Park, an area of Sacramento long considered synonymous with prostitution, drugs, and drive-by shootings, has changed somewhat. Thanks to an enormous amount of financial investment fueling urban gentrification and a huge push on the part of Sacramento city officials to increase police presence in the last ten years, portions of Oak Park are looking a lot better. A popular coffee shop chain store and an art gallery are now occupying the former apartment building where I lived when I had my last psychotic episode. Oak Park is still not a great neighborhood to live in, by any stretch.

My stepfather Tim, at long last, received a portion of his comeuppance. Over the years he had suffered work-related falls that partially disabled his back. He has irreparable damage to his left elbow which somewhat limits his range of motion with that arm. During courtship with his soon-to-be second wife, she discovered his mental illness and irrational rages when she caught him bullying his own two children during a routine weekend visit.

Bless her heart, she called the police and had him arrested. At which point he was dragged off to a psychiatric hospital for evaluation. After his second arrest for domestic violence, and subsequent psych assessment, she terminated their relationship and kicked him out for good.

Only once did I catch up with Sam, my stepbrother. He had the haunted look, sunken eye pits and the thousand yard stare of a child in a war zone. I had tried, unsuccessfully, to shield him from the negative influence of the others until our family was split apart.

Sam always wanted to fly. He figured his best route would be through the Air Force, but which he eventually flunked out of. Afterward, he became a thoroughly unsuccessful thief, con artist and stolen goods reseller. He has taken brand new cars for a test drive and never returned them to the dealerships.

Last I heard, he combs though people's mail, looking for personal information he can use to defraud them. Several times he's tried to get other people in my family involved in his bad check writing and loan defaulting schemes. He has since repeatedly spent time in jail. Sam owes thousands of dollars in restitution fees and can not keep the most basic, unskilled job for very long.

My stepsister Alice's eating disorders only got worse over time. She eventually left my mother's house to enter college. During her freshman year she began cutting herself and became suicidal. She was hospitalized, diagnosed with bipolar disorder type I and medicated with lithium. She left the college life as fast as she got into it and is now disabled by her depressions and mood swings. Last I heard, she was living in an adult group home, where she is slowly "coming to terms" with her illness.

My brother Byron has fared much better. He was once diagnosed with ADD and briefly medicated for it with Ritalin in the 1980s. Today, you would never know he supposedly had a "neurobehavioral developmental disability." He is an autodidact and taught himself small engine repair, basic electronics, basic computing and process engineering. As a result he has had successful ventures as the lead mechanic or chief technician in various sectors of the machine industry.

Byron learned an important lesson about mental health treatment from hearing about what happened to me. He never became overtly suicidal, nor did he shoot himself in the foot repeatedly like I did. He mostly stayed out of legal trouble and rarely got into fights. He kept most of his issues bottled up inside.

He was not exposed to additional abuse, forced drugging and seclusion, or life in a lockdown, once he got kicked out of the Hell House. He rebounded, I think, much faster than I did, at first. He didn't need to go on a spiritual quest to get over the things he went through growing up. But he's never been the kind of a person who would do that sort of thing anyway.

He is largely a loner by nature. His chief love is skydiving, which is as close to religion and spirituality as I have known in him. No one on this planet understands me as well as he does. He's probably the only person I've ever met in my life whose mind works in similar ways. He is definitely his own person though. There is no one quite like him.

My father Andrew never fully understood what was going on with me back then, nor did he have any idea how much I suffered once I was receiving mental health treatment. He was under a lot of pressure to get me some help and the experts he paid told him that I would get it while inpatient. He made some other decisions and came to some conclusions about me which I resented for a long time. I know he loves me, and over time I have come to love him more, as I see myself in him and him in me. Our relationship, once rocky, has steadily improved over the last ten years.

As for my mother Sarah, she eventually married a man that would never threaten her physically or intellectually. A man who is on permanent physical disability and spends his time drinking quietly to ease his pains. Sarah never got her dream home of a cottage in the woods by the side of a lake with a white picket fence. In divorcing my father Andrew, she left the only husband out of the three she had had who could have ever afforded to build her one.

She is still depressed, but from what I hear, she has settled down quite a bit and has gained some level of introspection over the years. Sarah does not like to talk too much about "The Olde Days." She continues to go to church when it suits her. She had two more children, twin girls, from her new husband. I have no contact with them or her at all. Besides occasional contact with my brother and father, I've had nothing to do with either side of my family since 1995.

I do not consider myself "recovering" or "in recovery." By slowing myself down enough to pay attention to what was going on inside me, I became sensitive to how my own thoughts and emotions actually work. Certainly, I had some guidance in the form of those meditation seminars and all of the teachers and students who took some time to give me honest advice about my practice. But I took personal responsibility for my own mental health recovery. I did about ninety-eight percent of the work on my own.

During my recovery I had no psychological or psychiatric help. Nor did I have any kind of mental health support group which might have continuously reminded me, month after month, year after year, that I had these different incurable mental illnesses that would always be there, necessitating that I be "in treatment" forever.

The combination of distance and seclusion saved me, in many ways, from being caught up in the culture of endless recovery that currently surrounds the bipolar and schizophrenic communities. The grim prognosis for people with severe thought disorders and emotional dysregulation is due, in part, to the current popularity of biological psychiatry (which reduces the experience of the mind and moods to a series of malfunctioning chemical switches) as well as the unsatisfactory treatments for these kinds of problems.

I am not a scientist, so I can't explain how I was able to cure myself of such crippling mental illness with any certainty. I do have some theories and ideas about how that happened.

Perhaps, consistently stacking so many factors in my favor early on in my adult life reversed the stresses that had been accumulating since my formative years, which had led to all the things that were going wrong in my mind. It may be a lot harder for people in their forties and fifties, with life-long histories of mental illness, to reverse it and heal like that themselves, but you never know. It's a scientific fact that the brain has a great neuroplasticity to it that can allow even brain damaged people to learn new skills into old age.

A lot of research in the last twenty years has demonstrated the positive effects of prolonged meditation practice on the prefrontal cortex, an area of the brain fingered by some neuroscientists as being underdeveloped in people with bipolar disorder and schizophrenia.

The prefrontal cortex is hardwired with a great many connections to the limbic system and consequently receives input from, and sends output to, all of the deeper brain structures responsible for anger, panic, sadness, aggression and other emotions and impulses. The prefrontal cortex strongly interacts with the amygdala, an area of the brain where emotional memories and patterned emotional responses are stored long term.

From what I understand, meditation causes the prefrontal cortex to create a denser mass of intricate connections into the rest of the brain. I conclude that every hour I spent in solitude, meditating, was the mental equivalent of strength training in the area of the brain that can process and rule over emotional impulses. Over the months and years, I trained my brain to control all of those wild mood swings and racing data-streams that occupied my mind, noisily informing me of and distracting me with a trivia overload of sensations, observations, and thoughts of grand portent.

I purged myself of the behavioral conditioning stored alongside the abuse memories. I defused the triggers, the rage, and the need for vengeance, which were slowly leading to the path of becoming a psychopathic serial killer. I was able to fully get over the traumas that happened to me, from the loss of my family and freedom as a teen, to the assault, dehumanization and coercive drugging that I suffered while in psychiatric care. Over time, I learned how to forgive the people that had caused those things. Eventually I discovered self-love and have never suffered from major self-esteem or self-confidence issues since then.

The disease model of psychiatry that so thoroughly dominates the arena of mental health care in this country right now, blames malfunctioning brain chemistry and faulty genetics as the cause of mental illness symptoms. Consequently, there is no need to really analyze and develop insight into one's own thoughts and behaviors. Certainly don't investigate whether it's actually true that there is nothing you can do about your mood swings and racing thoughts, but take pills or otherwise self-medicate.

For a little over five years I worked directly with what I perceived as the cause of my mental illnesses. I focused on trying to overcome obstacles in my mind, body and heart that were preventing me from being at peace with myself on a here-and-now basis. And through the alchemy of meditation and a religious adherence to keeping my stress minimal, I achieved lasting changes in my personality. I don't experience "bipolarity" or the "bipolar life" that my psychiatrist predicted for me twenty years ago.

For a long time the idea of suicide was never far from my mind. Now, I find it unthinkable. I am totally healed of depression. I don't have manic episodes. I don't experience nightmares and flashbacks or any other post traumatic stress symptoms, like anxiety and hypervigilance, nor am I triggered by reading about child abuse or watching dramatized violence on television anymore. I don't have "thought broadcasting" delusions, paranoia or other kinds of intrusive thoughts.

These illnesses and their myriad symptoms are completely gone as though these things had never happened and dominated every facet of my life for seventeen years. And yet, my inspired creativity and the intensity of my energy remain intact to this day. It is like a controlled fusion reaction now, as opposed to the unpredictable fire that would come without warning and burn me up (and out) and leave exhaustion and depression in its smoldering remains.

For some adults, especially those who do not receive their bipolar disorder diagnosis until their thirties or forties, the moment of acceptance of the label becomes an "Ah ha!" experience that finally explains away many of their previous episodes and breakdowns. With this new bias in mind, they reinterpret certain behaviors or events in their past as being a "manic phase," a "depressive phase" or a "mixed episode."

In this telling I've tried, with some exceptions here and there, to avoid pigeonholing one experience or another as being emblematic of this diagnosis or that. I never felt like I had three (or more) different diseases in my head. I experienced all of the craziness and dysfunction together, undifferentiated. Subjectively, it was just one big problem with my mental operating system. In curing myself, all of my symptoms gradually impacted me less and less as meditation installed a dimmer switch on my extreme moods and behaviors.

Since the diagnosis of manic depression, schizophrenia and post-traumatic stress disorder is currently based on subjective, self-reported symptoms, I feel empowered to use the word "cure" very confidently. But I know that kind of claim flies in the face of everything that patients are told about these conditions nowadays. Why do you suppose that is?

Award-winning medical journalist Robert Whitaker, in his phenomenal book *Mad in America: Bad Science, Bad Medicine, and the Enduring Mistreatment of the Mentally Ill* (2002), tells us of the times when madness was curable. The early 1800s saw the rise of the Quaker retreats that were based on the "moral treatment" of mental illness. These retreats were small communities that were based on the novel idea that if you took a distressed person and placed them in an esthetically pleasing, calming and nonthreatening environment and you treated these patients with the utmost dignity and respect, their minds might slowly but surely heal.

Patients who had gone mad or had a nervous breakdown needed to take a step back from the stress of their normal life, and places like England's York Retreat provided a safe environment to take that respite. By the mid-1800s these moral treatment asylums had spread to America, and some of them boasted 50 percent, 60 percent or even 80 percent cure rates of previously insane patients within one year.

Sure, there were always some unfortunate hard cases, people who never got better. But once upon a time, physicians and caretakers recognized that patients who had been certified insane could, given the right kinds of nurturing and therapy, be cured and made sane again.

Psychiatry, for all its boast of modern progress, has actually gone backwards in efficacy when compared to the success of the moral treatments of "nervous disorders" in the mid-nineteenth century. Psychiatrists fractured vague terms like "insanity" and "madness" and replaced those concepts with a rigid, scientific-seeming compilation of symptoms of biological diseases. These so-called experts have yet to explain to my satisfaction, why those forms of madness have become incurable in the early twenty-first century in the face of our supposed advances in science and medicine.

Despite having unraveled the Human Genome years ago, scientists continue to fail to show exactly how manic depression or schizophrenia are genetic disorders or what the implications would be if they really were. A few years ago, *Unquiet Mind* author and *Manic Depressive Illness* coauthor, Dr. Kay Redfield Jamison, (herself a sufferer of bipolar disorder) admitted in an announcement, posted to the Johns Hopkins University website:

> *"The decades long search for the bipolar gene is over. No longer do we believe that this disorder is the product of one defective gene. It is now believed that a complex assortment of genes will someday reveal the origins of this terrible disease."*

Well, good luck with that, Dr. Jamison.

Practitioners of the reductionist model of biologic psychiatry have omitted one very important part of the human equation from the DSM, that is involved in the experience of suffering from mental illness. The biological perspective does not allow for the possibility that the manifestation of spirit through the force of will can impose changes on the state of the mind, and through its bio-electrical connection via the nervous system, the body too (*which, one might suppose, could progressively alter the chemical expression of your genes, put your neurotransmitters back in balance and change the firing of your brain patterns*).

What I did with my healing lifestyle was not all that different from the concept of those "archaic" nineteenth century Quaker retreats which dismissed the prevailing medical model of insanity in favor of treating the person, their mind and spirit in a safe and respectful environment. It was with the spiritual and ontological factors of my suffering equation that I focused on, which I believe lead, albeit gradually, to the path of real healing.

Did I miss out on anything by taking the road less traveled? Sure, lots of things. Spending so much time in solitude did not teach me political correctness, nor did that lifestyle accelerate my social development, or enhance my communication skills. I didn't get rich working blue-collar, living paycheck-to-paycheck, spending my meager earnings on mind-body training at every opportunity.

I missed out on Nietzsche, Proust, Atwood, Plath, and Byron (the Lord-poet, not my brother) as well as the whole cap and gown thing. I've never seen a single episode of *Seinfeld*, *Sex in the City* or *Survivor* which I am told were fairly popular evening television shows in the late '90s and early 2000s. I was always (and continue to be) a bit behind hip new culture, and out of step with the latest fashions.

In a lot of ways, I am still playing life skills catch-up with adults my own age because of all the things that I didn't learn or do as an adolescent and young adult. But I do not regret taking the path that I took, for in the final analysis, it truly made all the difference.

344 Jane Alexander

AFTERWORD

Contained within these pages and in the essence of my writing are my notes, describing how mental illness began, progressed and was reversed. This narrative details a comparative analysis of the efficacy of my choice of alternative methods of healing versus modern psychiatric treatments.

I have, from time to time, been strongly encouraged to write a book about my ordeals and my journey of self-healing. But I didn't believe that people would be receptive to a book about recovery or spirituality, by a twenty-something, when it was first suggested to me.

It occurred to me also that some readers would mistakenly conclude that I was looking for pity or catharsis or trying to get back at people from my past. I didn't think those were good reasons to write this book. Besides, if I was truly over it all, what was there to say? That line of reasoning snuffed any interest I had in writing about my life. So a few more years went by, and I gave no further thought to sharing my story. I was content to simply put the past behind me and move on.

All of that changed on the morning of my thirty-first birthday. While browsing the BBC online, I whimsically took an online depression screening. When I had my depression test results scored, it alleged that I was not only not depressed but that I must have discovered the "secret to happiness." I started chuckling then, because for the longest time happiness had nothing to do with me.

I opened another internet browser, typed in the words "bipolar disorder" just to see what would come up. I ran into websites representing organizations that I'd never heard of, like NAMI, the National Alliance for the Mentally Ill, and DBSA, the Depression and Bipolar Support Alliance, not to mention the endless-seeming bipolar disorder support forums and discussion boards. I had been out of touch with the mental health community for thirteen years at that point and I was dismayed to quickly find out that the ineffective and debilitating drug treatments that I had been forced to take back then were still the *de rigueur* protocol for treating the condition.

While I had been off, doing tai chi and meditation in the woods around the American River year after year, unbeknownst to me, the illness itself -bipolar disorder- was going through considerable changes within the psychiatric and patient communities. The diagnosis of bipolar disorder with psychotic features split into softer versions, like Bipolar Disorder II, that required weaker symptoms. (*You don't need a suicide attempt and a psychotic episode to receive a bipolar diagnosis anymore.*) And more and more people, especially young people, even children, are getting labeled with it and summarily drugged. These kids are told that they have a permanent and incurable disease, a practice which deeply concerns me.

Bipolar disorder has become a fad diagnosis in the last decade or so. I lived through something similar in the '80s and '90s, when attention deficit disorder had attained a similar status as a fad. In the rush to diagnose better and sooner, the condition was blown up to the status of a nationwide epidemic.

The primary treatment (and for many people the only treatment) for ADD (ADHD) is drugs. There is no doubt that during the ADD diagnosing craze (which, some folks would argue, is still happening) a lot of "difficult" children, like my brother Byron, were caught up in that net, labeled for life, and unnecessarily medicated for their non-pathological condition. For them it is an effective form of behavioral control.

In September of 2007, the *N.Y. Times* online carried a report by journalist Benedict Carey, citing an apparent forty-fold increase in the diagnosis and treatment of children with bipolar disorder in less than ten years. This completely astonishes me. Frankly, I am appalled to hear about toddlers being forced to take four or five different toxic psychiatric drugs (leading to death in some cases) on account of their so-called "pediatric bipolar."

The giant elephant standing in the center of any debate about the validity of these diagnoses is, who is really benefiting from this increased diagnosing and treating of bipolar disorder? Certainly not the vast numbers of misdiagnosed children, whose social and physical development are threatened by the labels they are given and by the drugs administered to them. And there's no sign that psychiatrists and parents are going to come to their senses any time in the near future.

As crazy as it may sound to some, when I was a teenager, I preferred being miserable or manic to being sedated and unfeeling, day after day, as a consequence of the drugs. At least when I was depressed or euphoric I felt intensely real, and I retained my cognitive and artistic abilities. On psych drugs I was a powerless witness to the decay of my mental and physical prowess. I do not exaggerate when I say that I experienced the death of personality under those chemical effects.

It breaks my heart to know that children and teens are being experimented on with these drugs. Parents are either willful or ignorant accomplices (or both), in the chemically induced mind-crime that is being committed on the unassailable high ground of, "Wanting only what is best for our kids." I predict: Society as a whole is going to be negatively effected in ways that will only be apparent in hindsight, as a consequence of raising an entire generation of children, programmed since day one, into believing that they have uncontrollable mental disorders that need perpetual drug maintenance.

Clearly, these children have no one to speak for them. One day, these kids will be adults, and they are going to demand explanations as to why that was done to them and how it was possible that the mental health experts were able to diagnose an incurable genetic disorder (or two or three) merely by observing the behavior of a growing child (*honest answer: because several highly influential Ivy League psychiatrists, who were neck deep in Big Pharma money, were making their names and fortunes off of the "bipolar child" paradigm at the time*). They will ask why their developing brains and bodies were subject to the dangers of drug-induced neurological damage (*honest answer: because mood stabi-*

lizers and antipsychotics are considered the mainstay of "effective treatment" for patients with bipolar). And why no one would sit down and help them learn how to deal with the confusing thoughts and disturbing emotions that are wired into us as human beings (*possibly, because both their parents had forty-hour-a-week jobs and simply no time and energy left to coach them*).

While the popularity of schizophrenia as a diagnosis has not spread in the way that the current "epidemic" of bipolar disorder has in recent years, the treatment for the condition is, in my opinion, inhumane. Antipsychotics have been unequivocally proven to damage the frontal lobes of the brain. These poisons are the primary treatment for those with schizophrenia or bipolar with psychotic features. I don't accept comparisons of psychiatric drugs to insulin injections.

People who haven't been on neuroleptics, aka "nerve clamps," have no idea what it is they are insisting their friends and loved ones must take. Maybe you should try a Haldol or Zyprexa injection yourself so you can appreciate it firsthand. When the brain fog, body fatigue and slurred speech settles in and you realize that toxic feeling isn't going away after a night's sleep, ask yourself why it's acceptable that others suffer it. Tough luck? That's what you get because you are mentally ill? Be grateful because it's better than being chained to a wall in a dark cell, being sprayed with freezing cold high-pressure water, or whirled around in a chair until you upchuck and excrete everything you had eaten in the last few days, like the state-of-the-art scientific treatments of yore?

Before I started writing my first drafts, I did a lot of research on the origins and uses of the drugs that were so callously and irresponsibly administered to me as a teenager. For one, I learned that antipsychotics had been used in the Soviet Union as punishment. If you were an intellectual or a political dissident and you voiced dissatisfaction with the government regime, you were incarcerated or hospitalized and forcibly injected with Haldol or other neuroleptic drugs. Sooner or later you were no longer protesting or thinking very much about anything.

What I found out about Trilafon, the antipsychotic that was used to punish me, was even more disturbing. According to the

Trilafon concentrate pharmacology information, found at Pharmacycode online:

> *Perphenazine is a piperazinyl phenothiazine, acts on the central nervous system, and has a greater behavioral potency than other phenothiazine derivatives whose side chains do not contain a piperazine moiety. It is a member of a class of drugs called phenothiazines, which are dopamine D1/D2 receptor antagonists. Perphenazine is 10 to 15 times as potent as chlorpromazine; that means perphenazine is a highly potent antipsychotic. In equivalent doses it has approximately the same frequency and severity of early and late extrapyramidal side-effects compared to haloperidol.*

In a nutshell, what that means is: Trilafon (perphenazine) is significantly stronger than Thorazine (chlorpromazine) and has the same basic side effect profile as Haldol (haloperidol) along with a few of it's own peculiar effects due to the piperazine component. (*piperazine is also used in plastics and solvents.*) Perphenazine is one of the more powerful of the first generation so-called "typical" antipsychotics (*as opposed to the next generation "atypical" antipsychotics*).

Trilafon is an analog of phenothiazine which is an industrial chemical that has been used in solutions for making dyes. Phenothiazines are also noted for having a profound and "useful" disruptive effect on the central nervous system of insects, and so it is sold to the agricultural industry as a viable pesticide. The drug certainly had profoundly disruptive effects on my system. The liquid form of Trilafon comes with a warning: *Do not allow this liquid to come into contact with clothes or skin.* Are you going to try to convince me that this same chemical is good for you if it is introduced orally or injected into muscle and adipose tissue? How did this toxic compound ever become associated with psychiatric treatment?

During the mid-to-late twentieth century, these industrial compounds underwent a thorough image makeover which resulted in being given new brand names. With great care, drug marketers excised all the previous association with "chemical lobotomies" while spinning a total fabrication about how these drugs were truly medicines, intentionally engineered to have "antipsychotic" and "antischizophrenic" properties. Here, one must take into account that the outcome of their drug efficacy studies is a commodity that can be bought.

It is an absolute deception to claim that antipsychotics are all that different from their industrial and agricultural versions. Should you ever get a good whiff of a liquid antipsychotic, you will notice right away that it smells like a solvent – if it quacks like a duck . . .

Neuroleptics scramble the functioning of your frontal lobes, warping your reality and skewing your subjective sense of self and being alive. From the moment those chemicals enter your body, you slowly start diminishing every hour of every day. And the FDA would actually have you believe that it is just fine to dope up growing children and teens with this stuff. Take it from someone who was on it, that no, it is *not* fine. These kinds of drugs, antipsychotics especially, take and take from you in a path that can only lead away from, and not towards, a sound mind in a sound body.

Having unchained, unscrambled frontal lobes was critical in understanding myself, my problems and eventually in using mindfulness to find my own path back out of madness. A practice made vastly more difficult and frustrating when your brain is stewing in chemicals that promote and induce mindlessness. The former produces cortical growth through neuroplasticity while the latter reduces frontal lobe activity, shrinking cell density, leaving pockets of interstitial fluid where useful brain matter formerly thrived. As a therapeutic modality, mindfulness and mindlessness are antithetical to each other.

If it were up to me, it would be unlawful to forcibly treat or psychologically coerce a child or teen into taking antipsychotics. At the very least, a human being should be allowed to develop fully without the constant threat of disabling iatrogenic complications or risking the irreversible injury to the brain and nervous systems that can be caused by these chemicals. Seriously, ask your doctor if Tardive Dyskinesia is right for your depression.

As an adult, you can ask for pills and make a reasonably informed decision if you take the time to ask questions and do some fact-checking about the medications your doctor is prescribing. You pay your money and you take your chances.

But kids just have to accept it. They can not meaningfully evaluate the risk-reward trade-off. Especially since they are routinely not fully informed (or outright lied to) about things like the distressing short and long-term extrapyramidal side effects (like drooling, slurred speech and akathisia). And until they reach a certain age (fourteen, fifteen or sixteen, depending on the state laws,) they can not legally refuse.

Most children and teenagers have not yet trained themselves to the same level of self-deception that some adults seem to possess. When they are made to take those drugs, they sense without bias or preconception what is really happening inside their minds and bodies. Consequently, they are not yet brainwashed enough to tell themselves that their diminished mental function, weight gain and uncoordinated muscle movements is a medicinal effect. They intuitively feel like they are being poisoned and turned into zombies.

I also think adult patients should demand better care and treatments for themselves. Considering that the options available, once psychotherapy has been exhausted, are: brain damage in a bottle, brain damage from a cattle prod applied to the head while under anesthesia or brain damage from an ice pick through the eye socket.

When people are diagnosed with bipolar disorder or schizophrenia, they ask the same question that I asked my psychiatrist over two decades ago. "What causes these conditions, and what is the cure?" People today are told the same thing that I was told in the late '80s:

"Scientists are still trying to figure it out. Give them time. For now, there is no known cause and no cure and you don't have to feel responsible because it's all about faulty genes and chemical imbalances (*and scientists will prove that, someday, wink, wink*). But hey, don't worry about it. Here is your scrip, now go take your meds like a good girl."

Compared to the steady rate of scientific advances in fields like astronomy, robotics and even other branches of medicine, psychiatry is experiencing some major lag. For those unfortunate enough to lose an arm or leg, prosthetic limbs have become high technology as of late. Nowadays, doctors can replace your heart and implant artificial eyes. They are using genetic recombination to treat Crohn's disease and create killer T cells that target some cancers. They can grow skin in vats and are developing nanomachines with the aim of cellular damage detection and repair.

But psychiatry's strategy for dealing with disorders of the mind continues to be: Blame the brain and then attack it chemically, electrically or physically, damaging it or artificially changing its natural chemical balance. And if the random number generator of chance results in the patient experiencing relief from their symptoms(in spite of the attending side effects), well than that's considered a successful treatment.

Having new drug treatments is not an advance in understanding mental illness, in my book. Endlessly treating the symptoms and never coming anywhere near a cure can not be considered worthy progress and certainly not something to boast about.

Scientists and doctors now believe that once your "chemicals" are "imbalanced," that's it, you're screwed. Like it's a one-way ride. All I am saying is: No. It isn't. Not necessarily. My guess is, it's going to take these experts decades more, perhaps even centuries, to unambiguously prove in a genetic assay or other lab test what I have asserted in this work about the subjective nature of the mind and its relationship to whole-person health. The same goes for the mind's obvious influence – both positively and negatively – over the chemistry of the body.

The reality is, aside from some colorful PET scans and a few well designed twin studies there have been no significant advances in understanding the genesis of manic depression and schizophrenia. Not just in the last twenty or thirty years, but not even in the last hundred years.

Some folks will disagree with me, stating that studies X, Y, and Z show one or two specific genes common to a wide sampling of people who've all been diagnosed with these conditions. So what? I guessed that would be the case from the time I was a teenager and lived with my mentally ill family. It still tells us nothing about what manic depression or schizophrenia really are at a molecular or chemical level and thus does nothing to further the objective understanding of root causes. Nor does it promote scientific cures. It's just another "tantalizing clue."

If you ask the leading experts in genetics right now how close we are to accurately pinpointing a cluster of genes responsible for just say, depression, they will tell you that scientists are only now just realizing how many genes are involved and that they are no-where near understanding how genes effect the wiring of the neurons in the brain – which itself is still being mapped. I believe that science will eventually figure it all out, but it's unlikely to happen any time soon or at least until your average genetic lab has access to a lot more computing power than what is available these days.

Because of what I know about the current state of genetic re-search, I would be extremely suspicious and distrusting of any genetic tests for schizophrenia or bipolar disorder that may come out in the near future in the next two or three decades. Having said that, if I thought these tests were accurate I might take one out of sheer curiosity. Do I have the genes and they are just in the "off" position now, thanks to my training and lifestyle? It might be interesting to know from a medical and psychological standpoint.

I think if a behavioral researcher was ever genuinely interested in the science of how I was able to cure myself, the best place to start would be a PET scan of my brain. Then compare it to those that were performed on experienced Buddhist monks and also to the available scans of patients who are actively suffering from manic, depressive or schizophrenic symptoms. I wonder what we'd see. I have my own speculations.

At any rate, there are significant problems with the practice of psychiatry in America right now. With as little as a single phone call, a psychiatrist can have you stripped of your civil rights and confined to a hostile and dehumanizing environment where you can be forcibly treated in ways that violate mind, body and dignity.

It's unthinkable that a doctor would have the police deliver a patient to a hospital in handcuffs, only to be summarily knocked out, operated upon and then forced into seclusion for a broken limb with complete disregard for the patient's wishes on the matter.

Yet psychiatrists are empowered to do that to someone with a broken mind. They can have you restrained physically and chemically or have your brain shocked on a regular schedule whether you want it or not.

That's the real stigma of mental illnesses as opposed to physical ones. Your value as a human being is lessened in the eyes of others. Your judgment is suspect because your thoughts are considered the result of a diseased brain. You somehow magically no longer know what is best for you. A person would have to be crazy, not to see how beneficial a trip to mental health services could be on their journey towards wellness.

It's very unlikely that you can achieve real healing or be cured of your existential misery by being subjected to the institutional experience. It's added insult to ongoing injury and becomes something else you have to get over. In light of what I've witnessed first-hand, it's very difficult to take the profession seriously, yet there is every reason to be wary of it's far-ranging influence.

The bottom line is this: The psychiatric toolkit is quite limited. If you are not willing to endure polypharmacy roulette or lie down for some electroshock, then (referrals aside), there is not a whole lot they can do for you.

And as for cures for mental illness? Scientists these days don't even talk about them. Whenever we see reports in the media that a new study has revealed a possible set of common genes in a certain population, a spokesperson for the study manages to conclude the report with the sentiment that: "With further study new drugs can be designed which will take advantage of the genes under investigation to create better, more effective treatments." This can be roughly translated as: *We hope this leads to a new patented blockbuster drug which will rake in billions of dollars to our shareholders.*

There are a variety of psychological modalities out there that I never got to partake in. I didn't get any couch sessions in Freudian analysis or dialectical behavioral therapy while the State was footing the bill. I rejected the therapies that had been imposed on me, like group and art therapy. I had never even heard of Gestalt psychology or hypnotherapy or EMDR (Eye Movement Desensitization and Reprocessing) until I was an adult. I didn't want counseling. I never had a deep subconscious desire for one-on-one validation of my suffering with another person back then.

As a teenager, concerned relatives like my aunt Myra would say things like, "You were an abused child. You got abandoned. You need to be in therapy, sweetheart." And I would whirl back around and snort defensively, "I don't want to talk about it. I've moved on and I'm okay." when it was obvious to just about everyone that no, I was not okay.

But my pain was private, and even if I had had the financial resources, entering an open-ended therapeutic relationship with a counselor (assuming I could even find one I liked) never had any great appeal to me. Compared to the rate of my daily, even hourly progress once I got serious about meditation, monthly or even weekly face-to-face therapy sessions would have been too pedestrian. I made so many discoveries and changes to myself and was evolving so fast, that a clinician wouldn't have been able to keep up. I was keeping my own schedule with regards to the pace of my recovery. So I forged a therapeutic alliance with myself.

I've been fascinated by the study and training of the mind since my early teens. Being diagnosed with incurable mental conditions in my youth had a way of strongly motivating me to learn about how my mind works. It is my belief that the work I turned to in healing myself enabled me to conduct effective psychoanalysis and self-psychotherapy in the private laboratory of my own mind.

Despite my experiences, I am not anti-psychiatry or anti-drugs. There is nothing to gain by boxing myself into (and having to defend) such an inflexible position. It should be obvious that I am very much pro-science and pro-medicine and I love reading about it. I am not a Luddite "psychiatric denier" that refuses to accept that the practice has in fact helped some people and saved some lives. I do think modern chemistry has a lot to offer and perhaps there will someday be better treatments that are not quite as unhealthy for the brain and body as the ones available today.

In the meantime, until psychiatry does some significant catch-up and reform, one would do well to understand the full extent of their current lack of understanding, and realize what they might be in for if psychopharmacology or an inpatient stay is an avenue they are considering exploring.

People have a right to be fully informed and should be about the possible short term effects and lasting ramifications before getting involved with modern psychiatry. Unfortunately, children and teenagers usually are not and have no one at their age with firsthand experience of that kind of treatment to advocate for them. I certainly had no idea what I was in for and, as a former "bipolar child" myself, some of the chapters in Part One of this book entail my testimony of just how fun and enriching that experience was.

Psychoanalysis and psychotherapy were more en vogue during the '70s and early '80s. Since the '90s and the deregulation of the pharmaceutical industry, there has been a strong shift towards a reliance on psychiatric drugs. The entire basis underlying the drug treatment regime is that all cognitions and emotions are caused by chemicals and if you don't like the way you feel or behave, go ahead and take other chemicals until you feel only what you want to. In that way, psych meds are not all that different from so-called "street drugs" as both kinds of drugs are used to escape from or alter the experience of reality.

While that may be therapeutically valuable to some people short-term, over the long term it divorces you from the real -you-inside. The experience of the "real you" may just be anxiety, irascibility or depression, and all of the "anti-this" and "anti-that" medications impose chemical distortions that obfuscate the most subtle levels of your consciousness. Sure, you can get a little bit of benefit by combining drugs and doing entry level meditation or relaxation breathing. But the effects of psychiatric drugs (*or any kind of mind-altering drug really*) ultimately become an insurmountable barrier if you were to ever get seriously involved with stillness and deep meditation.

In the course of navigating my way through the field of alternative medicine, I found some very helpful therapies, whereas other modalities did not live up to their hype and expectation. St John's Wort and fish oil supplements, taken to alleviate depression, didn't do anything for me. A gluten-free diet did not noticeably affect my moods or thoughts in any appreciable way. Crystal healing, essential oils and homeopathy did little or nothing to change my inner landscape.

Becoming sensitive to and respecting my stress triggers. Learning to get enough sleep, to eat healthy and live simply. Having a physically vigorous lifestyle that included manual labor, mountain biking and martial arts training. Adhering to the seventy-percent rule of moderation as an approach to my personal endeavors. All of that helped. Learning how to be content within myself and with my lot in life had profound stabilizing effects on my mind and body. I would not say that those other experiments were useless, because their efficacy (or lack thereof) provided useful clues to solving my personal depression puzzle.

Abuse and neglect, both domestic and institutional, still occur all over this country as a hard fact of life twenty years after it happened to me. This situation perpetually populates our country with people with PTSD. The abuse can also trigger comorbid conditions, like mood and thought disorders or substance addictions, in people who have a hereditary disposition to them. If these illnesses materialize during a person's adolescence, they may be forced into treatment and locked down in psychiatric facilities and group homes.

I've tried to spotlight some of the many shortcomings of social workers employed by Child and Family Services. I had three different social workers during my youth. My placement coordinator, Earlene, the child abuse investigator, Ms. Hafidi, and ironically, my stepfather, Tim (*who was a former case worker before he married my mother*). All three of them had chances to show their quality and all three of them dropped the ball because of character flaws, procedural red tape plus lack of training and rampant mental illness.

My perspective is that social workers (intentionally or otherwise) actively work against, not for, the best interests of the children in their admittedly overworked caseloads. There are far too few of them for the total demand of the functions they preform, like investigations and court dates and transportations. They are not very well-paid for what can be a frustrating job, playing handler between families, government agencies and abused, violent or otherwise disturbed children. And they have an enormous amount of power to make your life miserable if you happen to get one of the bad apples in the social worker bushel.

Whenever you see on television, or read in the news, about parents who abused their children, you're told that their children are automatically removed from the home and placed elsewhere. My anecdotes should give the reader a realistic picture as to what eventually happens to some of those abandoned or warehoused children and teenagers when they get caught up in forced mental health care and state-sponsored social services.

This book does not just document my own problems, but also what it was like growing up with my mother Sarah and stepfather Tim, both of whom clearly had mental illness that progressed over time. My brothers Sam, Byron and my sister Alice eventually became mentally ill as well, with many of us sharing a range of symptoms and behaviors that are indicative of manic depression and PTSD.

Other symptoms, like my sister's cutting and overeating, and my little brother's inability to stop committing crimes, point to a broader range of causes for mental dysfunction than just chemical imbalances. Hereditary disposition and modeling, how we were treated, as well as the environment that we grew up in together. These explanations confirm my own personal theories about the genesis of mental illness.

Namely that we are not dealing with hundreds of different kinds of mental illness. It's more likely that most mental illnesses start from psychological stress and how we handle it. Stress is everywhere: being a child and rearing children is stressful, growing up and changing is stressful too.

Repeated exposure to threatening environments and the effects of inescapable physical, emotional and verbal assault create stress reactions which, combined with poor coping mechanisms, insidiously corrupt you. These effects stay with you for years. They can grow to overshadow or limit everything you try to accomplish in your life. Over a long enough period of time, it becomes exceedingly challenging to even comprehend, much less appreciate, just how messed up you have really become.

Mental illness, like physical sickness, can strike any of us. Not just those with a hereditary disposition. It's a matter of pressure and vulnerability and duration of exposure to destabilizing forces. At any age, stress that overwhelms us can wreak havoc on our psyche and our body.

It is my belief that if you take care of your mind like you would your body, by resting it and treating it respectfully, then you may be able to remedy the process that led toward your breakdown. I think that most people stand a decent chance of a natural recovery from mental illness, just as they would a physical one, as long as they take time out to heal their mind and bring their life back into balance.

If people take anything away from this, it should be that hereditary disposition does not necessarily mean unalterable destiny. If it was, I would never have been able to write this book because I'd probably be in solitary confinement by now, or dead.

What happened collectively with regards to myself and my family's mental illness grants a glimpse into all the manifest ways a mind can break down under stress. Although a few of my relatives had suspicions now and then, no one ever had any idea just how mentally unwell all of us children were becoming, nor how emotionally and physically out-of-control our parents were.

Indeed, my experience demonstrates conclusively that having mentally ill parents was a severe setback for our psychological, emotional and social development. I consider myself lucky because, through fate or by calling, I slowly developed the resources to overcome my past. As of this writing, two of my other siblings still haven't even begun to recover from what happened back then.

During the 1980s, mental illness was a plague in our house, and no one that lived there was spared. In my years of living in residential facilities, group homes and foster families, I met dozens upon dozens of children and teenagers who had gone through similar circumstances (and far more horrific ones).

There are tens of thousands of these kinds of placements across America. And the money that quietly sustains the staff salaries and residential living necessities as well as their lackluster life-skills programs (plus the over-medicating to control and sedate their inhabitants, going on unmonitored within their cloistered walls even as I type this), is paid for by the sending state, which pulls those funds from tax money that came out of your pocket. This situation does not seem likely to change any time soon.

Generally, people with mental illness are encouraged to do the opposite of what I did. The advice is usually to maintain family contact, hold on to an active social life, and make use of psychological services as well as "evidence based" treatments like psychiatric medications. At this point in time I am the only one in my family to have learned meditation from a master, practiced it until my supposedly incurable mental and emotional problems were gone, and authored a book chronicling the entire healing process.

I'm not telling people to dump their pills and quit going to therapy. But I think there is a growing percentage of consumers who are dissatisfied with or have been damaged by the range of treatments for mental illness that currently exist and they wonder what else is out there that might help. You simply can't ignore the growing body of science and statistics that shows that the physical health outcomes of those mental health patients who rely primarily on polypharmacy over the long term are considerably poorer than those who went without.

At a time in our culture when a person can jack in wirelessly to the Net from almost anywhere, anytime and occupy themselves with high-speed music and video downloads, "twittering" status updates to their global social network while sipping a double-shot latte, it is vastly easier and more stimulating to pop a pill and move on to the next interesting thing than it is to sit vigil on the motion of your mind, hour after hour, month after month developing a real-time intimate and accurate understanding of how your thoughts and emotions actually work. Or how you might change your reactions to stress or stimulus with certain kinds of cognitions.

If you are one of those people, like me, for whom psychiatric drugs were intolerable and unacceptable, you either continue to suffer or you find a different path to healing. I was fortunate that meditation was that path for me, but I don't believe meditation is some kind of miracle cure for the masses. If it were easy to do, everyone would be doing it by now. But with that said, practicing meditation has brought about mental clarity and emotional stability in its adherents for thousands of years. And science is just now catching up in its understanding of how and why it works.

Meditation, when practiced correctly, has the power to change your cognitions, stabilize your emotions and improve overall brain function as well. And like with any other therapy or treatment, there are significant caveats involved. Meditation is difficult to do properly, and there are a lot of false ideas about it to navigate your way through when trying to learn the real thing. Meditation is also very time consuming. It's a long-term investment, not a quick fix.

You will find that deep meditation can periodically exacerbate your symptoms before lasting inner stability becomes hardwired into your brain and nervous system – that is part of the ride on the journey to connecting with the real you. The best preparation for this turbulence is knowing that it is going to happen sooner or later. Meditation requires a great deal of patience, perseverance and presence of mind. There are no guarantees that you will succeed in healing yourself with it.

In all humility, I'd like to think that the data that I provided in this work could, in its own small way, contribute meaningfully to the actual study of the mind, its weaknesses, strengths and capabilities. I am not sure if that will happen in my lifetime so, perhaps this is for posterity.

I hope I have shed some light on the shortcomings of today's social and welfare systems and the problems inherent in the mental health treatment machine in an era of our society when more and more it seems, normal variations in human character or behavior are pathologized as symptoms.

Most of the memoirs in this genre highlight one person's struggle with one mental illness. My account deals with the subject of dual-diagnosis and comorbid conditions. My intent was to illuminate what a struggle with that kind of mental illness is like and what recovery from that can be, as a counterpoint to today's climate of fifteen minute mental health assessments and the inevitable dispensing of "maintenance" treatments for the predictable "chemical imbalances." A concept which sounds plausible and makes a kind of sense but ultimately has yet to be proven conclusively on paper.

There are a lot of mental health memoirs out there already, some of them very good. One of the things that I felt that I had to offer was some detailed and practical insight into why and how I did and felt the things that I did. As well as some situational awareness as to why certain things happened to me and how I brought many of those things upon myself as a consequence of my madness.

The skill to realize the extent of my bad programming was hard-won insight which led to the ability to take responsibility for my faulty thoughts, emotions and behaviors. The facility to interface with, edit and recompile said bad code, was a resource that I cultivated in the long process of introspection into my flaws and failings. It was a process that naturally developed from spending so much time, voluntary and imposed, abiding in solitude with only the company of my thoughts.

If you read this from one end to the other and managed to stay with me to this point, I'd like to thank you for having taken the time to read Possessing Me: A Memoir of Healing. If this book inspires someone to similarly go within and heal themselves of their demons, solve their depression and find a lasting measure of inner happiness, then it was worth writing.

Acknowledgments

The persons and places in this memoir are real but I have taken the liberty of changing certain names, places and descriptions to protect their anonymity.

Thanks to my father Andrew for that memorable trip to Hong Kong which exposed me to tai chi as well as Buddhist monasticism and Taoist philosophy at an impressionable time in my teenage life. Thanks to my aunt Myra who gave me a book on Hatha yoga when I was thirteen. Your fascination with spiritual healing was a great inspiration to me when I was growing up.

A great big thank you goes out also to certain people in the mental health blogging community, whose candid experiences, poignant writings and resource links were all crucial to me in learning about what is going on right now in mental health treatments and politics in this country. And thanks also to my former boss Paul and his wife Jody and everyone else who suggested (in some cases, demanded) that I share this story.

I would like to thank Darsie, Robert, Oz, Marian, Stacey, Brian, Gerold, Sudeep, Lisa and Laura and everyone else who reviewed my manuscript at various stages and gave me much appreciated feedback and suggestions. I also wish to give a very special thanks to Gerold for his brilliant editing and advice during the long and often frustrating revision process. You helped me create a better book than I believed I was capable of.

Finally, to Master Bruce Frantzis, who made the Water Method school of Taoist meditation available to Westerners. From the moment I saw that black and white picture of you in China with Liu and your ba gua palm radiating from inside the covers of a certain chi gung book that I pulled off the shelf at a tiny Waldenbooks outlet in a mall in New Hampshire when I was fifteen, I somehow knew deep in my gut, that you were the real deal. Back then training with you was just a pipe dream that I'd had.

You may or may not remember me dropping in on a few of your courses later on and I wanted you to know that I was deeply inspired by and appreciative of your work. In my twenties, I often fantasized that you were my personal trainer. An imaginary Bruce hologram existed in my mind constantly demanding me to be honest and realistic about my capabilities and progress as I trained on my own. Practicing that material saved me and profoundly changed my life and I sincerely thank you from the bottom of my heart.

Related Reading

The Myth of the Chemical Cure: A Critique of Psychiatric Drug Treatment by Joanna Moncrieff

Mad in America: Bad Science, Bad Medicine, and the Enduring Mistreatment of the Mentally Ill by Robert Whitaker

Anatomy of an Epidemic: Magic Bullets, Psychiatric Drugs, and the Astonishing Rise of Mental Illness in America by Robert Whitaker

Toxic Psychiatry: Why Therapy, Empathy and Love Must Replace the Drugs, ECT and Biochemical Theories of the "New Psychiatry" by Peter Breggin MD

Your Drug May Be Your Problem by Peter Breggin MD, David Cohen MD

Blaming the Brain: The Truth About Drugs and Mental Health by Elliot Valenstein PhD

Manufacturing Depression: The Secret History of a Modern Disease by Gary Greenberg

Shyness: How Normal Behavior Became a Sickness by Christopher Lane

The Mind and the Brain: Neuroplasticity and the Power of Mental Force by Jeffrey M. Schwartz MD, Sharon Begley

Mental Health Politics

"Harvard researchers fail to reveal full drug pay" by Gardinier Harris, Benedict Carey *NY Times online*, June 2008

"Dr. Robert Spitzer criticizes the secretive collaboration of the DSM V" by Benedict Carey, *NY Times online*, December 2008

"Backlash on bipolar diagnosis of children: Joe Biederman PhD" *(bipolar) can be present the moment a child opens its eyes* by Scott Allen, *Boston Globe online*, June 2007

"Bipolar labels for children stir concern" by Carey Goldburg, *Boston Globe online*, February 2007

"Selective Publication of Antidepressant Trials and Its Influence on Apparent Efficacy" by Erick H. Turner, M.D., Annette M. Matthews, M.D., Eftihia Linardatos, B.S., Robert A. Tell, L.C.S.W., and Robert Rosenthal, Ph.D., *New England Journal of Medicine online*, January 2007

"Outrage! Preschoolers used as guinea pigs for psychotropic drug testing" by Mike Adams, *Natural News online*, May 2006

Meditation and Brain Science Articles

"Imaging technology makes it possible to study brains of meditating monks" by Curt Newton, *MIT technology Review online*, February 2004

"Meditating monks give clues on how to override the brain's basic responses" *BBC online*, June 2005

"Meditation helps you preform better and alters the structure of your brain" by Alison Motluk, *New Scientist online*, November 2005

"Meditation can change the workings of the brain" by Mark Kaufmen, *Washington Post online*, January 2005

"Meditation promotes neuroplasticity in the prefrontal cortex are the findings of Dr Sarah Lazar, Harvard Medical School" *PhysOrg online*, January 2006

"Zen does help clear the mind" by Charles Choi, *LiveScience online*, September 2008

"Mindfulness-based cognitive behavioral therapy for bipolar disorder: a feasibility trial" by Weber B, Jermann F, Gex-Fabry M, Nallet A, Bondolfi G, Aubry JM, *PubMed online*, June 2010

Meditation

TAO of Letting Go: Meditation for Modern Living by Bruce Frantzis

Relaxing Into Your Being: The Water Method of Taoist Meditation by Bruce Frantzis

About the Author

PHOTO BY LISA LIPPINCOTT

Jane Alexander spent over a decade working blue-collar jobs in the industrial sector. In recent years she has become involved with mental health activism and advocacy and was inspired and encouraged to write about her unique story of recovery. Jane is a dedicated practitioner of *chi gung* (qi gong) and *nei jia*, the internal martial arts, in which she has almost fifteen years experience. She currently resides in the Bay Area. You can reach her at www.possessingme.com.

CPSIA information can be obtained
at www.ICGtesting.com
Printed in the USA
LVOW13s1937211216
518303LV00014B/284/P